MEMORY
KEEPSAKES

MEMORY KEEPSAKES

43 PROJECTS FOR CREATING AND SAVING CHERISHED MEMORIES

THUNDER BAY
P·R·E·S·S

San Diego, California

Thunder Bay Press
An imprint of the Advantage Publishers Group
5880 Oberlin Drive, San Diego, CA 92121-4794
www.thunderbaybooks.com

All notations of errors or omissions should be addressed to Thunder Bay Press, Editorial Department, at the above address. All other correspondence (author inquiries, permissions) concerning the content of this book should be addressed to Rockport Publishers, Inc. 33 Commercial Street, Gloucester, MA 01930-5089. Telephone: (978) 283-9590; Fax: (978) 283-2742; www.rockpub.com.

ISBN 1-59223-030-X

Library of Congress Cataloging-in-Publication Data available upon request.

Grateful acknowledgment is given to Connie Sheerin and Janet Pensiero for their work from *Treasures Forever* on pages 10–15, 40–53, 66–79, 82–95, 110–123, 144–157, and 272–295; to Barbara Mauriello for her work from *Making Memory Boxes* on pages 16–33, 54–59, 128–139, 158–177, 200–243; to Betty Auth for her work from *Stamping Tricks for Scrapbooks* on pages 34–39, 62–65, 104–109, 142–143, 186–197, 254–271; to Kathy Cano-Murillo for her work from *Making Shadow Boxes and Shrines* on pages 60–61, 80–81, 140–141, 178–185, 244–253; and to Livia McRee for her work from *Easy Transfers for Any Surface* on pages 96–103 and 124–127.

Cover Images: Kevin Thomas; Bobbie Bush Photography
         www.bobbiebush.com

Studio Photography by Bobbie Bush www.bobbiebush.com, Brian Piper, Saunders Photography, and Kevin Thomas

Printed in China

1 2 3 4 5 07 06 05 04 03

Sierra
&
Stephanie

Contents

8 INTRODUCTION

11 THE BASICS
    12 Basic Tools
    14 Basic Techniques
    16 Box Making Basics
    34 Scrapbooking Basics

41 BABY MEMORIES

67 GROWING UP

83 FAMILY MEMORIES

111 IN REMEMBRANCE

145 LOVE AND FRIENDSHIP

199 EVENTS, TRIPS, AND FAVORITE THINGS

273 GALLERY

292 PATTERNS

296 SUPPLIES AND RESOURCES

300 CONTRIBUTORS

302 ABOUT THE AUTHORS

Introduction

Memories are certainly one of a kind, but at the same time, they are similar for each and every one of us. They begin with the moment we arrive in this world and continue throughout our lifetime. Each day holds a souvenir for us to take to the next day, next decade, or next lifetime. As time travels on, memories become even more precious as we collect the treasures associated with these moments. Some of my fondest memories were etched in mere moments, but they remain a part of who I am for a lifetime. The bond we all share with our treasures and memories creates many friendships that grow even stronger as we bring these artifacts of our lives together in a creative manner to display, share, and enjoy.

Now in my Goddess Years (as I choose to call my current stage of life), I have grown to understand why I have schlepped so many of these little treasures from home to home, with each and every move. Every time I unpack them, another memory is relived. It seemed to me that it was time to assemble these things in some order—creatively is my favorite way.

These thoughts and remembrances are all marvelous and become the real ties that bind us to our family and friends. Even strangers, who may never have known us, gain a clue about our lives and may find inspiration to create new memory pieces. Whose hand will run over the work I have done and wonder what was going through my head while creating this piece? Whose lives will be touched in the future by these things I have created? I think of that often and smile at the thought that one day they will be artifacts for them to ponder.

Through the years, these treasures capture our "firsts," such as something as small as the first curl cut from a baby's head or a fond memory of a day at the beach. Everything that we do is special to us, unique to us, even the smallest event. These memories make up a map that helps another person understand our time, our journey, our contributions during our time here. These memories certainly help us become more aware of how much the important moments really stay with us, although celebrating or remembering these moments changes with the advance of technology. Remember that you are never alone when you have a memory that is treasured forever—all you have to do is look at it and just remember.

Always creating something,
Connie Sheerin

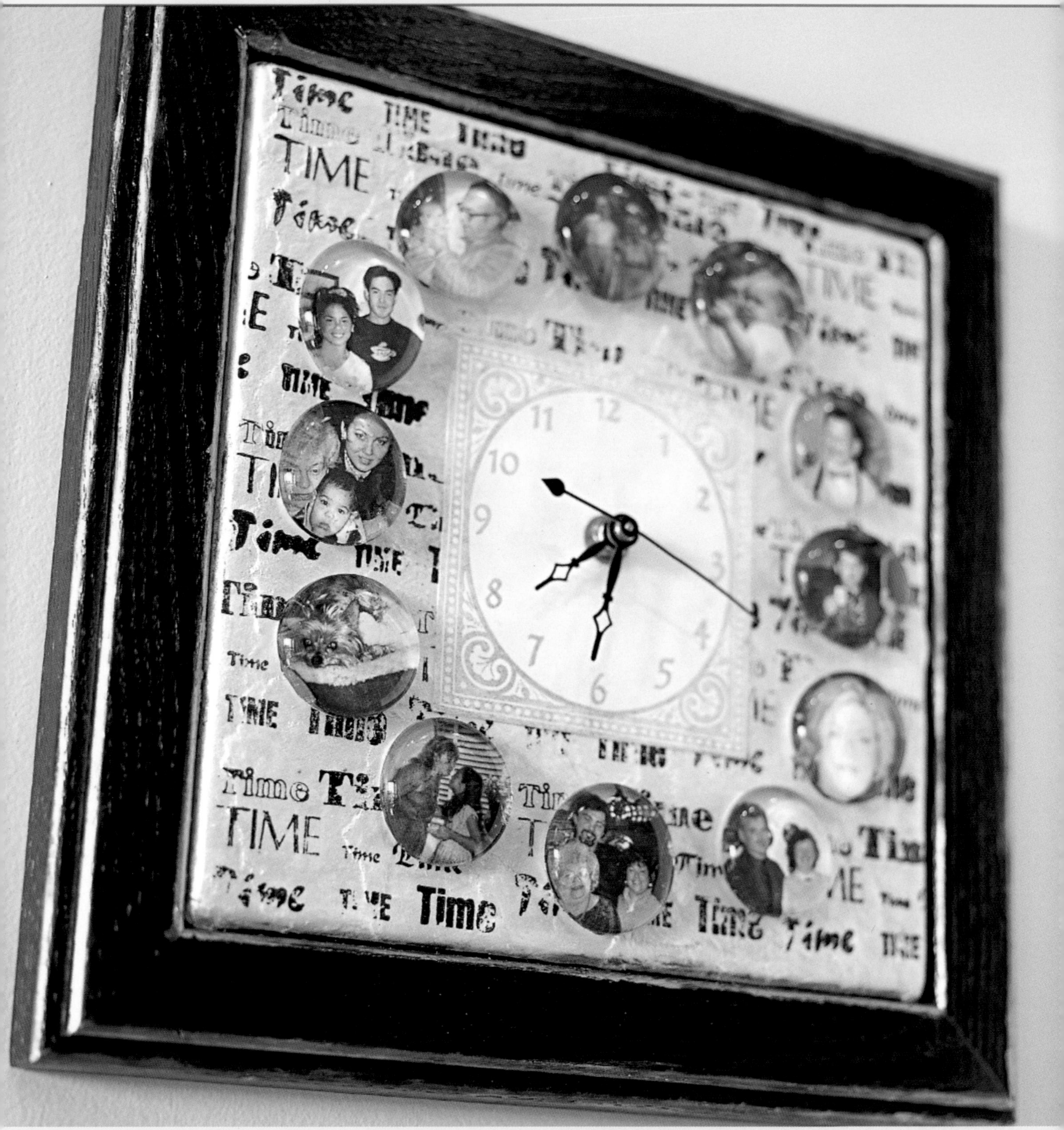
TIME
Time
TIME
Time

Basics

YOU WILL USE many different techniques to make the projects in this book. The basic materials you should have on hand to create these projects are listed in this chapter, along with general information on a wide variety of craft techniques.

Basic Tools

*H*aving the right tool allows you to make a project with ease. For the projects in this book, you'll need the basics—pencils, erasers, scissors, and masking tape—as well as some specialized items:

A **ruler** and a **grid-lined cutting mat** help you make straight cuts and square corners with little effort.

A good 7" (18 cm) or 8" (20 cm) pair of **straight scissors** is indispensable for crafting. Decorative scissors are also very popular and are great for putting fancy edges on photocopies and photos.

You'll need a **mat knife** to cut mat board or heavy-weight cardboard.

Use a **craft knife** instead of scissors when you need to cut precise measurements. The blades are replaceable, and there are many different sizes and styles available. Always be sure to use a sharp blade.

Needle-nose pliers and **wire cutters** are essential for wire crafting. Use the pliers to make smooth curls and loops. The pliers are also very helpful for holding small items securely when positioning them.

Washable fabric-marking pens are very handy for transferring patterns to fabric. Disappearing ink pens are also available—the marks usually fade after a day or two, but always test the pens on a scrap piece of fabric first.

Permanent fabric markers are available in an array of colors and are perfect for transferring lettering to fabric. You must set most of them with an iron for them to be permanent.

A **hot-glue gun** is great for attaching odd-shaped items to flat or curved surfaces. The glue sets quickly as it cools. Be sure to read the directions for the glue thoroughly before you use it—the temperature to which you need to heat the glue varies from brand to brand, and for the materials you are gluing.

Double-sided adhesive sheets are used for bonding large, flat pieces of paper or cardboard together. The sheets are thin and have a waxed paper carrier sheet on either side to protect the adhesive. Pull one carrier sheet off, and press the adhesive sheet in place. Then remove the other waxed sheet to finish the bond. For smaller areas, use double-sided clear tape.

Spray adhesive can be used on just about any surface for a stain-free, smooth, even layer of glue. Spray adhesive dries quickly, but you can still reposition items after it has dried.

PVA (polyvinyl acetate) is an excellent all-purpose, acid-free adhesive that you can use for most projects. Also known as white glue, it is a quick-drying, plastic-based adhesive that keeps paper flat and dries clear. When diluted, it can also be used for sealing porous surfaces. Apply the glue with a brush, brushing it from the center out to ensure all areas are covered.

Acrylic matte medium is opaque when wet and translucent when dry. It can be used for collages and also works well in adhering paper to glass. It produces a matte, nonreflective finish.

Permanent, quick-grab glue, such as Fabri-Tac and E-6000, is absolutely essential. There's nothing worse than waiting for glue to dry or watching objects slip and slide because the glue hasn't firmed up yet. Quick-grab glues are usually formulated for a variety of surfaces and can be used on almost anything.

Liquid Laminate is an all-in-one laminating product that acts as both the adhesive and the protective covering, and it dries crystal clear. Be sure to test it with each material you are going to use, however, so you can avoid any bleeding of color or writing. Liquid Laminate is great for decoupage. It also bonds, coats, and seals fabrics and papers onto glass, plastic, wood, cardboard, and more.

Archival glue is acid-free and nonstaining, which is important for ensuring your projects are preserved for generations. Archival glue works well with photocopies, photographs, paper, and paper trims for all of your memory work and crafting, collages, and even glitter writing. It is fast-setting and dries clear, without wrinkling or curling your paper or photos.

Epoxy glues—such as Glass, Metal & More—are clear-drying, all-purpose glues that you can use with several materials. Make sure your surfaces are clean and dry, and be sure to protect your work area. Test the glue on a scrap area first, and then apply it evenly with light pressure. This glue sets in about 30 minutes and fully cures in 24 hours.

Several of the projects are made with **handmade paper,** which can be found at craft and rubber-stamp stores, by mail order, and on the Internet. You can also find unique papers for computer printers at office supply stores in a range of colors and textures. Both handmade and computer paper work great for the pages of handmade books and as accents in decoupage projects. Tracing paper is useful for copying artwork and transferring lettering.

Rubber stamps offer an assortment of ready-made artwork for crafters. You can also find alphabet stamps, which are handy for telling stories, in many styles and sizes. You can press the stamps into polymer clay for a 3-D effect or into embossing ink and powder to create the effect of raised engraved type. Sprinkle the powder over the stamped image, and shake off the excess. Then heat the image with a heat gun (specially designed for this use) to achieve a raised, glossy image.

A few good **brushes** are all you'll need to do these projects—a $1\frac{1}{2}$" (4 cm) flat brush to paint large areas, a #8 or #6 round brush for any detail work, and several foam brushes for the acrylic sealer and decoupage finish. Brushes designed for special purposes, like stenciling, are also available. Remember, you'll get the best results using a high-quality brush.

A few other tools you might want to have ready include a screwdriver, tweezers, cotton swabs, rubbing alcohol (for cleaning your brushes), newspapers (to cover work surfaces while painting), clear adhesive tape, and straight pins.

Basic Techniques

Cutting Paper Products with a Knife

Always use a sharp blade and work on a cutting mat. Cutting mats are useful because they help you align and measure your pieces and protect your work surface. Hold the paper down firmly with a straightedge, and cut along the straightedge with the blade. Keep your fingers away from the path of the blade to avoid any accidents. Don't remove the straightedge before checking that you have completely cut through the paper—you may need to run the blade through twice.

Decoupaging

Decoupage is a Victorian art that continues to find easier ways to keep itself current and less time-consuming. Having a good pair of decoupage scissors is very important. The real trick to cutting is to guide the paper into the scissors rather than to force the scissors into the paper. Wonderful prints of every description and theme are available. Wrapping paper offers some great designs—keep your eyes open!

Decoupage medium is a water-based glue, sealer, and finish that can be used for applying paper to all surfaces. It can be applied with a brush or a sponge, and once it dries, it provides a strong, fast-drying, permanent surface. Decoupage medium is available in a variety of finishes, from matte to satin to gloss. You can even find decoupage medium with a slight sparkle that you can use to add a little pizzazz to your piece.

Using Polymer Clay

Polymer clay is a manmade material. It is much more user-friendly and versatile for the home crafter than ceramic clays. To cure polymer clay, bake it in a convection oven, toaster oven, or your own home oven at temperatures ranging from 265° to 275° F (130° C). Read the directions that come with the clay to determine the actual temperature and curing time.

Before using the clay, you must first condition it. You can do this either by kneading it and warming it in your hands, or by rolling it through a pasta machine. Simply fold and roll the clay through the machine until it is soft and pliable. As a general rule, tools that are used for polymer clay should be dedicated to clay and not used in food preparation.

Using Finishes

Add a coat of protective finish to projects that will receive wear and tear, such as furniture or other functional pieces. The finish will protect and waterproof the surface of your project. Apply the finish with a sponge or bristle brush, taking care to follow the specific manufacturer's instructions. Multiple coats are usually recommended for the best protection.

Acrylic varnish is a water-based finish, which can be used to coat and protect any paper project. It is available in matte and satin varieties. It dries quickly, before dust and particles can settle in it, so it is usually not necessary to sand between coats.

Polyurethane is a durable polymer-based finish. Use paint thinner or mineral spirits for cleanup. Polyurethane dries more slowly than acrylic varnish, so you will need to lightly sand your project between coats to smooth out any dust that adheres to the finish.

Making Papier-Mâché

You can either purchase papier-mâché paste in a craft store or make it from scratch by using the recipe for basic flour paste in the book (see page 34). If you store the paste in an airtight container in a cool place, it will keep for several days. Wheat paste, which is used for hanging wallpaper, also works well. Papier-mâché is an easy technique, but remember to allow for drying time between making the layers. Because it can be a messy process, cover your work area with newspapers to keep it clean.

Lettering

If you have beautiful handwriting, by all means use it on your projects. If not, you can print out your text in a variety of typefaces and almost any size from your home computer. To transfer your lettering to a transparent surface, like glass, slip the printout with the lettering behind the surface and trace it with a pen designed for decorating glass or plastic. Some of these pens need to be heat-set to be permanent. Lettering can be transferred onto fabric by placing the printout behind the fabric and holding the two pieces up to a light source. Then you can easily trace the text. To transfer your lettering to opaque surfaces, rub the back of the paper with the lettering with the point of a graphite pencil (a #2 pencil works well). Place the lettering with the graphite rubbing facing the surface to be lettered, and trace the lettering with a sharp pen or pencil. The lettering can then be painted or filled in with marker.

Sewing

The projects in this book that involve sewing are designed for a beginning sewer on a home sewing machine. In addition to the sewing machine, you'll need large and small hand-sewing needles, and thread in the color of your choice. If you can sew on a button, you can do the hand-sewing required to complete these projects.

Stenciling

Ready-made or hand-cut stencils are easy to use and readily available. Choose a stencil brush in a size appropriate for the stencil you're using. Oil-based "dry" stencil paint is designed specifically for stenciling, but you can also use acrylic craft paint. If you use acrylic paint, make sure that your brush is slightly dry.

Painting

Acrylic craft paint is easy to use, it dries quickly, and you can clean it up with water. Make sure the surface you're painting is clean and dust-free. Always sand rough wood before painting. It's best to use two or three light coats of paint to cover a surface. Use a water-based polyurethane to seal the paint. If you use an oil-based paint, be sure to let it dry for 24 hours between coats. Seal your painted project with an alkyd-based polyurethane.

Laminating

You can laminate documents and photos with clear self-adhesive laminating sheets that you can find in craft and office supply stores. If you're laminating something precious, make sure the laminating sheets are acid free or archival quality. For a less expensive, nonarchival effect, clear contact paper works well. If you're not sure about using the self-adhesive sheets, copy centers can laminate documents and photos for you.

Transfering Images

Iron-on photo transfer paper designed for a home ink-jet printer is great for transferring photos and artwork onto fabric. You can easily create designs on the computer using a graphics program (you may have one pre-installed on your computer) and print them onto the transfer paper. You can also use existing images—family photographs and original children's art can make your projects truly one-of-a-kind. To get your own images into the computer, photograph them with a digital camera or scan them. If you don't have a camera or a scanner available, take your pictures to a photo developer who can burn your favorite photographs onto a CD. Then you can easily transfer the images onto your computer. You can also work with images received via e-mail or through one of the photo Web sites that allow you store images online.

When your design is complete, run a test print on a piece of regular paper. Sometimes colors or design elements appear differently on paper than they do on the screen. Adjust your image until you get it just the way you want it. Print the image onto the iron-on paper using an ink-jet printer or copier. Follow the instructions on the package for ironing the image onto the fabric.

Find a copy center with a self-serve color photocopying machine. With this machine, you can enlarge, reduce, and adjust the color of the photos and documents you're copying. You can even make a color photo into a black-and-white copy or add color to a plain document. You can also ask the people at the copy center to transfer your image onto iron-on transfer paper.

box making basics: *tools*

The following tools are essential to making memory boxes:

AWL: A wooden-handled tool with a sharp, pointy metal shaft, used to punch holes; from bookbinding suppliers and hardware stores.

BRUSHES: For gluing: $1/2$" (1 cm) and 2" (5 cm) wide short-handled flat brushes (cheap) from the hardware store.
For pasting: $1 1/2$" round natural-bristle brushes (expensive but should last a lifetime) from Italy and France. Check out pastry brushes in cookware stores or go to your bookbinding supplier.

C-CLAMPS: A hardware store item, used to clamp boards to the workbench, to stabilize box parts as they are being glued.

CHISEL: Wood chisels from the hardware store, in a variety of sizes (to match the width of ribbons used as box closures).

CUTTING MAT: A self-healing mat board, imprinted with a grid pattern, on which endless cuts can be made with your knives; available in several sizes from bookbinding and art supply stores.

DRILL: A drill with small drill bits, to pierce holes in wood and plastic elements.

FOLDERS, BONE AND TEFLON: Folders are used to fold and crease paper, to turn materials over the board edges, to smooth down materials, to burnish board, and for about a hundred other uses. The essential bookbinder's tool, the bone folder, is a flat, smooth tool carved from bone in a variety of shapes and sizes. The most useful is a 6"–8" (15–20 cm) folder, with one pointed and

one rounded end. Teflon folders are generally thicker than bone folders and cannot fit into the narrow spaces where bone folders can slide. Their advantage over the bone tool is in smoothing down glued materials; miraculously, they do not mark or score the surface of cloth when rubbed directly on top of a cloth-covered board.

KNIVES: Utility or mat knives, X-acto knives or knives with snap-off blades are all acceptable and easily available at hardware and art supply stores. For most operations I prefer a surgical scalpel (#4 handle) and good-quality curved blades (#23), purchased through bookbinding or surgical suppliers. For cutting binder's board, a utility knife is best.

MICRO-SPATULA: A slender, metal surgical tool with flattened ends, used to push ribbons through narrow slits; from bookbinding and surgical suppliers.

POTTER'S NEEDLE: A sewing needle stuck into a metal or wooden handle. Finer than an awl, it is useful for making unobtrusive pinpricks on materials prior to punching or chiseling; from a pottery supplier.

PRESSING BOARDS: All of the projects in this book require gentle pressing—that is, under boards and weights rather than in a bookbinding press. Plywood, hardwood, and seasoned masonite boards, sheets of heavy-duty plastic, and leftover kitchen counter laminates in all sizes are useful. Boards must be larger than the item being pressed.

RULERS: A metal ruler or straight-edge is preferable to a plastic

one that can be nicked or shaved when used with a knife. The heavier the ruler, the more secure the action.

SANDPAPER: Used to smooth the seams of a box after gluing-up. To make your own sanding sticks, glue various grades of sandpaper to heavyweight binder's board; cut the boards into 1 1/2"–2" (4–5 cm) wide strips, 10"–12" (25-30 cm) in length.

SCISSORS: Make sure they're good and sharp. Used mostly for rough cutting of cloth, trimming corners, snipping ribbons, etc. Most accurate cutting is done with a knife and straight-edge or, for the truly fortunate, with a heavy-duty board shears.

SEWING NEEDLES: A variety of needles, with large and small eyes, is useful.

SPRING DIVIDER: A measuring device (similar to a compass in appearance) used to obtain measurements and transfer them to subsequent steps in the boxmaking process. This wonderful tool limits dependence on numbers (and on math in general). Next to the bone folder, it is the bookbinder's best friend; from bookbinding and architectural tool suppliers.

T-SQUARE: Used, with a knife, for cutting boards (and other materials) and maintaining right angles; from an art supply store.

TRIANGLE: You can't make boxes without a metal triangle. The smaller the better, to fit into the right-angled corners of little boxes; from a bookbinding or art supply store.

WEIGHTS: Anything will work: bricks wrapped in bookcloth to keep them clean, tins filled with pennies or with sand, small dressmaking weights, or hefty litho stones.

OTHER IMPORTANT SUPPLIES INCLUDE THE FOLLOWING:

- Waste paper: Vital in all steps of boxmaking, to keep both workbench and box surfaces free of adhesives. Must be thin and absorbent. The best paper is unprinted newsprint, available in pads from art supply stores or in bundles from packing and moving businesses.
- Pencils and pencil sharpener.
- Bowls, for glue and paste.
- Measuring cup and spoons, for preparing adhesives.
- Whisk and pot, for cooking paste.
- Paper towels.
- Plastic containers with lids, to store adhesives.
- Wax paper.
- Masking tape.
- Hammer or mallet, for use with chisels and punches.
- Trash can.

box making basics: *materials*

The basic materials of boxmaking are paper, cloth, board, and adhesives.

PAPER

The world of papers is large and magnificent. Art supply and stationery stores, Asian groceries, a trunk in the attic or at the flea market, today's mail—all are potential sources for treasures. Whether cheap and gaudy or handmade and elegant, nothing transforms a box from ordinary to extraordinary more swiftly than the right piece of paper.

Papers vary greatly in strength and durability and must be used appropriately. Papers too fragile to function as hinges work beautifully as box liners. Papers too thick to mold themselves around boards are simply scored and left to stand as paper boxes. Papers too sheer to hide the construction details of the box are either laminated or carded around lightweight boards to make them denser. All papers have a place in boxmaking.

CLOTH

The world of bookcloth is smaller than that of paper. Bookcloth is fabric that has been treated to accept the application of adhesives.

Most commonly, fabrics are backed with paper to provide a glue barrier. Older cloths, such as starch-filled muslins and lovely glazed buckrams, are slowly disappearing. Paper-backed rayon, silk, and linen, in dazzling colors and various textures, are taking over the market.

Cloth must be used wherever there is extensive hinging. In combination with decorative papers, cloth is often used in narrow strips to cover the joints of the box. To learn how to convert your own fabric into bookcloth, see The Picture Frame Box, page 54.

BOARD

Binder's board is an extremely dense cardboard and is available in an acid-free form. I use three thicknesses—60 point (lightweight), 80 point (medium weight), and 100 point (heavyweight) board.

Rag boards, such as museum and mat boards, are easier to cut than binder's board but are also easier to dent. Because of their high cotton content, rag boards are thirsty, slurping up the moisture from adhesives and thus are more likely to warp than binder's board.

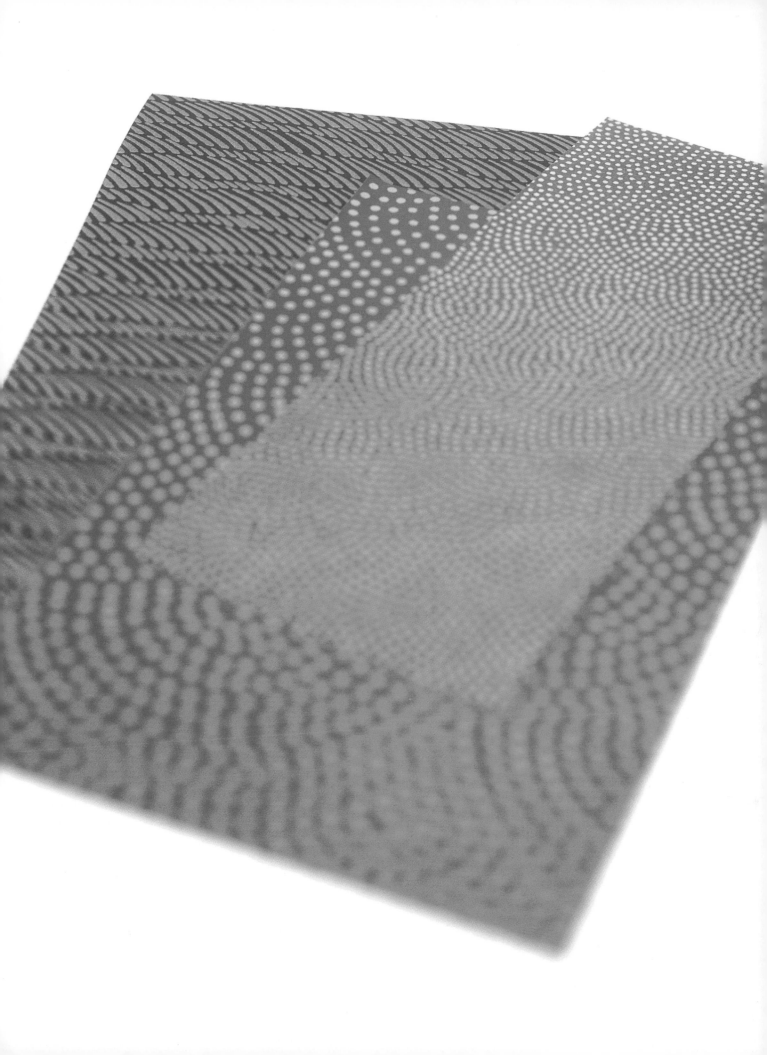

box making basics: *adhesives*

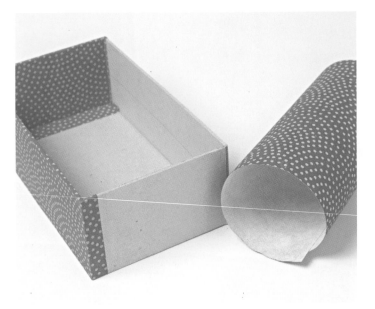

ADHESIVES

Most bookbinders have a love/hate relationship with adhesives: We need them, but they cause much heartache. The rules governing their use change according to the project. No two boxes, by either their materials or their size, ever seem alike. And the rules of adhesives are based completely on: (1) the properties of the materials (paper-covered boxes require an entirely different approach than cloth-covered boxes), and (2) the size of the box (large boxes have a different set of rules than small boxes). To tell you that experience must be your guide in the selection of the proper adhesive seems evasive. It is, however, the truest piece of advice I can give. I use four adhesives: Paste, glue, methyl cellulose, and assorted pressure-sensitive adhesives.

WHY ADHESIVES MATTER

Buckling and warping in boxes are due to either a miscalculation in grain direction or to the improper use of an adhesive coupled with inadequate drying techniques.

Most adhesives contain moisture. Moisture causes materials to stretch and expand. Materials that expand eventually try to contract. This contraction causes warping. Because warping cannot be avoided, it must be counteracted.

Try this experiment: Cut two pieces of paper and one piece of binder's board, all to the same dimensions and grain direction

(see page 24). Paste out one piece of paper. Notice how the paper has stretched in width (from spine to fore edge). Apply the pasted paper to the board. Observe the board. Within minutes, the board will begin to curve, first away from and then toward the paper-covered surface. At this point, all the pressure in the world will not flatten the board. Paste out the second piece of paper and apply it to the reverse side of the board.

Observe the board. Initially, the original warp will increase until, slowly, the board pulls back in the opposite direction and eventually flattens. At this point, pressing the board under a light weight will help stabilize it.

The lesson is this: Whatever you do to one side of a board, do to the other. Keep the moisture content consistent. In order to be consistent you must sometimes fool your materials. For example, if you are covering a box with cloth (using mixture) but lining it with a delicate paper (requiring paste), add an extra dollop of methyl cellulose to your mixture—make it wetter and thereby induce more warp, to counteract the reverse warp of the pasted surface.

PASTE

Paste, vegetable in origin, is a flour or a starch cooked with water. Rice starch, wheat starch, and the unbleached flour in your kitchen pantry all make fine pastes.

I use paste exclusively on paper—never on cloth or boards. Paste is the most luscious adhesive: Smooth and creamy in the bowl, it spreads like silk across the surface of a sheet of paper. Largely water in content, paste induces the immediate relaxation of even the crankiest papers. Fragile papers that tear under the weight of glue and stubborn papers (like gift wrap) that escape into sticky spirals unless they are thoroughly subdued with water are the best candidates for paste.

ADVANTAGES OF PASTE

- Paste is reversible with water. Stains can sometimes be removed with a damp sponge.
- Paste dries slowly. If you need the adhesive to stay active for a long time (as when covering a large box), use paste. If the paste is drying more quickly than expected, it can be reset by spritzing the pasted paper with water.

DISADVANTAGES OF PASTE

- Paste requires cooking. (There are some precooked flour pastes on the market, but they are somewhat gritty.)
- Paste has a short life once cooked.
  Since most preservatives are either toxic (thymol) or aggressively scented (oil of cloves, oil of wintergreen), I prefer to make small batches of paste daily rather than to use preservatives. Refrigeration prolongs the life of a bowl of paste, but it also makes the paste watery and less sticky.

INGREDIENTS Yield: Approximately I cup of paste.
- 4 tablespoons rice starch
- $1/4$ cup cold water
- $1/2$ to I cup boiling water
- (Note that these amounts are approximate. Can be thinned by adding cold water.)

Measure the starch into a saucepan. Add the cold water and whisk until the starch is completely dissolved. Add $1/2$ cup of the boiling water, slowly, as you continue to whisk. Place the saucepan over a medium flame and cook, stirring constantly and adding more water as necessary, until the mixture thickens and turns translucent. When the mixture comes to a boil, let it cook for a minute or so. Remove the saucepan from the stove and pour the paste into a bowl to cool. Stir occasionally to prevent a skin from forming.

GLUE

There are many glues, both animal in origin (hide, rabbit skin, fish) and synthetic. In boxmaking I use one of the synthetic glues, polyvinyl acetate (PVA). There are several PVAs on the market; select an acid-free one. Because it is extremely tacky and unspreadable, I rarely use full-strength PVA. For maximum bond in dealing with small details (as in tipping a ribbon tie into position), I dip directly into my jar of glue. But for most operations I dilute the PVA with methyl cellulose (see page 23). Methyl cellulose makes the PVA easier to spread and slows its drying time. This combination of PVA/methyl cellulose will be referred to as mixture throughout these pages.

ADVANTAGES OF GLUE

- PVA requires no preparation.
- PVA has a long shelf life. (It must, however, be protected from freezing.)
- PVA dries quickly.

DISADVANTAGES OF GLUE

- Most PVAs are not reversible with water. It is almost impossible to remove glue stains from cloth and paper.
- PVA dries quickly. If working time is required, the PVA must be diluted.

METHYL CELLULOSE

Methyl cellulose is a synthetic adhesive. Because it does not have especially strong bonding qualities, I do not use methyl cellulose as an independent adhesive. Its use in boxmaking is as an additive to PVA. This resulting mixture is used on all cloth work, on most board operations, and on many heavy-weight papers.

In the mixture you will use, the proportion of the methyl cellulose to the PVA will vary according to the strength of the prepared methyl cellulose (it comes in granular form and must be mixed with water) and the scale of the work involved. If more time is needed (as in covering a large box), add an extra dollop of methyl cellulose to your bowl of mixture.

ADVANTAGES OF METHYL CELLULOSE

- Once prepared, methyl cellulose can be stored in a sealed container for weeks.
- It is reversible with water.
- It makes PVA a workable adhesive.

DISADVANTAGES OF METHYL CELLULOSE

- It has limited bonding qualities.
- It requires (minimal) preparation.

INGREDIENTS

2 teaspoons methyl cellulose

1 cup cold water

(Note that these amounts are approximate).

Pour the cup of cold water into a container. Sprinkle methyl cellulose into the water. Whisk vigorously. Let stand several hours until solution becomes uniformly gel-like and translucent. Store in a lidded container. Shake well before using.

PRESSURE-SENSITIVE ADHESIVES

Pressure-sensitive adhesives are layers of adhesives backed on release papers. I depend on these adhesives when moisture must be kept entirely out of a project, for example, when mounting a photograph on a box cover. They are also convenient in assembling scored boxes.

ADVANTAGES OF PRESSURE-SENSITIVE ADHESIVES

- They are moisture free.
- Their bond is immediate—no pressing or drying time is required.

DISADVANTAGES OF PRESSURE-SENSITIVE ADHESIVES

- The bond is immediate, allowing no slip time to guide the materials into position.
- Many of them are not archival. Consult your supplier's catalog for specifics.

box making basics

THE PARTS OF THE BOX

A box is composed of several separate units: The case, the flaps, the tray, and the lid. The case, consisting of a front, spine, and back, is constructed by assembling the boards on the covering material, often leaving a space between the boards (called a *joint*) to act as a hinge.

The most basic box is a simple case with no flaps, no trays, and no lid.

Flaps are panels attached to the case at the top (head), bottom (tail), and side (fore edge). They can be made separately and glued onto the case, or they can grow from the case itself. Flaps keep the contents of the box from falling out.

Trays consist of base boards with walls glued to them prior to covering. Trays are three-walled or four-walled, depending on the style of box.

Lids, either freestanding or attached to the spine, are panels built to extend slightly beyond the parameters of a tray. They create a lip for easy accessibility and lifting and are often embellished with knobs, buttons, ribbons, and other fasteners.

GRAIN DIRECTION

Anyone who has ever torn an article out of a newspaper has had a lesson in grain direction: Pulled in one direction, the paper tears beautifully. But when pulled in the perpendicular direction, the paper rips jaggedly. The clean tear is with the grain; the ragged one, against the grain.

Grain is inherent in paper, cloth, and board. It is determined by an alignment of fibers. The direction in which most of the fibers are aligned is the grain direction of the material.

WHY GRAIN MATTERS

For the moveable parts of a box to work easily and without stress, the grain must run parallel to this hinging action. In a book, grain runs parallel to its spine, making it easy to turn the pages and manipulate the cover. The same is true in boxmaking. The grain must run parallel to the spine of the box.

Understanding grain direction is also important for predicting the stretch of materials as they come in contact with moisture (adhesives). Materials expand *opposite* their grain direction. If a piece of lining paper is cut to fit perfectly within a box, after pasting it will have stretched in width (against its grain) while having remained unchanged in height (with the grain). It is necessary to anticipate this stretch and to trim paper accordingly before pasting or gluing.

HOW TO DETERMINE GRAIN

The best way to determine grain is through your sense of touch.

For paper and cloth, gently bend (don't crease!) the material and roll it back and forth several times. Let the paper or cloth relax, then bend and roll it in the opposite direction. The direction in which you feel the least resistance is the grain direction.

For board, hold a corner in both hands and flex it, then release the board. Flex the board in the opposite direction. The flexing direction of least resistance is the grain direction.

box making basics:
measuring and cutting

MEASURING

All boxes start from the inside out. The first piece of board to be measured and cut is the base board, the piece on which your objects (books, photos, marbles) will sit. All of the other boards take their measurements from the base. The base has two dimensions: Height and width.

Height is the distance from top to bottom or, in the bookbinder's language (used throughout this book), from *head* to *tail*. *Width* is the distance from side to side or, more precisely, from *spine* to *fore-edge*. The third dimension of the box, its *depth*, is found in its walls. Depth refers to the thickness of the object to be boxed; the distance, for example, from the top card to the bottom card in a deck of cards.

My approach to measuring is more intuitive than mathematical; I rarely rely on numbers. I love my rulers for their straight edges, not for their numbered markings. Precision is achieved by paying attention to the relationships between the materials and the parts of the box. This book provides you with models to be altered for future projects. When you understand the relationships between the parts and the whole, you will be able to change my patterns and create entirely new boxes.

CUTTING

In addition to the hand tools described earlier, a wonderful piece of equipment is a paper cutter. Whether tabletop or freestanding, a paper cutter (or the more substantial *board shears*) makes the difference between easy and laborious cutting. A good cutter that has a bed with a true edge perpendicular to the cutting edge, a clamp to hold the material in place, and a pair of sharp upper and lower knives is a joy to use. If a cutter is not available, use a utility knife and a T-square.

To ensure accuracy in cutting, you must follow a four-step process.

1. Determine grain direction of the board. (Review Grain Direction on page 24 if you need help with this.) Grain direction must run from head to tail on all boards.

2. Rough cut the board to the approximate size needed for the box. An oversized board is difficult to handle and will not fit on a tabletop paper cutter.

3. Square the board by trimming one long edge of board and a perpendicular short edge to form a true right angle.

4. Mark the board by placing the object to be boxed on the squared corner and making penciled markings of desired height and width.

To determine the depth of the object to be boxed, crease a scrap of paper to form a right angle; slide this scrap under the object and make a parallel crease in the scrap paper, snugly enclosing the object within these two creases. Transfer this measurement—the distance from one crease to the other—to your board.

box making basics:
pasting and gluing

PASTING AND GLUING

Pasting refers to the use of any starch-based adhesive. Gluing refers to the use of both full-strength PVA and the more commonly applied mixture of PVA and methyl cellulose.

PAPER   Some papers demand paste; others are happier with the PVA/methyl cellulose mixture. In general, lightweight papers that tend to stretch and curl excessively prefer paste. The high water content in paste saturates the paper and makes it lie down and behave. Similarly, thin, long-fibered translucent papers—like many Japanese tissues—respond better to paste than to mixture. Use mixture on heavyweight papers, which are unlikely to curl and stretch.

CLOTH AND BOARDS   On cloth and boards, always use the PVA/methyl cellulose mixture. The only question is how much PVA? How much methyl cellulose? The answer is determined by the size of your box, the nature of your materials, and the consistency of both adhesives. Remember, a larger box requires more working time (i.e., more moisture) than a smaller box. I usually start with a combination of approximately 70% PVA and 30% methyl cellulose. If my brush drags rather than glides across the surface being glued, my adhesive is too dry. I stop brushing and add another dollop of methyl cellulose to the mixture.

HOW TO PASTE A SHEET OF PAPER TO BOARD

When covering a board with paper, the adhesive must be applied to the paper rather than to the board. If dry paper is pressed onto a wet board, the paper will wrinkle. To paste, place a few layers of newsprint on the workbench. The newsprint should be larger than the paper being pasted. Position your paper face down on the newsprint. Scoop up a generous amount of paste with your paste brush and apply it to the paper with a circular motion, starting at the center of the piece of paper and working outward in concentric circles. Be sure one hand anchors the paper firmly to the newsprint. Keep a paper towel nearby, as you will get paste on your fingers. As you approach the edges of the paper, stop making circles. Return to the center of the paper and brush outward, in radiating strokes, creating a sunburst pattern. Never hold the brush parallel with the edges of the paper: Bristles can slip underneath and stain the surface of the paper. Give the pasted sheet of paper plenty of time to relax before picking it up. If the paper is curling excessively, continue to work your brush across the surface, pressing and flattening. When the paper has been sufficiently saturated with moisture, it will lie flat. Pick up the paper and apply it to the board.

HOW TO GLUE CLOTH TO BOARD

Unlike adhering paper to board, the adhesive can be applied to either the board or the cloth. To glue, follow all procedures as described above, substituting your glue brush for the paste brush and adjusting the PVA/methyl cellulose mixture to suit your materials.

box making basics:
making the tray

HOW TO COVER THE TRAY WITH PAPER

COVERING THE OUTSIDE   Cut a piece of paper long enough to wrap around all walls, plus $^1/_2$" (1 cm). (If your decorative paper is not long enough, use two shorter pieces; plan the seam to fall at a corner.) In width, the paper should be twice the depth of the tray, plus $1^1/_2$" (4 cm).

Paste out the paper. Give the paper time to relax and uncurl. Position your tray, with the bottom of the tray facing you, approximately $^3/_4$" (2 cm) away from the long edge of the paper and $^1/_2$" (1 cm) away from the short edge. Crease the $^1/_2$" (1 cm) extension around the corner and onto the wall.

Roll the tray on the paper, pushing the tray snugly into each right angle as it is formed. Before making the final roll, check the paper for stretch. If the paper has stretched beyond the board edge, trim

HOW TO CONSTRUCT THE TRAY   C-clamp a wooden board onto your tabletop. Set down a piece of wax paper. Place the base board on the wax paper. Using full-strength PVA and a small brush, paint a thin line of glue along the edge of the head wall where it touches the base. Position this wall against the clamped wooden board and push the base against it. (The clamped board supports the wall and helps to maintain a right angle.) Wipe away excess glue with your bone folder. Glue the fore-edge wall, painting the glue along the edge touching the base and also along the edge that meets the head wall. Glue the tail wall, painting the glue along the edge touching the base and also along the edge that meets the fore-edge wall. Glue the spine wall, painting the glue along the edge touching the base and also along the two edges that meet the head and tail walls. Let the tray set until it is dry (15 minutes). Peel the tray off the wax paper, and sand any rough joints. The tray is now ready for covering.

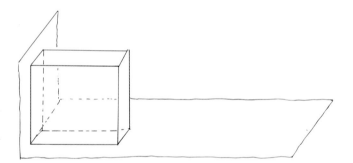

it to fit. Remember, wet paper tends to tear. To minimize this risk, place a piece of wax paper on top of the paper to be trimmed, and cut through the wax paper, using a sawing motion with your knife. Use your bone folder to crease the ³/₄" (2 cm) turn-ins onto the bottom of the tray. Clip the corners with scissors, and press the paper into position. You are now ready to finish the inside of the tray.

FINISHING THE INSIDE   (above left) To finish the inside of the tray, slivers of paper exactly one board thickness in width must be removed at each of the four corners. Position the tray on its spine wall, on a cutting mat. Place your metal triangle on the paper. One edge of the triangle should touch the board edge (thickness) while the triangle is slid firmly into the curve of the wrapped paper in the left-hand corner. With your knife, cut through the paper. Start the cut with the tip of the knife actually touching the board. Make a parallel cut, one board thickness away from the original cut. **Important:** Do not start this cut at the board. With the triangle repositioned, place the knife 1 ¹/₂ board thicknesses away from the board, and cut. With your knife, make a diagonal cut between the starting points of these two parallel cuts. This cut releases the sliver of paper—one board thickness in width—which allows the covering paper to be turned neatly into the inside of the tray. It also creates a mitered corner. Keeping the tray resting on its spine wall, repeat these cuts in the right-hand corner.

Turn the tray onto its fore-edge wall. Make the cuts, as described previously, in first the left and then the right-hand corners. **Note:** These cuts are made in only two of the tray's four walls. I have selected the opposite spine and fore-edge walls; you could pick the other pair of opposites, the head and tail walls. Your final cuts are made with scissors. Push the spine wall covering into the tray, pressing it against the inside wall and forcing the paper into the right-angle where the base meets the spine wall. Gently crease the paper by running your bone folder along this seam. Pull the paper back to the outside and cut away the two corners, removing 45-degree triangles of paper. Make sure the cuts stop at the crease mark made in the previous step. Repeat with the fore-edge wall.

(above middle) You are now ready to paste. Starting with the head, paste out the covering paper and push it to the inside, pressing it sharply into all seams. Rub with your bone folder to eliminate air bubbles and paste lumps. Repeat at the tail. (Since these two wall coverings have not had slivers of paper removed from them, they overlap the corners. This ensures that the cardboard seam will be covered.) Paste out the spine wall covering and press into place. Paste out the fore edge wall covering and press into place (above right).

box making basics:
corners and finishing edges

HOW TO COVER THE TRAY WITH CLOTH

When covering a small tray in cloth, I follow the same procedure described above, substituting mixture for paste.

When covering a large tray in cloth, I prefer to glue out the boards—one wall at a time—rather than the cloth, and to work a bit more slowly. Take care to press down the fabric well as you roll the tray on the cloth. Wrinkles in the cloth are more likely to develop if the cloth has not been saturated with the adhesive.

COVERING BOARDS: CUTTING CORNERS AND FINISHING EDGES

Cover papers and cloths are cut to extend $3/4$" (2 cm) beyond the edges of the board to be covered. This extension is called the "turn-in." Before the covering material is turned in, its corners must be cut. Both the angle of the cut and its distance from the tip of the board are crucial.

Apply adhesive to the covering material and press the board into position. Trim the corners at a 45-degree angle. The distance between the tip of the board and this cut should measure $1\,1/2$ times the thickness of the board. If you cut too closely, the tip of the board is exposed. If you cut too far away, the corner is klutzy. After cutting all corners, re-apply adhesive to the turn-ins if necessary.

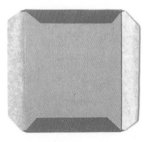

Starting with the head and tail, bring the turn-ins onto the board. First, using your bone folder, crease the material against the board edge. Second, flatten the material onto the board, pressing out any air pockets or bubbles. Use your thumbnail to pinch in the small sharp triangles of material at the corners. Press firmly so that the material hugs the corner and molds itself around the board tip. Now bring the spine and fore-edge turn-ins onto the board. With your folder, gently tap all corners, eliminating any sharp points or loose threads.

ALTERNATE CORNER COVERING FOR FRAGILE PAPERS

When wet, fragile or thin papers tend to tear. A universal or library corner involves no cutting and is recommended. This treatment is inappropriate for heavyweight papers or cloth; the resulting corner would be too bulky. After pasting the paper and centering the board on it, fold one corner triangle onto the board. Using your bone folder, shape the paper against the board thickness on both top (head) and side (fore-edge). Firmly press the remaining bits (right side of paper) onto the turn-ins below. Repeat at the other corners. With your finger, dab a dot of paste onto the turn-ins, near the corners. Complete the turn-ins (as in above directions). This corner covering yields a gentle, slightly rounded corner.

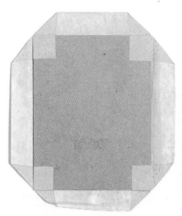

scrapbooking basics

BASIC STAMPING TOOL KIT

- **Stamps**
  Variety of images and sizes
  Alphabets

- **Inks and Inkpads**
  Dye-and pigment-based inkpads and reinkers
  Clear and tinted embossing inks and powders

- **Adhesives**
  Two-way glue pen
  Photo squares
  Paper adhesive
  Glue stick
  Removable tape

- **Cutting tools**
  Paper trimmer
  Paper edgers
  Straight blade 5" (13 cm) precision scissors
  Craft knife with extra blades
  Paper punches

- **Measuring and aligning tools**
  Transparent ruler marked in squares
  Cork-backed metal ruler
  Stamp positioner (optional)

- **Papers**
  Assorted cardstock in your favorite colors
  Handmade papers in a variety of textures
  Metallic and holographic sheets
  Inexpensive copy paper (the least expensive is usually the most absorbent)

- **Drawing and planning tools**
  No. 2 pencils, very sharp
  Art gum and white erasers
  Soft brush for eliminating eraser dust
  Fine-point black permanent marker

- **Miscellaneous tools**
  Stamp cleaner (spray or scrubber bottle)
  Long-handled tweezers
  Wooden skewers
  Heat tool for embossing
  Protective cutting mat
  Ink brayer or roller

photographs

The projects in this book might be considered art scrapbooks, and as such they utilize techniques and materials that are not always of archival quality. For that reason, you should not use your only copy of a photograph on the pages—save your priceless photographs in archival-safe storage boxes. If you have access to a home computer, with a good photo program and printer, use it with photographic paper or good copy paper to copy the photos. Today's copy centers and photo centers can be a great source of help with copying photographs in a variety of ways, and the personnel at these centers can often advise you on the best methods for obtaining great copies.

materials

The artists whose pages are presented here have used a wide range of stamping and scrapbooking materials for each project. Check the Resources section starting on page 296 for contact information about these products. In addition, you will need a basic kit of materials for constructing the pages. You may have most of these materials already, and others that work for you. The list at left is merely a suggested list of items that are handy to have on hand. By all means, substitute your own if you like.

stamping

Most of the stamping in this book is done with commercially purchased rubber stamps. They are readily available in stamp and craft stores, and through mail order and online merchants. You will find contact information for these companies in the Resources section starting on page 296.

Commercially manufactured rubber stamps come in an unlimited variety of styles, sizes, themes, and forms. The most common type is red rubber that has been mounted on a wooden block with the image illustrated on the opposite side (top) of the block. Some stamps are made of clear vinyl and mounted on Lucite blocks so you can see where you are stamping the image. Some stamps are sold unmounted, by the page; you can cut them apart and mount them yourself. You can also make your own stamps by carving into white erasers, foam blocks, potatoes, cork, and specially formulated stamp-carving blocks of linoleum or soft rubber.

To stamp an image, first pat the rubber side of the stamp on an inkpad or turn it rubber-side up and pat the stamp with the pad. Use an art pad, not an office inkpad. Pat until all the ridges are covered with ink. Turn it over and stamp gently on a sheet of non-glossy paper without moving the stamp once it has touched the surface. Let the stamp rest for a couple of seconds, then press over the entire wooden block with your fingertips to transfer the image. Lift the stamp directly up to avoid smears.

When finished stamping, or when changing colors, use a stamp cleaner to remove the ink and wipe with a paper towel. Baby wipes can be used as well, and glass cleaner in a spray bottle will work in a pinch. Don't immerse the stamps in water, or the adhesive may loosen and the stamp will come off the block. Always dry your stamps after cleaning and store them out of direct sunlight.

Keep your clean and dry stamps rubber-side down in a shallow container for easy access and prolonged life. Map chests with many shallow drawers are an excellent storage place for stamps. With care, your stamps will last for many years.

embossing

Embossed stamps are created with embossing ink, embossing powder, and heat with an embossing tool. Embossing inks are available clear, or with a tint so you can see where they have been stamped on the page. The tint will be covered completely, so its color will not show after embossing. The ink is sticky and stays moist longer than most other inks, but you need to work quickly for the best results. You may use pigment inks for embossing, although they don't stay moist quite as long as embossing inks and the result may not be as satisfactory.

To emboss an image, place your art paper on a large protective sheet of newsprint, cardboard, or other protective paper, then stamp with embossing ink. While the ink is wet, sprinkle liberally with embossing powder, covering all the ink. Check the labels for any special precautions or directions such as those found on extra-thick powders that are not recommended for detailed stampings. Pick up the sprinkled art paper and pour the extra powder back into the original container, tapping the paper to loosen the excess powder. This may be a lot easier with the help of a Tidy Tray (see Resources, page 296), which has a funnel built into one end just for this purpose. Turn on the heat tool and move it slowly across the embossing powder, holding the tool a few inches above the surface. The stamping will change before your eyes, and you can see when it's "done" because the powder will melt as you heat it.

There are many advanced techniques for embossing, and again the key is experimentation. Try new methods on scrap papers or cards before using them on your scrapbook pages.

tearing paper

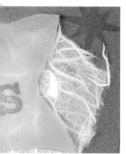

To create a ragged edge, use deckle paper edgers, or try tearing the paper. To tear, place a ruler on top of the paper where you want it torn and pull the excess paper up toward you while holding the ruler firmly in place. Different papers tear differently, and there are many metal and plastic rulers with deckle and other shapes made specifically for this edge treatment. Experiment on some blank papers, and try different tearing angles. To

simulate an aged look, sponge or lightly brush brown ink along the edges after tearing. Further age the appearance by wadding the paper then flattening it out to cause creasing.

shadow stamping

Although some artists define "shadow stamping" as the application of pale squares of color to a background, the term has evolved to include many other techniques. Before stamping an image, use the same stamp and very pale dye ink to create a shadow slightly to the right and below the position where the main image will go. Reink the stamp with pigment ink and stamp it over the shadow, allowing the shadow to show. For another method of shadow stamping, use pale inks on a background sheet to randomly stamp an image, then use a slightly darker color to stamp over the first impressions. Continue darkening or brightening the color as you stamp consecutive layers of the image, always allowing the palest images to show. This will create depth and interest.

faux batik

Batik is a decorative method traditionally used on fabric, but it can also be used on paper with a few simple modifications. Here is one method to try. On glossy cardstock, draw some linear designs with an Easter egg decorating crayon. (These are made with a much harder wax than the usual art crayons, and will form a better resist on paper.) After drawing the designs, paint or stamp some pigment inks over them. Place the paper on newsprint or several layers of paper towel, cover it with a sheet of typing paper to protect the surface of the iron, then iron the surface of the paper to melt the crayon. The paper will remain blank wherever the wax was applied.

monoprinting

Monoprints make beautiful and interesting backgrounds and middle grounds, as well as embellishments for scrapbook pages. They are one-of-a-kind artist prints that are much easier to create than their lofty name implies. The name "monoprint" is appropriate because each print is a single impression printed from paint or ink applied to a printing plate. For the pages in this book, the printing plate is a sheet of flexible vinyl and the color is often obtained from an inkpad or reinker.

GLUES AND ADHESIVES

Adhesives and glues that clean up with water are the best for paper because they are safe, convenient, and require no solvents. There are four basic types of adhesives for scrapbooks, and they come in several forms. The main types are dry, wet, heated, and sprays.

Dry adhesives include glue sticks, photo stickers and corners, and mounting tapes and sheets.

Wet adhesives may be applied with a brush or a toothpick, and some brands have fine-pointed applicators in their lids. Wet adhesives that are in liquid form may be thinned with water, or you can let them sit in an open container or saucer to thicken them. Easy-to-use glue pens resemble chisel point markers filled with glue instead of ink.

Heated glue is available in sticks that fit into glue guns. Sticks and chips can also be heated in electric dipping pots for large items. These pots were developed for the floral industry and are not generally recommended for paper projects because they are messy and the glue can leave a bumpy surface when cool.

Spray adhesives can be a good choice for mounting photos and other papers. Read the instructions to see if the glue sets immediately or if it needs to dry first. If possible, spray outdoors, using long-handled tweezers to hold and manipulate the item. Spray lightly on the back of a photo or paper shape. (Excess spraying is messy.)

stamp carving

There are many new products made specifically for carving stamps, including carving tools with comfortable wooden handles and interchangeable points. There are several sizes and types of carving blocks in craft and stamp stores, and these blocks are as easy as butter to cut. You can cut a stamp-carving block with a craft knife to make it a manageable size, and you can carve images on the front, the back, and even the edges. Start by lightly penciling a design onto the block—remember that it will be a mirror image of the impression—and then carve away the background. Use knitting needles, kitchen tools, awls, and other implements to make your carvings unique. Start with a simple design. You can draw it first on plain paper then use graphite paper to transfer the image to the block. You can also draw a design on paper, cut it out, and trace around it onto the block. Always try your hand-carved stamps on scrap paper first, to be sure the lines are clear and the background has been deeply carved.

craft knife cutting

It's always best to use a self-healing cutting mat with your craft knife. It will protect the work surface and make it easier to cut all the way through paper or matte board. If possible, stand up while cutting with a craft knife, and always use a sharp blade. To cut a straight line, use a cork-lined metal ruler and pull the knife toward you along its edge. For foam core or thick matte board, score the surface first, then go over the score lines with hard pressure.

paper edgers

There are dozens of decorative edges available in scissors-like paper edgers. Try a few in a variety of designs to get started, then add to your collection as you go. For the best results with these edgers, begin by cutting out a photograph or a shape with straight scissors or a craft knife just a little larger than you wish the finished piece to be, then trim the straight edge with the decorative blades. Cut almost to the end of the blade, then reset your edgers, matching up the curves in the blades with the part you've already cut, and finish the edge a little at a time.

air-dry modeling clay

When you need a special stamp shape, make your own from clay. A modeling compound made for kids will air-dry overnight with very little shrinkàge, and it remains flexible (see Resources, page 296). Knead this moist, white clay and roll it out between sheets of waxed paper to about ⅛" to ¼" (3 mm to 5 mm) thick. Use cookie cutters or a craft knife to form the shapes you want, then score them and add texture with a stylus. You can also impress the clay surface with things found around the house such as a tea strainer, a cheese grater, carved jewelry, pressed glass, or other object. Let the clay shapes dry overnight, then ink them and use as stamps. This technique is shown in the journal on page 267.

sponges

Natural kitchen and cosmetic sponges make interesting impressions, particularly for backgrounds. Dip them into paint or tap on an inkpad and apply to paper or cardstock. Use them as they come, or pinch off bits to create the shape needed or to disguise the straight edges of the sponges. Keep the sponge shapes simple and always try them out on scrap paper first.

mica chips

Mica chips, or embossing tiles, are available in large, intermediate, and small sizes. You can cut them, stamp on them, foil or paint them, or just enjoy them without altering their surface. Glue them on or drill holes and attach with screws or fine coiled wire. Transparent pieces of mica were used on the travel journal on page 268.

coloring techniques and tools

Colored pencils come in many forms, including oil, chalk, watercolor, and more. All are valuable tools for adding color to your pages, and most are sold with some instruction. Try them all and find the ones that you like best. Great backgrounds can also be created with direct stamping methods by lightly applying small cube or other inkpads directly to the cardstock or paper, using a slight twisting motion. This technique can be combined with brushing or sponging more ink over the top, or using daubers to refine the color on the page.

mesh

You can use metal screen from the hardware store, plastic canvas mesh, and various mesh materials from your kitchen or garage to create interesting patterns by spraying or daubing ink through the holes. The project on pages 194 and 195 is a beautiful example of this method. Meshes in a variety of patterns are available in stamp specialty stores and through on-line merchants.

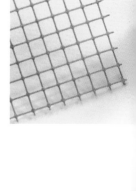

lettering methods

A variety of alphabet stamps are available, and their number is growing every day. Some are good for creating words and phrases because of their size and simplicity, and others are highly decorative, reminiscent of ancient illuminated manuscripts. You will find examples of both in the lettering chapter. Some of the most charming pages are those that include hand lettering. Your family and friends will treasure those pages the most because they impart a bit of yourself and they show that you care enough to take extra time. The quickest and easiest lettering method may be letter stickers or rub-ons, and with a little extra attention they can be very effective. Try embellishing them with stamps and dyes, and place shadow backgrounds around them with chalk or sponged ink.

scrapbooking basics

ARTIST: BETTY AUTH

Creating Layouts

There are thousands of possibilities for layouts on scrapbook pages, and a great number of ideas are presented in this book. The main element of a good scrapbook layout is simplicity. Even though the techniques may be complicated and embellishments applied layer after layer, the basic framework should remain simple.

Study the examples in the various chapters and notice how the page elements relate to one another, then adapt them to your own pages even if the themes are entirely different.

If you are designing a double-page spread where both pages are visible at once, plan the layout so some of the elements cross over from the left page to the right. This will help tie the two pages together and make them more cohesive.

To Make the Page at Left

Use a gold cat's-eye inkpad to stamp directly on a sheet of deep lavender cardstock, swirling the pad as you go over the page. Sponge on some burgundy pigment ink in the same way, folding the sponge to eliminate straight edges. Stamp the large, lacy leaves with purple pigment ink. Stamp the letters with purple ink on red cardstock and cut them out with paper edgers. Glue the letters onto a piece of gold cardstock and cut it into the shape of a banner. With a paintbrush and a dark neutral chalk or ink, stipple some shadows under the letters. Glue the banner onto the background.

QUICK TRICK

Make some inexpensive black and white copies of your photographs in several sizes. Use those to plan your page layout. Move them around and choose the most appropriate sizes before actually stamping or gluing the page.

To Make the Page at Right

Here is a wonderful idea for including many small photographs on a single scrapbook page. Small, round adhesive-backed ink-jet printer stickers are stamped with a diploma image then colored with markers. The photographs are cut into circles and stuck to the backs of the diploma stickers. A sheet of cardstock has been covered with background stampings and embossing. Slots are cut into the cardstock page with a craft knife and the photo circles are inserted into them. A matte board spine is attached to the page's left edge so it can be inserted into a three-ring binder.

Every page begins with a layout. You may have a plan, a sketch, or even a template to follow when placing the various parts on a page. Or it may all occur by just moving the elements around on a blank background and choosing what looks best. The arrangement of those elements—photographs, words, colors, and decorative additions like stamped images—makes up the layout. As you study the artist pages throughout the book, think about the construction of the page, and try to see the basic layout that each artist used. Look for simplicity, balance, and use of color.

ARTIST: SUSAN JAWORSKI STRANC

Stamp an image onto plain, adhesive-backed stickers.

BABIES CHANGE SO FAST. One day they're tiny infants cooing in a bassinet, and the next thing you know, they're toddling off in search of the remote control. Photos are a great way to document this exciting time, and most families keep busy snapping photos during a baby's first year. Most people choose to display their photographs freely in frames or on the fridge, but there are many ways to

Baby Memories

combine photos into a larger keepsake, such as in the First-Year Memory Frame.

In addition to preserving your memories from this time, we've also come up with some ways to save these earliest stories for the baby to look back at as he or she grows up. For example, the Baby Memories Envelope Book provides a wonderful place to stash handwritten family notes, newspaper clippings, and other memorabilia from that first year that will surely be enjoyed when explored in the years to come.

Baby's Stories

There are two kinds of stories to keep for babies. The first are the stories of the family's accomplishments, disappointments, and personalities that make up the baby's history. Surround your newest family member with photos of family and friends. Have members of your extended family write a story or wish, and bind them in a book or collect them in a box. Videotape or record the voices of special people for the little one to listen to and watch as he or she gets older. Write family quotes on fabric with textile markers and sew the fabric into a quilt or wall hanging. Convert some family photos into slides, and hang them from a lamp shade in the baby's room. Create keepsake boxes, which will become treasures to hold all these special things.

The second type of story is unique to the infant—his or her own story in the making. Parents, grandparents, and siblings can all collect and preserve items for the baby's story.

Save newspapers, magazines, and other printed material from the day and month of your child's birth. Pack a small suitcase with items that may be significant as he or she travels through life: the outfit her mother wore to bring her home from the hospital, crepe paper decorations her big brother made to celebrate her christening, pressed flowers from an arrangement at his bris. Growth and change can be fun to document, too. Press a tiny thumbprint into a soft lump of polymer clay, and bake it for a permanent reminder of the tiny hands long after they've grown.

Newborns don't usually have stories to tell, but the family who surrounds the crib listening to their coos and gurgles does. Encourage the members of your extended family—and friends, too—to write a special story or memory for your newest family member. Create this envelope book to hold the reminiscences for the day when your child can read them herself. You can also send the envelopes with blank paper and a request for a story to all your family members. Bind the envelopes—stamps, postmarks, and all—into a book. This book is made out of small square envelopes, but you can use any size you like. See page 286 for a variation of this project.

Baby Memories Envelope Book

MATERIALS

- pastel vellum paper
- square envelope templates
- Rollabind hand punch and binding rings
- ribbon
- clear plastic file folder (available at office supply stores)
- double-sided tape (clear)
- hole punch
- small piece of cardstock
- small sheet of coordinating solid paper
- rubber stamp, embossing ink, and silver embossing powder
- silver metallic marker
- diaper pin (optional)

1. Using a 5" (13 cm)-square envelope template, make approximately eight envelopes using the pastel vellum.

2. Cut a $5\frac{1}{4}$" x $5\frac{3}{8}$" (13 cm x 14 cm) piece of the plastic file folder for the cover. Cut a piece of cardstock the same size for the back cover.

3. Center the hand punch on the side edge of each envelope, and punch holes for the binding rings. Repeat with the front and back covers. Line up the holes, and insert the rings to bind the envelopes between the covers.

4. Create a 2" (5 cm)-square envelope out of a coordinating solid paper using an envelope template. Punch two holes in the center of the envelope, and insert ribbon ends from front to back, and then forward through the holes to end in the front. Using a rubber stamp, embossing ink, and silver embossing powder, create the raised baby pin art. Write your baby's name on the envelope.

5. Tape the small envelope in the center of the front cover using clear double-sided tape.

6. Stamp the baby pin with white ink on a piece of vellum the same size as the cover, to create an all-over effect. Insert the stamped vellum sheet directly underneath the clear plastic front cover.

7. Add a ribbon and a diaper pin to the disks by first drilling a hole in one ring with a small hand drill, and then threading the ribbon through the hole.

Keepsake Tip

Family members can write special stories and insert them in their own envelopes. Envelopes can be added or removed at any time.

family stories for Katie

Design: Janet Pensiero

I knew from the minute that I saw my first great nephew, Chase, that the camera loved his face. I created this project for his mother, Amanda, to document his first year, because babies change and grow so much during that time. You can adapt this idea for just about any subject—the first year of school, a sports season, or a memorable vacation or trip. You can be sure that it will be cherished forever.

First-Year Memory Frame

MATERIALS

- picture frame, for an 8" x 10" (20 cm x 25 cm) picture with 3" (8 cm) width
- spray paint (color of your choice)
- 12 glass squares, 2" x 2" x ⅛" (51 mm x 51 mm x 3 mm)
- one package of dried flowers and greenery
- self-adhesive silver foil tape, ¼" (6 mm) width
- 12 color photocopies to be cut to 2" x 2" (5 cm x 5 cm)
- photograph, 8" x 10" (20 cm x 25 cm)
- acid-free glue
- white glue
- scissors
- clear tape
- tweezers
- ballpoint pen

1. Spray-paint the frame, following the directions on the can. Cover the frame thoroughly.

2. Using a glass square as a template, draw a cutting line around each photocopy by tracing around the edge of the glass with a ballpoint pen. Then cut out each picture.

3. Use the tweezers to add the dried flowers and greenery to the corners of each picture with the white glue.

4. Secure each cut-out photocopy to a glass square with a small piece of clear tape on the top and bottom. Once the glass is in place, cut 2" (5 cm) pieces of the silver foil tape. You will need eight pieces of the silver foil tape per picture. Adhere one piece at a time to each side of the front of the picture. Then flip the square over, tape all four sides of the back to the frame, and seal each picture.

5. Carefully spread a thin, even coat of the acid-free glue to the back of each glass square and photocopy piece, and glue the squares over the entire frame.

6. Insert the 8" x 10" (20 cm x 25 cm) photograph in the frame.

Design: Connie Sheerin

I asked my mother to look through her collections to find items to inspire me for this book. Amazingly, she found the first curl that was cut from my locks when I was almost two years old. She had sent the curl to my grandmother, and it had eventually found its way back to my mother. Now that I'm in my "goddess" years, that first curl seems even more important. I especially loved my grandmother's handwritten date on the envelope and my pictures—both before the curl was clipped and after, at my second birthday. Embellish your shadowbox with any special objects, from a favorite toy to a tiny shoe to a baby spoon.

Baby Keepsake Shadow Box

MATERIALS

- color photocopies of baby's memorable events
- small items symbolizing infancy
- textured acid-free background paper
- Plexiglas box frame with a white cardboard box insert
- archival glue
- white craft glue
- one package of dried flowers and greenery
- tweezers
- craft knife
- lace and trim
- double-sided tape
- sawtooth hanger

1. Cut out the front of the cardboard box insert with a craft knife, and use the archival glue to cover the inside of the box with the textured acid-free paper. Make sure to cover up to the edges of the box—you can use lace and trim to hide any rough edges. Be careful not to make the edge too thick because the cardboard insert needs to fix back inside the Plexiglas frame when you are finished.

2. Arrange and glue down all of the pieces you have gathered. Use the archival glue for photocopies and a thick white glue for the small objects.

3. Use the tweezers and the archival glue to attach some dried flowers and greenery for embellishment.

4. Clean the Plexiglas carefully, and slide the cardboard insert back inside the box frame to finish the shadow box.

5. Use double-sided tape or glue to attach a sawtooth hanger so you can hang the box on wall. You can also prop it up on an easel.

Keepsake Tip

These inexpensive box frames are available in many discount and craft stores in a wide selection of sizes. To determine the size of frame that you'll need, lay out all the items and photocopies that you want to include.

Design: Connie Sheerin

Chase Joseph Cole came into this world in September 2000. His mother, my niece Amanda, gave the family the first baby in 22 years—what a joy! A new baby truly warms the heart and brings everyone together to celebrate life. This is a special box for my grandnephew to help his mother begin saving the wonderful things that make memories. This box can be customized to fit just about any special moment in life to hold the trinkets that mean so much as the years go by.

Chase's Memory Box

MATERIALS

- hinged wooden box, 11" x 4" x 3" (28 cm x 11 cm x 8 cm)
- baby-motif floral container
- three bags of ¾" (2 cm) tiles (one each of baby blue, white, and yellow)
- mosaic glue
- craft stick
- tile nippers
- baby blue acrylic paint
- black permanent felt-tip marker
- one bag of miniature star and moon decorations
- four white drawer pulls
- one white button
- buttercream sanded grout
- sandpaper
- graphite paper
- clean soft cloth

1. Lightly sand the wooden box, and apply two coats of baby blue acrylic paint, both inside and out.

2. To create the mosaic pattern for the top of the box, first nip the floral container into small pieces to create the main animal images. Arrange these pieces, leaving space between them to fill in with the colored tiles. When you are happy with the design, glue the pieces to the box using mosaic glue.

3. Fill in the spaces with the blue, white, and yellow tiles, nipped into the appropriate size, and secure them with mosaic glue. Finish off the edge of the box by alternating the colored tiles cut to fit around the lid edge.

4. Mix the grout according to the directions on the package until it is a fudge-like consistency. Then add the baby blue paint to the grout, a few drops at a time, and continue to mix it until you get it the shade you desire (the grout will dry a bit lighter). The grout is ready to use when its consistency is firm, but moist. Grout the mosaic, let it dry for 15 minutes, and then wipe with a soft cloth. Wait another 15 minutes, and you will see a haze appear. Clean off the rest of the excess grout, and polish the mosaic with a clean soft cloth. Allow the grout to dry overnight.

5. Make a paper pattern of the side of the box, and hand-letter the child's name on the pattern. Then use the graphite paper to trace your lettering onto the box. Go over the lettering with a black permanent felt-tip marker.

6. Glue the white button to the lid of the box to create a handle. Glue the decorations for embellishment. Glue the four white drawer pulls to the bottom of the box to act as feet.

Keepsake Tip

Check out yard sales and thrift stores for baby-motif floral containers or drawer pulls for the feet. If the drawer pulls aren't the right color, you can always paint over them to coordinate with the broken tiles used on the top.

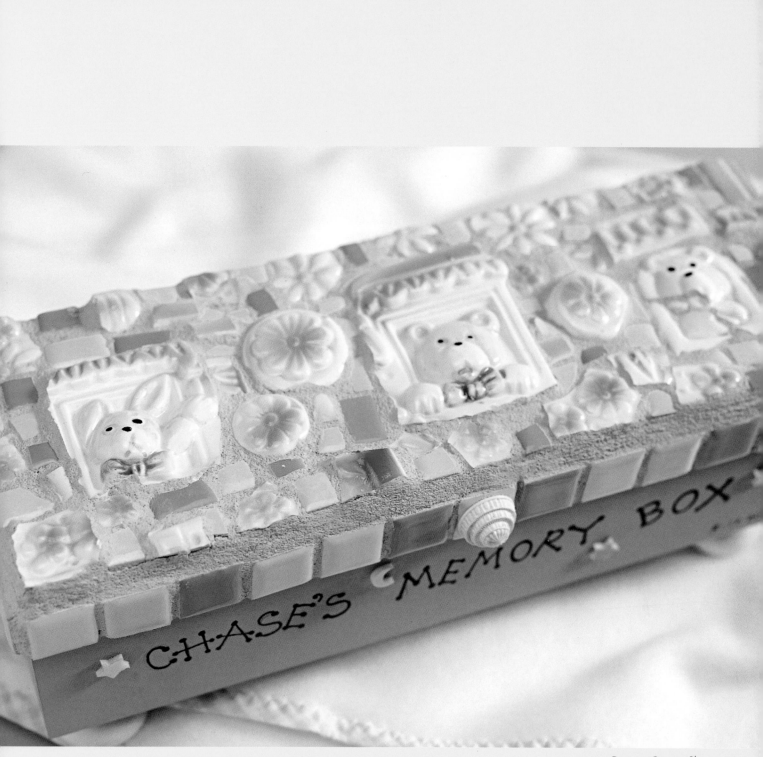

Design: Connie Sheerin

Everyone has some pictures that they'd like to frame in a special way. A unique and lasting method of displaying a favorite picture is to put it into a paperweight that can be propped up on an easel or just placed on a desk or end table. For a unique twist, try starting with black-and-white pictures, and hand-color them first.

Baby's Paperweight

MATERIALS

- glass tile, 4" x 4" x ³⁄₄" (10 cm x 10 cm x 2 cm)
- color photocopies of pictures and smaller head shots
- Liquid Laminate
- rubber gloves
- decoupage scissors
- mat board, cut slightly smaller than the glass tile
- felt for backing or round felt feet
- black, fine-line, permanent, acid-free pen
- damp paper towel
- metal easel (optional)
- archival glue

1. Make color photocopies of your pictures. Then cut and arrange the photocopies on the mat board, working from the background to the foreground.

2. After you have arranged your pictures and trimmed them to fit, glue the design together using the archival glue.

3. Use the black fine-line pen to add any written comments or memories.

4. Put on the rubber gloves and quickly cover your composition and the glass tile with the Liquid Laminate. Lay the glass tile over your composition, and press down, using the damp paper towel to wipe up any excess Liquid Laminate. Force the extra liquid from the center of the glass out to the sides. Wipe the tile clean, and let it dry.

5. After the Liquid Laminate has dried, cover the back of the composition with a piece of felt or add felt feet.

6. You can display this little masterpiece on a metal easel or on your desk.

Design: Connie Sheerin

Some photographs, such as these four of a sweet boy named Nicholas, are meant to be displayed rather than hidden away in albums. The Picture Frame Box is a wonderful way to celebrate a specific event—a birth, a graduation, a marriage. A cross between a book and a box, this extended case unfolds, accordion-style, to reveal the four photographs framed within. Make the interior as decorative as possible, and freely mix other mementos, such as birth announcements or fragments of letters, in with the photographs. My preferred covering material is a specific Japanese paper called Momi, *which has the strength and the folding qualities of cloth.*

picture frame box...
memories of a special child

MATERIALS

Two-ply museum board, for mats	Decorative papers (mats)	Grosgrain ribbon
Binder's board, for case	Decorative papers (linings)	Mylar
Momi paper	Two bone clasps (also called *tsume*)	Glue, mixture and paste

getting started:
cutting the boards and windows

- Cut the museum board to make four mats. Cut board to desired height and width. Make sure grain runs parallel with the spine edge.
- Cut out the windows in the mats. The windows should be approximately ¹/₂" (1 cm) smaller in both height and width than the photos.

ABOUT MOMI PAPERS   These papers are tough enough to be substituted for fabric, but they require special handling. The beauty of these color-saturated papers is in their crinkly surface. If the paper becomes too relaxed—for example, by the application of paste—the crinkles flatten out and the wonderful texture is lost. The solution to this problem is threefold: (1) use mixture instead of paste; (2) apply the mixture to the board rather than to the paper; and (3) don't be too aggressive with your bone folder.

1

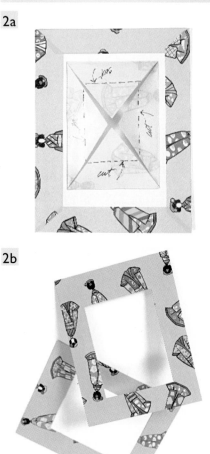

2a

2b

1   Cover the mats. Cut four pieces of decorative paper:

Height = height of mat plus 1¹/₂" (4 cm)
Width = width of mat plus 1¹/₂" (4 cm)

2a   PASTE OUT THE PAPER. Center the mat on the paper and press into place. Cut the corners and finish the edges. (see The Basics, page 32). To finish the interior of the mat, make two diagonal cuts, from corner to corner, through the paper in the windows. Remember that wet paper tends to tear when being cut. If your paper is saturated with paste, give it a few minutes to dry before cutting.

2b   Prior to pasting these flaps into position on the back of the mats, trim away excess paper with your scissors. Paste. Place the covered mats between sheets of newsprint, and under a board and a weight until dry.

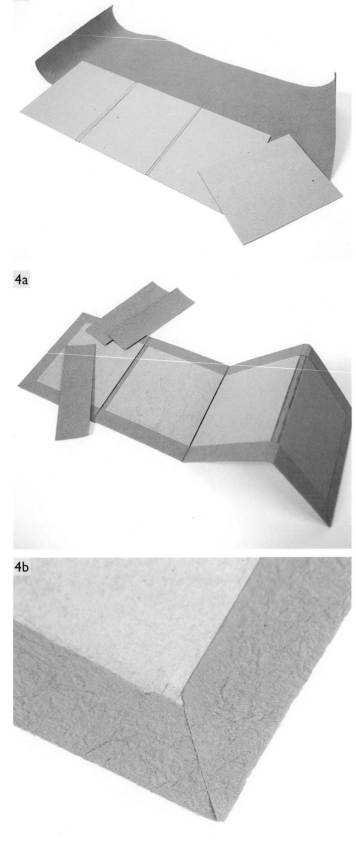

3

3 CUT THE BOARDS FOR THE CASE. Cut four pieces of binder's board:

Height = height of mats plus two board thicknesses
Width = width of mats plus two board thicknesses

From your scrap board, cut two joint spacers. Different spacers are required because, as the accordion closes, the first and the last joints must accommodate more bulk than the middle joint.
Spacer 1 (for first and last joints) = two binder's board thicknesses plus two mat thicknesses plus $^1/_{16}$" (.15 cm)
Spacer 2 (for middle joint) = two binder's board thicknesses

4a CONSTRUCT THE CASE. Cut a piece of Momi paper large enough to accommodate the four case boards and the joint spacers. Add a $^3/_4$" (2 cm) turn-in allowance around all four edges. Brush mixture onto the case boards and gently press them into position on the paper, leaving the proper joint spaces between the boards. Cut the corners (see The Basics, page 32). Applying your mixture sparingly, glue the head turn-in.

4b Bring the paper onto the boards and, with the edge of your bone folder, gently press the paper into the three joints. Pinch in the paper at the corners. Repeat with tail turn-in. Complete the spine and fore edge turn-ins.

CUT THREE HINGE STRIPS FROM THE MOMI PAPER.
Height = height of case boards minus $^1/_4$" (.5 cm)
Width = 2" (5 cm)

Stipple the mixture onto one hinge strip and, centering this strip, gently press the paper into the joints and onto the boards. Repeat with the other two hinges. Put the case aside to dry, flat, under a light weight.

5a

5b

5c

5d

5a ATTACH THE BONE CLASPS. Position the four mats on the case and close the case. Thread the ribbons through the slits in the bone clasps and place the clasps in the desired location on the front of the case. Mark the front of the case with four pinpricks, one on each side of the two clasps directly below their slits. (To make sure the clasps end up level with each other, make all marks on a pattern and then transfer these marks to your case.) Open up the case, remove the mats, and place the case right side up on a scrap board. Select a chisel to match the width of your ribbons.

Holding the chisel vertically, make four parallel chisel cuts (two per clasp), starting at the pinpricks and chiseling downward.

5b Angle the ends of two short pieces of ribbon and push down through the cuts, to form receiving loops for the clasps. Slide the clasps into the loops. Adjust the ribbons for a snug fit. Guide the main ribbons to the back of the case; mark for their insertion (again, with a pinprick or pattern). Make one vertical slit per ribbon.

5c Adjust the ribbons to make them taut. (Be sure the mats are inside the case

as you make these adjustments.) On the inside of the case, spread the ribbon ends in opposite directions.

5d With your knife, trace the outline of the ribbons, cutting and peeling up a shallow layer of board. Glue the ribbons into these recesses, using undiluted PVA. Make it as smooth as possible.

6

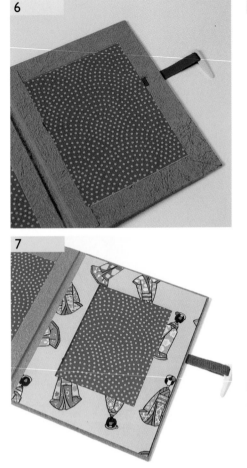

7

8

6 LINE THE CASE. Cut four pieces of decorative paper to fit within the case turn-ins. Paste out the papers and apply them to the case. Press the case, between newsprint and boards, under a light weight.

7 ATTACH THE MATS. The mats are glued to the case along three edges; the fourth edge is kept unglued, to allow for the insertion of the photographs. Glue backs of mats as follows (see diagram):

Mat 1: Glue out the head, tail, and the long edge of the mat that will sit near the outer edge of the case (i.e., away from the joint). Use undiluted PVA, masking off areas of the mat to be kept glue free with narrow strips of scrap paper. Brush the glue approximately ¹/₂" (1 cm) onto the mats. Center the mat on the case board, pressing down along the edges with your bone folder. Carefully scoop away any seeping glue with a micro-spatula.

Mats 2 and 3: Glue out the head, tail, and the long edge of the mat that will sit near the middle joint. Continue as with mat 1.

Mat 4: Follow the process as with mat 1.

When all four mats have been glued to the case, press the case by placing it between newsprint and boards, and under a light weight.

8 CUT FOUR PIECES OF MYLAR, approximately 1" (3 cm) smaller than the mats in both height and width. Slide the Mylar under the mats. Insert photos under the Mylar.

Apply glue to shaded areas.

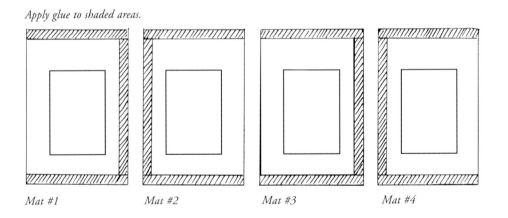

Mat #1   *Mat #2*   *Mat #3*   *Mat #4*

Tip: *How to Back Fabric*

MATERIALS   Cloth (lightweight cotton, handkerchief linen, silk)

Japanese tissue, such as mulberry paper

Paste (thick!)

Water, in a spritzer bottle

It is thrilling to transform special fabrics—
a piece of a wedding dress, a quirky 1930s
cotton print, an old silk scarf—into bookcloth.
The method is simple, involving a bowl of
paste and a sheet of Japanese paper. In contrast
to the whimsically patterned silk used here,
the case was lined with discarded pages from
a botanical book found at a flea market.

1. Test your fabric for permanency of dyes.
Wet a small piece. If the colors run, stop!
Check out alternative backing techniques,
such as those involving heat-set tissues.

2. Cut away the selvage from the fabric.

3. Cut a piece of Japanese tissue approximately 1" (3 cm) larger than the fabric on
all four sides. Make sure the grain direction
of fabric and paper is the same.

4. Place the fabric, right side down, on a
non-porous surface (glass, Formica, Plexiglas).
Spritz the cloth with water until it is fully
saturated. Straighten the grain and smooth
away wrinkles.

5. Paste out the sheet of Japanese tissue.

6. Hold a ruler over the short edge of the
pasted paper, approximately $1/2$" (1 cm) and
parallel with that edge. Give the ruler a quick
press onto the paper. You are, briefly, pasting
the ruler to the paper so that when you
pick up the ruler the paper will adhere to
it and be easily lifted off your workbench.

7. Lift and position the paper (pasted side
down) on the fabric and slowly lower it onto
the material. Don't place it down all at once,
or you will trap huge air bubbles.

8. Draw a stiff dry brush across the surface
of the paper, pressing to ensure a tight bond
and to remove air bubbles.

9. Paste out the four edges of the paper
that extend beyond the edges of the fabric.
Stick down, onto one of these edges, a small
piece (1"–2"; 3–5 cm) of heavyweight
paper. This will become a lifting tab when the
fabric has dried.

10. Carefully peel the backed fabric off
your workbench and reverse it onto a drying
surface. (Keep a sheet of Plexiglas in your
studio for just this purpose. It can be put aside
while the fabric is drying and not occupy
valuable workbench space.) Make sure
the four pasted edges are well adhered to
the surface.

11. When the fabric has dried, slide the
micro-spatula behind the paper tab and peel
the fabric away from the board. Wash the
drying surface with warm, soapy water.

Newborn Baby Box

The moment the cheery stork delivers that special package to a doorstep, a baby memory book follows right behind. Packed with pages documenting all the pertinent details, the scrapbook becomes a crucial aspect to mommies and daddies who want to preserve the miracle. Somewhere in the mix of sorting the memorabilia, there are always leftover items such as wrapping paper from gifts, the baby's first diaper pin, shower party favors, and cake decorations. These tiny, underestimated odds and ends are the perfect adornments for a loving shadow box specially designed for that tiny bundle of joy.

Materials

8½" × 8½" × 1" (22 cm × 22 cm × 3 cm) shadow box

Miniature dollhouse dresser

Handmade papers

White, pink, yellow, and blue glue

3 miniature baby photos

2" (5 cm) baby photo

Photo ornament

Baby shower keepsakes: wrapping paper, cake decorations, diaper pins, and party favors

Cotton handkerchief

Craft foam

Ribbon

Wood banner

Acrylic paint in white

Acrylic accent paint in pink or blue

Scalloped scissors

Basic craft supplies

1) Apply a base coat of white acrylic paint to the entire box and the miniature dresser. Sand the edges if desired to give it an aged look. Use scalloped scissors to cut the handmade paper into strips. Use a glue stick to apply these to the border of the box's frame.

2) Adhere the wrapping paper by decoupage to the interior of the box. Take the mini dresser and stock it with some of the keepsakes. Cut the handkerchief into small squares and fold them to look like diapers. Accent the dresser with the pink or blue paint.

3) Glue the dresser in the box center and the banner at the top of the frame. Gently rip a circle from the handmade paper and attach it to the back of the 2" (5 cm) baby photo, then place it in the center of the banner.

4) Cut small images from wrapping paper and adhere them to the craft foam to create a colorful border edge. Carefully glue these along the banner and around the frame, interspersed between more small baby pictures.

5) Attach the hanging ornament with a ribbon at the bottom of the box. Add a sawtooth picture hanger for displaying.

TIPS
• Make color copies if you prefer not to use originals.
• Apply the photos to wood discs to create a lifted, dimensional effect.

VARIATION
Instead of a square shadow box, use a circular wall hanging and line with it with lace or beads.

Dimensions 8½" X 8½" X 1" (22 cm X 22 cm X 3 cm)   **Artist** Kathy Cano-Murillo

Birthday Boy: Embossed Background Page

ARTIST: DAWN HOUSER

This lively and cheerful background is perfect for portraying the mood and theme of a child's first birthday—it practically sings with joy and celebration.

To Make the Page at Left

To make the background, first use thinned acrylic paints or watercolors to paint a band of color at the top and the bottom of the background cardstock. Allow the paint to dry. Cut a mask of copy paper or cardstock the size and shape of the photograph and stick it to the center of the page with removable adhesive. Choose a square stamp with a small, allover pattern and cover the entire page, a little at a time, by stamping and embossing one area then moving on to the next. Be sure to stamp over the edges of the photo mask. When the page is covered, remove the mask. Mount the photo on a slightly larger block of cardstock and mount it in the masked-off area on the page. Stamp and emboss the letters and other elements separately, then cut them out and glue in place.

STAMPING TRICK

Plan ahead when making background paper and stamp an entire page (or several pages), even if you only need part of it for the page you are constructing. Put the extra pieces into your stash of scraps for later use.

Embossing Help

A tray with built-in funnel can be very helpful when embossing. Stamp the paper or cardstock with embossing ink, then place it in the tray and liberally pour on the embossing powder. Pick up the paper, holding it over the tray, and tap the excess powder into the tray, then use the funnel to pour the powder back into its original container. Wipe off the inside of the tray and put the paper back in while you use the heat tool to emboss the piece. For 8 ½" × 11" (22 cm × 28 cm) sheets, choose the larger tray.

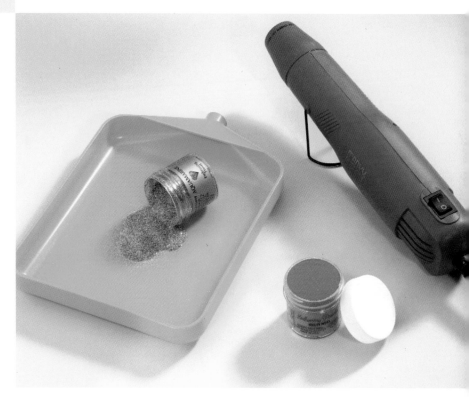

Flower Babies: Accents as Frames

ARTIST: SANDRA McCALL

You can embellish a frame by adding one or more paper appliqués. Here, single and multiple images are stamped on a separate sheet of paper, then cut out and glued partially over the edge of the photographs and the background. The pink and fuchsia flowers surrounding the sweet faces enhance these adorable baby photos.

This method allows the freedom to experiment with colors and shapes before committing to a particular design. You can stamp many flowers, hearts, stars and other shapes on white paper, cut them out, then sprinkle them on the pages of your scrapbook, only gluing down the ones you like.

MATERIALS

- **Stamps**

  Small flowers

  Large oak leaf, leaf spray and fern

- **Ink and ink pads**

  Small petal shaped and Cat's Eye pigment ink pads

  Magenta to green dye inks

- **Papers**

  One sheet plum cardstock

  Two sheets white cardstock

  One or two sheets pale yellow paper

  Two or three sheets white copy paper

- **Miscellaneous**

  Scissors

  Household bleach

  Paper towels

  Large nylon paint brush or brayer

QUICK TRICK

When making copies of your photographs, print several different sizes, including some as small as postage stamps, so you can arrange them in a variety of ways before affixing them to the page. Repeating the same image in several sizes can be used to focus the eye where you want it to go for maximum impact.

Getting Started

Step 1

Protect your work surface and wear old clothing since you'll be using bleach. Start with a sheet of light colored cardstock. You could also try a matte copier paper or art paper.

Step 2

Press the small pigment ink pads directly on the paper, alternating and turning them as you work to swirl the colors all over the page. Rub the colors into the paper with paper towels.

Step 3

Paint or brayer dark magenta to green dye ink over the surface, covering the pigment ink.

Step 4

Pour the bleach into several layers of folded paper towels in a dish and pat the stamps on the bleach as you would use an ink pad. Stamp off most of the dye ink, revealing the leaf patterns in pigment ink underneath. The bleach will lighten as it dries, and you can speed the process with a hair dryer or heat tool. Rinse stamps immediately in cool running water and dry them.

Making the Flowers

Stamp the flower images on white cardstock using dye ink, and cut them out leaving small white margins around them so they will stand out from the page.

Finishing the Page

Up to seven layers of paper are used in some areas of this precious scrapbook page. Layer successively smaller sheets of plum, yellow, and faux batik papers. Mount the photographs in various sizes on white cardstock and cut them out with a narrow white margin. Place the photographs on the background and sprinkle flowers around the page to tie it all together. Make the labels from pale yellow cardstock.

Every year and for
every occasion we
buy Pop a couple of
ties. And every time
he gets dressed up he
wears one of the ties
that we got him.
Matt Carr

PHOTOGRAPHS, ARTWORK, AND OTHER CHERISHED ITEMS can bring back memories of celebrations, of milestones, and of difficult times—all of which make up the experience of growing up. Turning these items into household keepsakes—such as pillows, bowls, and doorstops—not only gives you time to relish the memories that they help you recall but also gives a whole new life to objects that might

Growing Up

otherwise have been cast away and forgotten. These memories of childhood can spark the fire of youth and vitality in your crafts, which can then be passed to others who share in your treasures.

The Family Home

The projects in this chapter represent the "crevices" in the tree trunk of life—those odd things that you discover as you delve through old boxes, which may seem insignificant but still remind you of deeply rooted experiences. From children's artwork to favorite books, this chapter will certainly remind you of some of those growing-up memories, as well as inspire you to create some very special projects. Adapt the projects so that you can use the unique items found among your own possessions.

The doorstop made of a brick from the house I grew up in is one of my all-time favorite projects. Including the general history of the house in the final project greatly interested my entire family, especially the grandchildren. They are now young adults, and as children they played for many hours in that house, but they never really knew its history. My mother, now in her eighties, is such a great storyteller, and fortunately for me, she was able to straighten out and fill in facts to many family stories for me. Special thanks to our family matriarch! Take the time to discuss your memories with older members of the family to see what unique details they can add—you may discover startling and wonderful details.

Houses are so special, especially when families have spent several decades in them raising more than one generation. Something is always happening in these homes—the first day of school, a prom, a wedding day, and the bringing home of the first grandchild. This special doorstop means a great deal to my family, and it can make a wonderful housewarming gift for anyone of any age. After all, your home is your castle for storing treasured memories. What objects remind you of your first home? Perhaps you have also saved some part of it, or some of the treasures that had a place there. Those objects can help you get started on projects reminiscent of your early years.

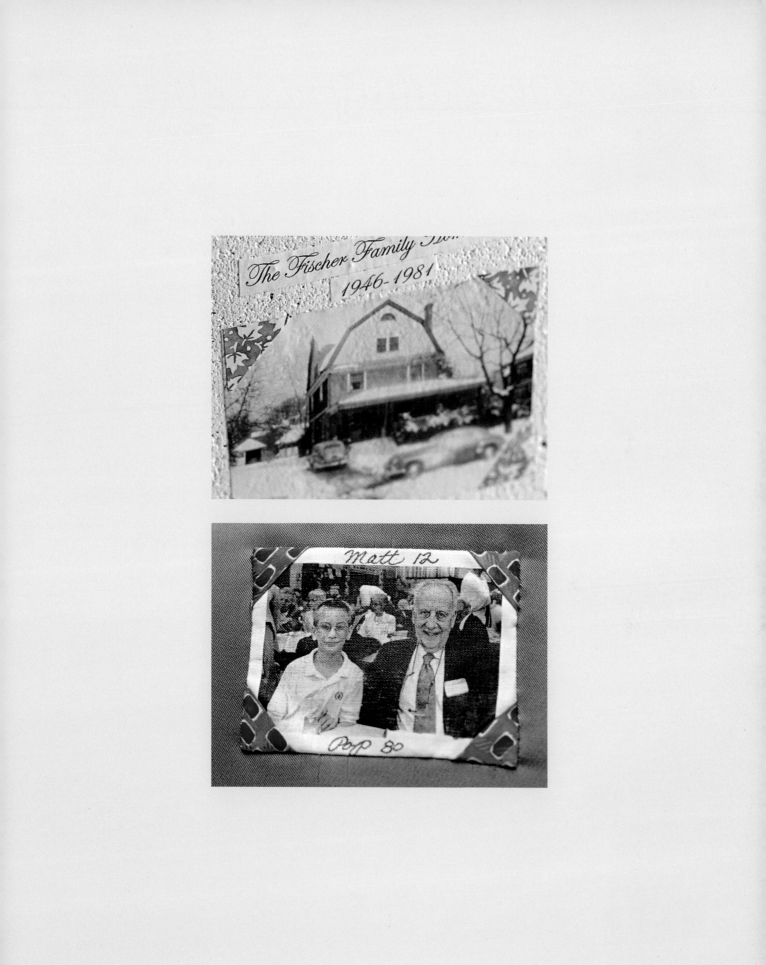

The clothes we wear become a large part of who we are. Some men have a closet full of clothes; others are happy wearing the same T-shirt and jeans over and over. Take that special item and create a keepsake that is certain to generate memories. If your dad or grandfather prefers work shirts or flannel shirts, a patchwork of several patterns would make a lovely pillow cover as well. Sew a pocket from the shirt onto the center of the pillow to hold your written remembrances or even tiny keepsakes. My nephew Matt wrote a story about his Grandpop's ties, and we wrote it onto fabric for the center of this pillow.

Grandfather's Tie Pillow

MATERIALS

- 10 to 12 neckties
- permanent fabric marker
- small scrap of white fabric
- 17" (43 cm) square piece of coordinating fabric for the pillow back
- pattern (see page 293)
- needle and thread
- seam ripper
- scissors
- ruler
- iron
- 16" (41 cm) square pillow form
- cotton fringe trim (optional)
- photo transfer (optional)

1. To prepare the ties, first take them apart with a seam ripper or scissors. Remove and discard the lining and interfacing. Iron the ties to remove the creases. Cut off the point of each tie. Cut each tie to a length of 20" (51 cm), starting at the wide end, and then cut each of these pieces in half lengthwise.

2. Sew the tie pieces together along the long edges in a pleasing arrangement to create a sewn piece approximately 30" x 20" (76 cm x 51 cm).

3. Enlarge the pattern (page 293) on a copy machine so that the long seam line is 16" (41 cm) long. Cut four from the sewn tie piece.

4. Sew along the four angled edges, and iron the seams open.

5. Cut a 4" (10 cm) square of white fabric for the center of the pillow front. Write a message or memory on the square with the permanent fabric marker.

6. Iron the center seams of the tie pieces under, and hand-stitch the white square in place. You can stitch some trim over the seam for a decorative touch.

7. Cut a piece of coordinating fabric 17" x 17" (43 cm x 43 cm) for the pillow back. With the right side of the fabric to the front of the pillow, stitch around three sides of the square. Turn the pillow cover inside out, and insert the pillow form. Hand-stitch the open seam closed. You can sew fringe trim into the outside edge seam if you'd like.

8. If you have a longer story to tell, you can use the entire back of the pillow to write your remembrances. Permanent markers work best on smooth fabric with no nap, like a plain polyester-cotton blend.

Keepsake Tip

Make an iron-on photo transfer at a copy shop or with your computer printer. Iron it onto a small piece of fabric and hand-stitch the fabric to the back of the pillow.

On the pillow's handwritten label:

Every year and for every occasion we buy Pop a couple of ties. And every time he gets dressed up he wears one of the ties that we got him.
Matt Carr

Design: Janet Pensiero

Every family has a refrigerator or bulletin board covered with wonderful finger-paint and construction-paper creations made by the children in their lives. The paint that young children use is not permanent and the paper is not very stable, so their artistic treasures don't hold up very well over time. By combining a classic children's craft technique—papier-mâché—and high-tech color copies, you can preserve their masterpieces for years to come, and create a unique decorative bowl that you and your little artist can both be proud of. A paper bowl can be made from color copies of almost anything—photos, postcards, newspaper clippings, first-grade handwriting samples, report cards.

Precious Art Papier-Mâché Bowl

MATERIALS

- color copies of children's art—preferably 11"x 17" (28 cm x 43 cm)
- papier-mâché art paste or homemade flour paste (see recipe below)
- newspaper
- large bowl (such as a smooth plastic salad bowl)
- vegetable oil or petroleum jelly
- one sheet handmade paper (optional)
- water-based polyurethane sealer

Basic Flour Paste

½ cup flour
1 teaspoon salt
1 cup warm water

1. Mix the paste to a thick, creamy consistency. It will keep several days if sealed in an airtight container and kept cool. Lightly coat the inside of the bowl with vegetable oil or petroleum jelly so the papier-mâché will be easier to remove.

2. Tear the newspaper into 1½" (4 cm)-wide strips. Dip the strips one at a time into the paste, and remove the excess paste with your fingers. Lay the strips one by one on the inside of the large bowl, slightly overlapping them.

3. After the inside of the bowl is completely covered, let the first layer of paper dry. Once dry, repeat this step 3 or 4 more times to create a sturdy paper bowl. Let dry thoroughly.

4. Carefully remove the paper bowl from the inside of the large bowl.

5. The inside of this paper bowl is lined with some torn pieces of handmade paper. If you like this look, use a torn brown paper bag or any solid-color, colorfast paper.

6. Cut out the copies of the children's artwork, and lay the cutouts inside the bowl in an arrangement that you find pleasing. Glue the cutouts in place using the papier-mâché paste.

7. When the bowl is completely dry, seal it with several coats of water-based polyurethane finish.

Keepsake Tips

- Don't forget to include the artist's name and the date on the bottom of the bowl. (This project features artwork by my niece Katie.)
- You can start small by making smaller bowls using individual salad bowls as your molds.

Design: Janet Pensiero

We know that books have stories to tell. Even children too young to read understand that wonderful stories live on the pages of the books that are read to them by their parents and older siblings. Special books also trigger personal memories and stories—the history of the book itself, happy times spent reading and being read to, or in the case of a cookbook, meals enjoyed. Get the kids involved in creating these hand-me-downs for their younger brothers and sisters by writing their own personal book review. Handmade slipcases inscribed with personal stories will become treasured heirlooms as time passes and the books travel to another generation.

Memory-Wrapped Books

MATERIALS

- favorite books
- acid-free paper or cardstock
- archival glue
- acid-free adhesive mounting sheets
- acid-free pen
- ruler
- scissors
- craft knife
- rubber stamps, acid-free ink, embossing powder (optional)

1. To make the slipcase, first measure the width of the cover and the thickness of the book. Double this measurement and add 2" (5 cm) for the overlap. This measurement is the length of the paper or cardstock that you will use for the slipcase for your book. Determine the height by measuring from the bottom to the top of the front cover.

2. Cut the paper or cardstock to size with the craft knife, and mark off the points on the top and bottom edges where the paper will fold. Connect the points with a pencil, and score the paper along these lines with the dull side of a small scissors. Wrap the cover around the book, and glue the overlap with archival glue.

3. Add pieces of contrasting paper on which you have written your story in acid-free pen or have created some rubber stamp art. If you prefer, you can print the story out using your computer printer and acid-free paper.

4. To make the wraparound cover, measure as above, but fold the ends of the paper around the edges of the front and back covers of the book. Tack the edges of the paper to the inside of the covers with archival glue.

Keepsake Tip

All paper, glue, and ink used on books should be acid-free or pH neutral. Acid-free supplies are readily available in the scrapbook area of craft stores.

Amy Vanderbilt's
COMPLETE
COOKBOOK

ABOULAYE'S
FAIRY
TALES

This book belonged to your Grandpop when he was a boy. His parents bought it when he was a baby. He read it to me when I was little and your father and I read it to you. Someday you'll read it to your children.
Love,
Mom

Design: Janet Pensiero

Built in 1910 by a Mr. Schilling as a custom home for his daughter and her husband, 321 Owen Avenue stood proudly on its half-acre of land for all to admire. My father, F. Theodore Fischer, Jr., was the second owner, purchasing the 17-room house in 1946 for $16,500. The deed included the fact that the cost of wallpapering the three floors in 1910 was $75. It also included the stipulation that no farm animals were to abide within the house. We obeyed the deed! I don't know why, but I kept a brick from that house when we left—and now that simple object has become a fun accessory in our new home. If you're moving from or even remodeling your own home, consider saving some architectural remnant, to turn into a keepsake down the road.

Brick House Doorstop

MATERIALS

· one standard size brick (even better if you can get one from the house)

· white acrylic paint

· paintbrush

· self-adhesive home-themed stickers

· color photocopy of the house (front and back views)

· color photocopies of home-related saying and pictures

· archival glue

· damp paper towels

· scissors

· Liquid Laminate

1. Paint the top and bottom sides (the two largest sides) of the brick with two coats of white acrylic paint. Leave the sides of the brick in their natural state.

2. Trim the color photocopies of the house pictures so that they fit in the center of each painted side of the brick. Attach them to the brick using the archival glue. Pat the photocopies with a damp paper towel to remove any air bubbles and to make sure the glue fills all the nooks and crannies in the brick. Be sure not to rub the picture or the ink from the color photocopy may rub off.

3. Arrange the self-adhesive stickers as a border at the top and bottom of the brick.

Add the little sayings and pictures to enhance the piece.

4. Print a short history of the house, making sure the entire story will fit on the top side of the brick. Then glue it to the top of the brick using the archival glue. Also, print out the family name and address of the house, and glue them to the front of the brick underneath the picture. You can also add the year the house was built.

5. Cover both painted sides of the brick with two coats of Liquid Laminate. Be sure to coat the trim at the top and the bottom, being careful not to get any on the natural brick.

Keepsake Tip

Use the top of your doorstop to include some historical details about your architectural remnant, such as when the house was built, how many families lived there before you, and any interesting stories about the house.

On the road between the houses of friends grass does not grow.

The Fischer Family Homestead

1946-1981

Design: Connie Sheerin

Almost everyone has a junk drawer—that place in your home where the odd bits and pieces of your life end up. With an old desk or end table drawer, either from the trash or from a thrift store, you can create your own homage to "junk." The items in this project don't have to be fancy. In fact, the kids will enjoy gathering up the things that are meaningful to them and helping to arrange them in the drawer. This shrine contains a small sampling of the junk I've accumulated since moving into my house in 1984. I've written the date I moved in with a metallic paint pen on the outside of the drawer.

Junk Drawer Shrine

MATERIALS

· small empty drawer, or unfinished wooden display box

· acrylic paint (optional)

· hot-glue gun and glue sticks

· white glue or decoupage medium

· E-6000 glue or any one-part epoxy

· assorted tchotchkes

· sandpaper (optional)

· paper, such as take-out menus, receipts, old wallpaper, and greeting cards

1. Thoroughly clean your drawer if you got it from the trash or purchased at a thrift store.

2. You can leave the wood unfinished or do more decorative painting, depending on your taste. If you are going to paint the outside of the drawer, lightly sand the unfinished wood before painting it. Then, cover the back surface and sides with paper—take-out menus, receipts, and old wallpaper. You can also use greeting cards, kids' artwork, or appliance warranties.

3. Gather your tchotchkes, and arrange them in the drawer. Glue the items in place using hot glue for most items, white glue for paper, and E-6000 or one-part epoxy for the odd-shaped, hard-to-hold pieces.

4. Try a little ball fringe for the bottom edge, or if you like sparkle, add some sequins or even tiny Christmas lights.

Keepsake Tip

Tchotchke (also spelled chotchke, and pronounced "choch-key") is a Yiddish word meaning something pretty and decorative, but basically useless.

Design: Janet Pensiero

"My Little Muffins"
Children's Toy Box

Why a muffin pan? Why *not* a muffin pan? When it comes to kids and having crazy, wild, and goofy fun—anything goes. But that isn't always what Mommy is thinking when she steps on spiky playthings in the middle of the night. Before *that* happens again, make a clean sweep through little junior and missy's bedroom to confiscate the guilty little playthings. Don't feel bad, because you're about to transform them into art. A standard muffin pan is equipped with twelve wonderfully roomy spaces to house everything from toothless smiles to action figures. Invite your child to help you create a playful wall piece that will hang nicely in their bedroom. However, don't forget to use the glue. You never know when the kids will have the urge to reclaim the toys, no matter how artfully they are arranged.

Materials

Standard muffin pan

5 or 6 small pictures of kids

Mini toys and candies

Party streamers

Spray paint

Construction paper

Foam board

Scalloped scissors

Picture-hanging attachment

Basic craft supplies

1) Clean the pan of debris. Spray paint in desired color in a well-ventilated area. Line the various muffin cups with construction paper.

2) Cut out pictures with scalloped scissors and glue a border from a crumpled party streamer around the edge. Using hot glue, adhere a small piece of foam board to the back of the pictures and mount into the muffin cups.

3) Take time to arrange the toys in the remaining cups until you find an assemblage that is balanced. Glue the items down and let dry. (See tip below).

4) Using industrial-strength craft glue, adhere a hanging attachment to the back.

TIP
Stick with industrial-strength craft glue when adhering items directly to the pan (hot glue will not bond properly).

VARIATIONS
- If you do not have a muffin pan, use another box that has many small compartments.
- Instead of school photos, take the children to a self-service photo booth at the mall. This will add even more whimsy to the box.

Dimensions 10 ½" X 14" (27 cm X 36 cm)   **Artist** Kathy Cano-Murillo (concept by Jenny Ignaszewski)

NEARLY EVERYONE HAS A COLLECTION of family photos, either filed

in a shoebox or lovingly arranged in a photo album. But what do you

do with all of those things that trigger memories and family stories but

don't quite fit neatly into a picture frame or a scrapbook?

Use these projects as a guide and a source of inspiration. If you

don't have a collection of kitchen tools to display, hang a few of

Family Memories

the screwdrivers and wrenches that your uncle used to tune up his

first roadster. Or you can display a few of those hand-woven loop

pot holders that your mother painstakingly created when she was a

young girl. Whatever objects you choose to preserve and display

will surely be cherished for years to come, and more important, their

stories won't be forgotten.

Memorabilia & Collections

When gathering memorabilia to save, think about what makes your family special.

What quirks do your family members have? Do they collect anything? What objects remind you of them or trigger family stories? Keeping the stories alive can be as simple as gluing a handwritten note inside a drawer or on the underside of a special piece of furniture explaining how and why it's important to your family history. Or you can be more creative and assemble a collage of objects that are special to a family member, or memorialize a time in your own history with photos and stories. You can turn fabric that has special memories into a pillow, wall hanging, or quilt. Imagine a quilt made of squares of worn denim from all the jeans you've worn over the years—with embroidered dates, even. Or, you can make a baby quilt using squares of fabric from your maternity clothes.

If you are lucky enough to inherit someone else's collection, your only dilemma is how to display it. Painted racks, shelves, and boxes are great for this, but don't forget to include the stories that are attached to the objects. Collections come in many shapes. The collection of empty wine bottles that your grandfather kept in the basement could become a picture of your grandfather in a picture frame beautifully decoupaged with wine labels, recalling his love of good wine.

Sometimes the simplest things remind us of the best stories. If your family spent rainy days in feverish battle over board games that are now too worn and missing too many pieces to use, consider gluing a game board and some pieces to a tray or tabletop and sealing it with polyurethane. Every time you use it, it will remind you of the wonderful times you had playing the games together. And remembering is what it's all about.

Travel scrapbooks are great, but they tend to be put away and looked at only on special occasions. Take some of those paper keepsakes that you can't bear to throw away, and preserve them between glass to create functional and memorable coasters. Almost any paper item can be used—photos, ticket stubs, receipts, menus, even foreign money. Tuck a manila envelope or plastic bag in your suitcase to collect the paper memories of your next trip.

Vacation Memory Coasters

MATERIALS

- 4" (10 cm) square plate glass—two pieces for each coaster
- self-adhesive silver foil tape, ¼" (6 mm) width
- photos, ticket stubs, stationery, and any other paper memorabilia from your trip
- self-adhesive cork squares (optional)

1. Clean and dry the glass.

2. Cut and arrange several pieces of trip memorabilia on a single piece of glass for each coaster. Carefully cut the paper to the edges of the glass. When you have an arrangement you're happy with, place a second piece of glass on top of your arrangement.

3. Hold the two pieces of glass together, with the photos and paper sandwiched in between, and tape around the edge of all four sides with the silver foil tape. If desired, attach the self-adhesive cork squares to the bottom of the coasters.

Keepsake Tip

Make these with your kids using craft foam and self-adhesive cork squares. Laminate copies of photos, and place on the adhesive side of the cork squares. Arrange geometric shapes made from the craft foam around the photos, and fill in the spaces with tiny glass beads.

MOUNT KENYA Safari Club

Mount Kenya Safari Club Ltd. P.O. Box 35, Nanyuki, Kenya

British airways

KENYA

KENYA 3'50

African heritage
KENYATTA AVENUE,
P.O. BOX 41730,
...OBI, KENYA

Design: Janet Pensiero

Every family has its favorite recipe, one that is passed down through the generations, either strictly followed or tweaked just a bit to add new twists. Whether your family's recipe is for apple pie, green bean casserole, or chocolate cookies, you can document it with this easy platter project—a great accessory for any kitchen and fun to pull out for all those family gatherings. My mother made this recipe when we had special company for dinner.

Favorite Family Recipe Platter

MATERIALS

- wooden platter
- polymer clay
- stencil
- acrylic paint
- alphabet stamps
- printed-out or handwritten recipe
- white glue or decoupage medium
- E-6000 glue, any one-part epoxy
- spray acrylic sealer
- craft knife
- gel ink or paint pen
- sandpaper
- damp cloth
- scissors

1. Lightly sand the wooden platter. Wipe with a damp cloth to remove all dust. Apply one coat of paint in the base color of your choice. Let the paint dry, and apply one or two additional coats of paint to completely cover the wood.

2. Print out your favorite recipe from your computer, or hand-write the recipe in a shape to fit the platter. Test the ink with the spray sealer before gluing the recipe in place. Cut out the recipe in an oval shape, and glue it in the center of the platter using the white glue.

3. Roll out a small piece of polymer clay to a thickness of $1/8$" (3 mm). Press the alphabet stamps into the clay, and cut the letters into tile shapes with a craft knife. After you've made the alphabet tiles for the name of your recipe, bake them according to the directions for the clay. When the tiles are cool, glue them to the platter with E-6000 glue.

4. Choose a stencil or two, according to the ingredients in your recipe. Stencil the ingredients in the empty spaces on the platter, around the recipe, or on the rim. Add polka dots or other design elements to complement your design.

5. Write a personal memory of the recipe on the platter with a gel ink or paint pen. Seal the entire plate with several light coats of a spray acrylic sealer.

Keepsake Tip

Make color copies of your original recipes, and decoupage the copies to the center of an old china plate or platter with liquid laminate. Cut some colored paper with decorative scissors to use as an accent. Seal the plate with several coats of liquid laminate.

PEARS AU VIN

8 Bartlett pear halves, canned in light syrup
¾ cup red wine
½ cup sugar
½ stick cinnamon

Cook above until sauce thickens. Refrigerate overnight.
Allow 2 halves per serving.
Serve with whipped cream if desired.

for dessert when we had company

Design: Janet Pensiero

As soon as children are old enough to realize that they're part of a family, they start trying to figure out how they fit in. I made this simple four-generation chart to illustrate for my niece and nephew where they came from. To add information and stories, you can pin some badge holders onto the wall hanging with copies of relevant photos—from grandparents' wedding, for example—and documents to illustrate the stories.

Family Tree Wall Hanging

MATERIALS

· 2 yards (1.8 meters) of white polyester-cotton fabric

· acrylic paint, four or five different colors

· leaf shapes (real or fabric leaves)

· black permanent fabric marker

· heavy-weight adhesive plastic laminating film

· grommets

· vintage buttons (optional)

· clear plastic badge holders (optional)

· scissors

· foam brush

· iron

· family tree information, with family lists on separate pieces of paper

· tape

· sewing machine or needle and thread

1. Cut eight pieces of fabric 8" (20 cm) square and three pieces of fabric 10 ½" (27 cm) square. Trace the leaf shapes, and enlarge them to fit on the individual squares of fabric. When they're large enough, trace the shapes onto the adhesive laminating film, and cut out the leaves. Press the adhesive leaves onto the fabric squares, and paint around the leaf shapes with acrylic paint, using a foam brush. Let them dry, and then iron flat.

2. Gather your family tree information, and lay out each family list on a separate piece of paper. You can hand write the names, or print them from the computer, using a typeface that you like. Place the fabric over the printout, and tape it to a light source, like a light table or a window. Use a permanent fabric marker to trace the names through the fabric.

3. Stitch all the squares together, and join the family members with dotted lines. Sew a border around the edge.

4. Cut a piece of fabric for the back. Place the good side of the fabric against the front side of the wall hanging, and sew around 3 sides. Turn the wall hanging inside out and insert a layer of batting between the front and back. Stitch up the open edge. Hand-tack the layers together at the corner of each square using vintage buttons, if desired.

5. Add grommets to the top and bottom edge to hang.

Keepsake Tips

• Pin on badge holders with photos and documents that help tell the story.

• There are several Web sites that will help you trace your family history.

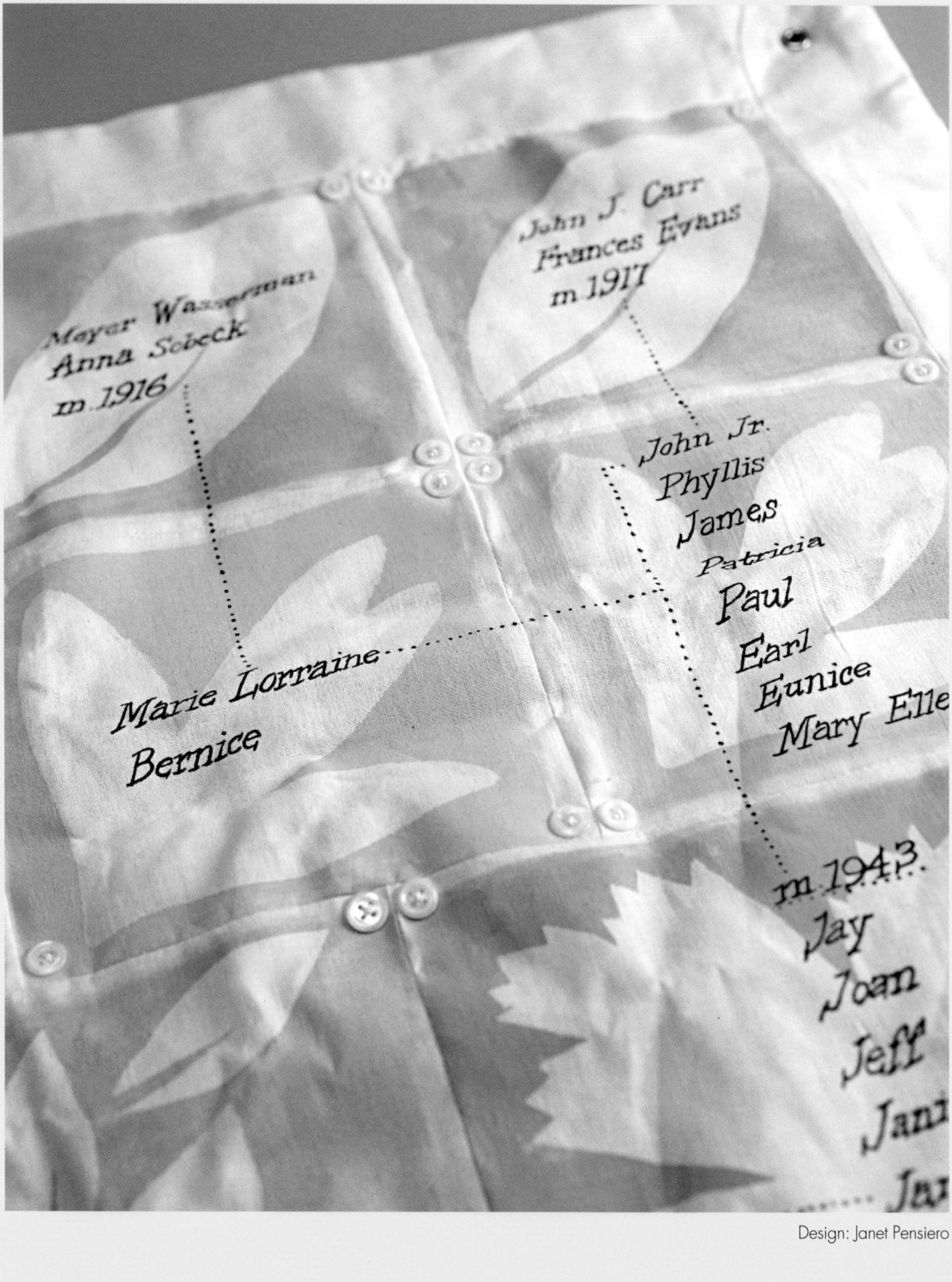

Meyer Wasserman
Anna Sobeck
m. 1916

John J. Carr
Frances Evans
m. 1917

John Jr.
Phyllis
James
Patricia
Paul
Earl
Eunice
Mary Elle

Marie Lorraine
Bernice

m. 1943
Jay
Joan
Jeff
Jani
Jay

Design: Janet Pensiero

Family recipes can keep memories of holidays and informal gatherings alive for generations. My Aunt Fran published a cookbook filled with recipes, many going back over 150 years, from family and friends. This cookbook has helped my family retain its Pennsylvania Dutch and German heritage by reminding us how to prepare the dishes our ancestors loved. There is nothing like the aroma of a home-cooked meal to warm the soul and bring back loving memories of family meals and gatherings.

100-Plus Years of Family Recipes

MATERIALS

- metal or wooden recipe box
- miniature rolling pin
- kitchen-themed cutouts and stickers
- utility knife
- Liquid Leaf copper enamel paint
- Liquid Laminate
- archival glue
- hot glue
- recipe cards
- laminator (such as Xyron) (optional)
- small paintbrush
- sponge brush
- color photocopies of your family's "historical" cooks

1. Use the sponge brush to paint the recipe box with two coats of Liquid Leaf Copper Paint, pulling brush lightly over the wood to create the illusion of grain.

2. Arrange the kitchen-theme cutouts and stickers. When you are happy with the design, glue the paper to the box with the archival glue. Make sure you do not leave any air bubbles under the stickers. Allow the glue to dry thoroughly, and then use a utility knife to trim the paper where it hangs over the top and bottom.

3. Write a short history about the family recipes, and print it out on a computer printer. Glue it to the bottom of the box with the archival glue.

4. Apply two coats of Liquid Laminate over all of the paper designs with a small paintbrush, including the history on the bottom of the box.

5. Hot-glue the miniature rolling pin onto the lid of the box to act as a handle.

6. Prepare the recipe cards. You can use one card for each of the family contributors. You can even add a small picture of each contributor on the upper right-hand side of the card, with a short story about that person and their relationship to you. You can laminate the cards to protect them, or not at all—whatever suits your taste.

Design: Connie Sheerin

I created this clock using family pictures under glass nuggets so that every time I looked at the clock, I would remember my family. The same concept could take on many ideas and themes, like baby's first year, your favorite pet or pets, first-year anniversary pictures, and so on. The amber-colored glass nuggets give a slightly mellow look to the old black-and-white pictures of my mom's sisters. What a special little gift to give to anyone you love!

Family Photo Clock

MATERIALS

- 11" (28 cm) square wooden frame
- 8" (20 cm) tile with a hole for the clockworks
- 12 1½" (4 cm) diameter clear glass nuggets
- 12 color photocopies of photographs
- clock face rubber stamp
- *time* rubber stamp
- white textured paper
- metallic white pearl acrylic paint
- gold pigment stamp pad
- gold metallic paint
- high-gloss black spray paint
- archival glue
- Liquid Laminate
- black permanent ink stamp pad
- damp paper towel
- white craft glue
- set of black clockworks
- sawtooth picture hanger

1. Cover the wooden frame with two or three coats of high-gloss black spray paint until it is completely covered.

2. Tear the white paper into irregular pieces, about 2" (5 cm) square. Glue the paper pieces to the 8" (20 cm) tile with archival glue, overlapping the pieces to cover the front of the tile. Be sure to poke through the hole in the center (from the front side) before glue the dries.

3. Glue the color photocopies under the glass nuggets using Liquid Laminate. Push out any extra liquid with your finger, and wipe off the excess with a damp paper towel.

4. When the Liquid Laminate has completely dried, apply a coat of the metallic white pearl paint over the torn pieces of paper.

5. Stamp the word *time* all over the front of the tile. Stamp the clock face with the gold metallic paint, and glue it to the center of the front of the tile. Poke a hole though the center of the clock face to line up with the hole in the tile.

6. Use the archival glue to attach the picture nuggets around the outer edge of the tile to represent the hours on the clock.

7. After all the glue under the nuggets has dried, glue the tile into the wooden frame, and allow it to dry overnight.

8. Highlight the black frame using gold paint. You can either use your finger or a cosmetic sponge.

9. Attach the clockworks, following the directions on the package. Attach the sawtooth hanger to the middle of the upper back of the frame. You can now hang and enjoy your family clock.

Keepsake Tips

- Practice using the *time* stamp and permanent black ink on scrap paper before using it on the clock. Don't forget that this project is handmade—it doesn't have to be perfect to be just right.

- I found more pictures than I needed, so I added a magnetic strip to the back of the extra glass nuggets to adorn the refrigerator and the filing cabinets at work.

Design: Connie Sheerin

Family *Tree*

This family tree is easily updated anytime there is a marriage or birth, because the photographic panels are a snap to make using inexpensive, easy-to-cut balsa wood. Arrange the panels on a wall to visually suggest a tree, or lay them out in a traditional genealogical pattern. Skeletonized leaves can be used in many ways to accent the panels and are available in several colors at craft and art supply stores. Also try using pressed foliage or flowers. To add names, first print them out from a word processing program, then have them reversed and copied to a heat transfer sheet at a copy shop.

MATERIALS

- *balsa wood planks*
- *skeletonized leaves*
- *decorative papers*
- *white pickling gel or water-based stain*
- *heat transfer paper*
- *craft knife*
- *cutting mat*
- *glue stick*
- *sponge applicator brush*
- *fine sandpaper*
- *iron*

Starting *Out*

Use a glue stick to quickly and easily adhere the paper and leaves to the photo panels.

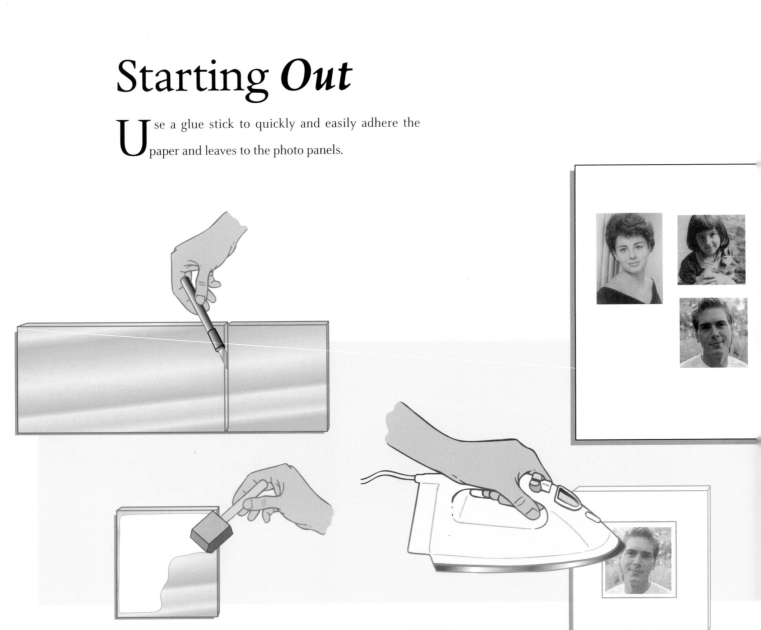

STEP 1

<u>Cut and stain the panels</u>. Cut the balsa wood planks into squares or rectangles. The ones here are 6" x 6" (15 cm x 15 cm) and 6" x 7" (15 cm x 18 cm). Smooth the cut edges with fine sandpaper. Then, apply a transparent white wash to the panels with a sponge applicator brush. Let them dry thoroughly for several hours or overnight; any moisture in the wood will prevent the transfers from adhering properly.

STEP 2

<u>Prepare and iron the transfers in place</u>. Compile the photographs to be used, then size them using a color copier or a computer. Photocopy or print artwork onto a heat transfer sheet, following the manufacturer's instructions. Fit as many as possible on each sheet. Carefully trim around each photo using scissors or a craft knife and cutting mat. Next, preheat the iron on a low to medium heat setting. Adhere the transfers to the centers of the panels. Use a straight up-and-down motion when ironing, rather than a side-to-side or circular motion, to prevent the image from smearing. This should only take a few minutes. Check adhesion frequently as you iron, and be sure all the edges of the transfers are secure. Let the transfers cool completely before peeling the backing paper off.

[Tip:]

Use a glue stick to quickly and easily adhere the paper and leaves to the photo panels.

Variation:

Make panels to celebrate and commemorate special occasions, such as a special anniversary, family reunion, or graduation. Silver-coated leaves and metallic papers were used to complement the black-and-white photograph used here.

STEP 3

<u>Decorate the panels with leaves and paper</u>. Arrange and adhere the leaves as desired on the panels. Then, measure and cut squares of paper that are 1/2" (4 cm) larger all around than the transfers. Cut out the centers of these paper squares to create a 1/4" (5 mm) border for the transferred photographs. Position them over the transfers and adhere to the panel. To cover the edges of the panels, cut 6" (15 cm) strips; determine how wide the strips should be by measuring the thickness of the wood, then add 1/2" (1 cm). This will ensure a 1/4" (5 mm) border around the front and back of the panel. Lightly score the strips lengthwise, 1/4" (5 mm) in from both sides, using a craft knife. Fold the strips in to a *U* shape and adhere them to the edges of the panels. Finish the panels with a coat of water-based acrylic varnish, if desired.

Memory *Art Canvas*

A prestretched canvas is the perfect choice for creating a commemorative photographic compilation like this one, which chronicles the fun, romantic weekend one couple had in Venice Beach, California. So dig up all those vacation, party, or holiday photos and start photocopying or scanning them to make the perfect gift for friends and family. Liquid transfer medium is the best choice for stretched canvas, which is awkward to iron evenly. Also, color copies work best with this method. To finish the project, try painting the edges of the canvas for a quick faux-frame.

MATERIALS

- *prestretched canvas*

- *clear liquid transfer medium*

- *craft knife or scissors*

- *sponge brush applicator*

- *large sponge*

Starting *Out*

Tinting photos in various, fun shades is easy to do with any image-editing program. Consult the application's guidebook for specific methods, or have a photocopy clerk adjust the hues.

STEP 1

Prepare the transfers. Photocopy or scan and print out the photographs to be used. Play with the size and arrangement of the photos, and lighten or darken the images if necessary. The colors of the images can be manipulated with a copier or a computer. Next, get a color copy of the prepared artwork. If using an inkjet printer, use a high-quality matte-finish paper and the paper's corresponding setting for the printer. Then have a color copy made of the print out. Don't forget to flip the image, if desired. Let the paper dry for thirty minutes before proceeding.

STEP 2

Brush the medium on the canvas and adhere the transfer. Cut the transfer out along the edge of the image with scissors or a craft knife. The canvas used here is 8" x 10" (20 cm x 25 cm), so only one piece of paper was needed. For a larger canvas, tape together the pieces of paper on the reverse side. Be sure to align the seams carefully. Brush a thick, even coat of transfer medium on the canvas using a sponge brush applicator. The coat should be about $1/16$" (1.5 mm) thick. Next, lay the artwork face down on the medium. Use a bottle or a brayer to gently smooth the transfer and press it into the medium. Let the transfer dry for twenty-four to forty-eight hours, depending on humidity.

Variation:

Experiment with image-
editing "filters" to modify a
single photo. The watercolor
filter in Adobe Photoshop
Elements was used here for
a painted look.

STEP 3

<u>Remove the paper transfer with a sponge.</u> Moisten the entire transfer
with a damp sponge and wait a few minutes for the water to saturate
the paper. Then, use the sponge to rub the paper off the canvas
using a circular motion. Let the surface dry. If there are any clouded
areas, which indicate residual paper, rub the surface again with a
damp sponge.

Ferdinand and Lily: A Heritage Page

The ink used here is platinum, and it takes on a colorful patina when stamped on black cardstock. Try stamping in different colors on various papers to discover what works best with the photograph or artwork you wish to frame.

STAMPING TRICK

Stamp the frame with a bright, vibrant color of pigment ink, and apply the photograph separately to a layer of white cardstock. Cut out the photo and glue it over the stamping to preserve the clarity and contrast.

ARTIST: DAWN HOUSER

MATERIALS

- **Stamps**
  Color block
  Tag block
  Fancy flourish Bollio
- **Ink and Inkpads**
  Eggshell white, platinum, and black pigment
  Metallic bronze embossing powder
- **Papers**
  Black cardstock
  White cardstock
  White paper
- **Miscellaneous**
  Markers
  Metallic pen

Getting Started

To make this very simple page, stamp a border around the edges of a sheet of black cardstock using a flourish Bollio and eggshell white pigment ink, although platinum might be interesting for variety. Stamp three platinum or eggshell frames directly onto the page, allowing space for nameplates at the top and bottom. The two upper photos were stamped with a smaller frame stamp than the single one below them. Size the photos to fit into the stamped frames, and mount them on white paper before placing them on top of the stamping.

Adding the Names

To make the nameplates, first stamp the images with embossing ink on white cardstock, then emboss them and write the names with a metallic pen. Cut them out and place them above or below the appropriate photographs.

The frame stamp is composed of a background block with a built-in frame around it. It can be stamped with pigment ink, as on this page, or with dye ink, markers, or embossing ink and powder. Each treatment will produce a very different look and mood.

Mothers and Daughters:
Stamped Family Pages

A frame doesn't have to be four-sided to be effective. Stamp a crown or other image and attach on only two sides of a photograph, as shown here on the photo of the grandmother with her granddaughter. This design adds just enough elegance to convey the heritage quality of the photograph—any more embellishment would detract from the face.

Frames needn't be conventional in shape. The dress form image acts as a frame when the photographs are cut out in its shape and no other frame is applied, anchoring the photo to the page. To create a unique photo edge, first stamp a shape such as the dress form on thin white or tracing paper and cut it out. Lay it over the chosen photograph and pencil around the shape, then trim the photo. Here, a montage of several photographs is used to make an image large enough to fit the dress form. This treatment adds interest and character to the entire page and could be used to accentuate a particular theme by using the appropriate icons.

Five Generations: Hand Lettered Pages

These two pages illustrate the beauty and intimacy that are possible with hand lettering. If your penmanship could use some help, it's worthwhile to invest some time and energy improving your hand. Many books on the subjects of calligraphy and hand lettering are available in bookstores.

ARTIST: VICKI SCHREINER

- **Stamps**
  Nostalgic key
  Nostalgic pocket watch
  Liquid amber leaf
- **Ink and Inkpads**
  Copper metallic inkpad
  Honeydew metallic inkpad
- **Paper**
  Natural parchment cardstock
- **Miscellaneous**
  Medium olive green and ochre fine-tip markers
  Squares and ovals templates
  Ivory vintage paper napkins
  Paper glue and glue pen
  Seagull paper edgers

QUICK TRICK

Should you decide to use your computer and printer for a faux handwriting font, try several different ones in various scripts and look for a style that is easy to read. When it comes to labeling your photographs, clarity is more important than ornamentation, and it's very easy to be carried away by the creativity that is found in fonts.

Getting Started

On a sheet of natural parchment, lightly draw the ovals for the names. Write the captions with the ochre fine tip marker, then go over the words again with the green. Make the green lettering slightly to the left of the ochre to create the illusion of shadows. Draw a green line around each oval and add dashed lines just inside it. Cut the ovals out and set aside for the final step.

Making the Pages

To make these vintage pages, stamp the background with the liquid amber leaf stamp and the honeydew pad on natural parchment cardstock. With the copper metallic ink, stamp about twenty keys on parchment cardstock, and stamp about fifteen pocket watches. Draw square and rectangle template shapes onto olive cardstock and also onto parchment. Make them about ½" (1 cm) larger all around than the photographs, then trim the parchment shapes slightly smaller than the olive. Mount the parchment shapes on the olive ones, then trim and mount the photographs on top of the parchment. Glue the small, framed photos to the background, cut out the keys and the pocket watches, and mount them at the sides and edges of the photos. To mat each of the large photographs, cut triangles from the corners of a paper lace napkin and butt them together to form a square. Tape lightly in the center to hold the square together, then mount the framed photograph on top. Glue the assemblage to the page. Add the captions to the appropriate photos. With seagull paper edgers, cut strips of olive cardstock and glue along the outside edges of the pages.

Time Flies By: A Heritage Divider Page

ARTIST: BETTY AUTH

Getting Started

Beginning with the lightest ink color, randomly stamp some dragonflies on a sheet of green cardstock, turning them in various directions. Continue stamping dragonflies with successively darker and brighter colors until the page is covered. Stamp and emboss three or four more dragonflies on white cardstock. Color the embossed images with watercolor pencils and daub some of the background colors on the bodies. Cut out the embossed dragonflies.

QUICK TRICK

To make an element stand out from the background, use foam-centered sticky dots to mount it, raising it above the surface of the page.

MATERIALS

- **Stamps**
  Dragonfly
- **Ink and Inkpads**
  Pink, fuchsia, lavender, and purple pigment cubes
  Clear embossing ink and sparkle powder
- **Papers**
  One sheet of medium green cardstock
  One sheet of white cardstock
- **Miscellaneous**
  Double-sided sticky dots
  Watercolor pencils
  Small paintbrush
  Sponge or sponge dauber
  Computer with script font or black fine-tip marker
  for hand lettering

Finishing the Page

Print the words on white cardstock, by hand or with a computer, and cut them out as a banner. Trim the photos and mount them in the center of the page, overlapping and fanning them out. Mount the banner above them. Use sticky dots to attach the dragonflies so they will stand out.

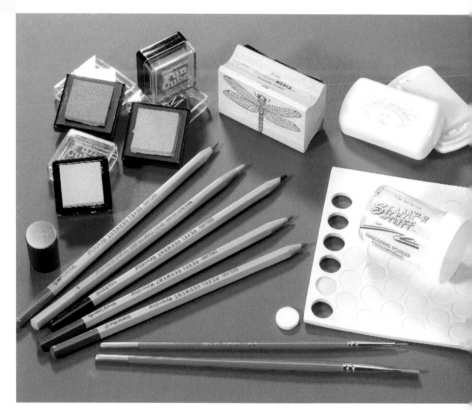

Watercolor pencils are effective tools for scrapbook pages because you can control the amount of water on the brush and avoid wrinkling the page.

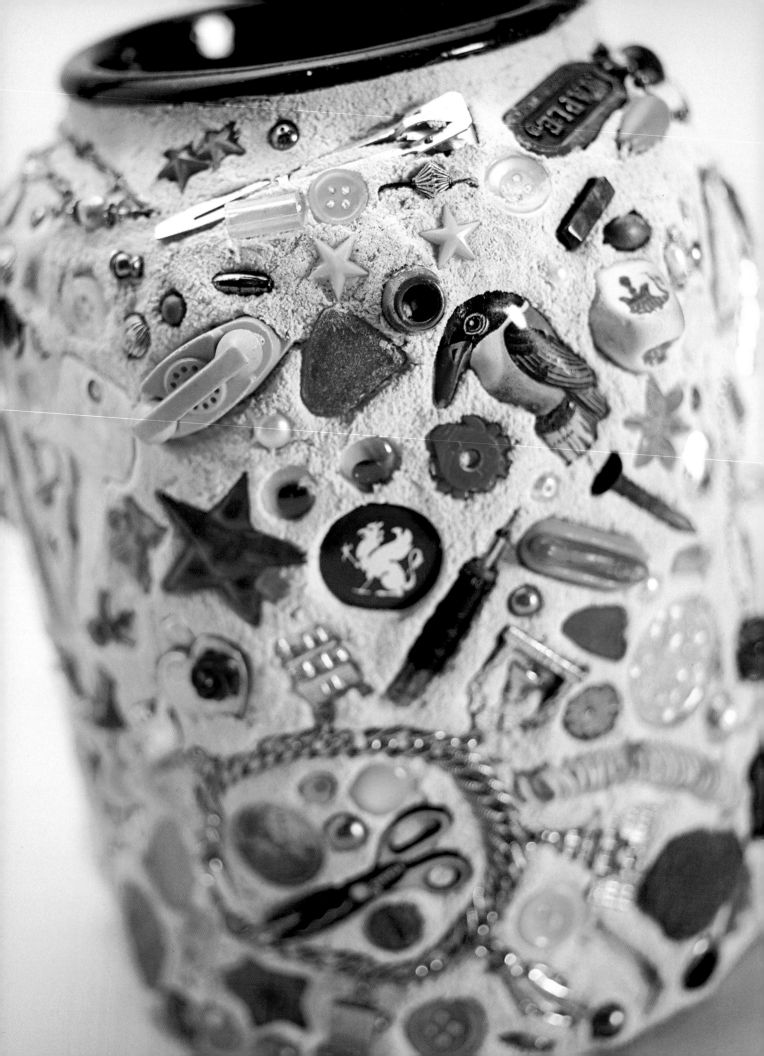

IN PRIMITIVE CULTURES, stories, proverbs, and cultural information were passed on orally from generation to generation. For example, the aboriginal people of Australia built their nomadic life around stories called songlines, which were told while walking and which served as maps, travelogues, and history lessons.

In Remembrance

In our high-tech culture, stories and information can be passed on with the click of a computer mouse. Crafters may be familiar with all the traditional crafting tools and techniques, but saving family treasures often presents the challenge of reproducing old, unique, and oftentimes fragile documents. To solve this problem, we used a combination of handcrafting techniques and modern technology, making computers, printers, and copy machines the new favorite tools to preserve history.

Cherished Memories

After losing someone close, it's sometimes difficult to face the items that have been left behind, but if done in the right spirit, you may find this experience rewarding and even therapeutic. Try to approach such a task as an opportunity to give these items a new life, one that will pay tribute to some very cherished memories. The projects in this chapter provide ideas for remembering some of those people who were dear to you. Each memory bears its own individual gift—another story told, another way to recapture our remembrances with both smiles and tears. Pulling those memories together in a creative way provides a special gift, one either to keep for yourself or to share with another person who has suffered this same loss. These physical symbols can be very powerful and immensely comforting as the grief subsides and the fond memories take its place.

A grandmother's button collection can become memory bracelets for all of her daughters and granddaughters. A few pieces of vintage costume jewelry can create a beautiful accent for a photo frame. A miscellaneous collection of small items can be transformed in a shrine, a collage, or a spirit jar. The simplest items, from handkerchiefs to kitchen utensils, can all be used as inspiration for your projects.

Sometimes it may seem as if there were years when nothing extraordinary happened—but just wait until you start really looking at and collecting the tidbits for these projects, and you will see that there was probably something worth remembering from every single day. There's a story behind every object. Take the time to share the stories and memorabilia of loved ones who have passed with the people in your life now. They will appreciate these tangible insights into your shared history.

A box of buttons can lead to a little journey through a lifetime. Special dresses, coats, baby clothes, and uniforms all come back to life when memories are triggered by these pieces of plastic and pearl. Our all-white version of this bracelet is made with pearls, mother-of-pearl buttons, and one glass shank button. This is a perfect way to turn a saved collection of buttons into special gifts for many members of a family.

Button Box Charm Bracelets

MATERIALS

- chain-link bracelet, either costume jewelry or sterling silver
- assorted vintage buttons (7 to 10 for each bracelet)
- 22-gauge wire
- beads or pearls (optional)
- wire cutter
- round-nose pliers

1. Cut a piece of wire $1\frac{1}{2}$" (4 cm) long for each button you want to attach to the bracelet.

2. Using the wire-twisting diagram as a guide (see page 294), attach the buttons at even intervals along the bracelet.

3. Secure the wire by twisting it with the pliers, and cut off any extra wire with the wire cutters. Add beads or pearls, if desired.

Keepsake Tip

You can make different types of jewelry, such button "charms" hanging on a chain necklace (see the wire-twisting diagram at the back of the book) or by stringing shank buttons on a piece of elastic with the ends knotted.

Design: Janet Pensiero

I inherited a collection of kitchen utensils from my grandparents, and for years I've had them scattered around my kitchen. I wouldn't dream of throwing them out, but because the utensils really aren't functional, they needed to take a decorative place in my kitchen. This project works well for displaying kitchen utensils, but it would also work for other collections, such as tools, pot holders, mugs, or anything else that can hang. A small, tiered shelf or shadow box frame, painted and decorated with stories, is a great solution for displaying objects that can't be hung.

Family Collection Hanging Shelf

MATERIALS

- wooden shelf
- acrylic paint, two or three colors
- cup hooks
- color copies of photos
- printed out or hand-written family stories
- spray acrylic sealer
- white glue
- toy fork and spoon (optional)
- wire brads (optional)
- sandpaper
- damp cloth

1. Sand the shelf, and wipe it with a damp cloth to remove the dust. Paint the shelf with the base acrylic paint color of your choice. Apply a second coat if necessary.

2. Paint some areas of the shelf with the acrylic paint to coordinate with the objects you want to display. Apply a second coat if necessary. I attached toy wooden utensils to the front of the shelf with wire brads.

3. Write your stories out by hand, or print them out from your computer. Make sure the type is large enough—16- or 18-point type works well.

4. Glue your color copies of the photographs with your stories to the painted shelf using white glue, and let it dry.

5. After it is dry, spray the shelf with acrylic sealer. However, make sure you test the spray sealer with your computer printout before you spray the shelf. (If the ink on the print-out runs, try a water-based polyurethane sealer). Screw in the cup hooks, and hang the items you want to display.

Keepsake Tips

- Make the stories short and to the point. They are most effective if they can directly relate to something that is displayed nearby.

- This idea can be adapted to be used on a hanging shelf or even a bookcase. Dedicate each shelf to a different family member. Decoupage the inside back area with photos and stories.

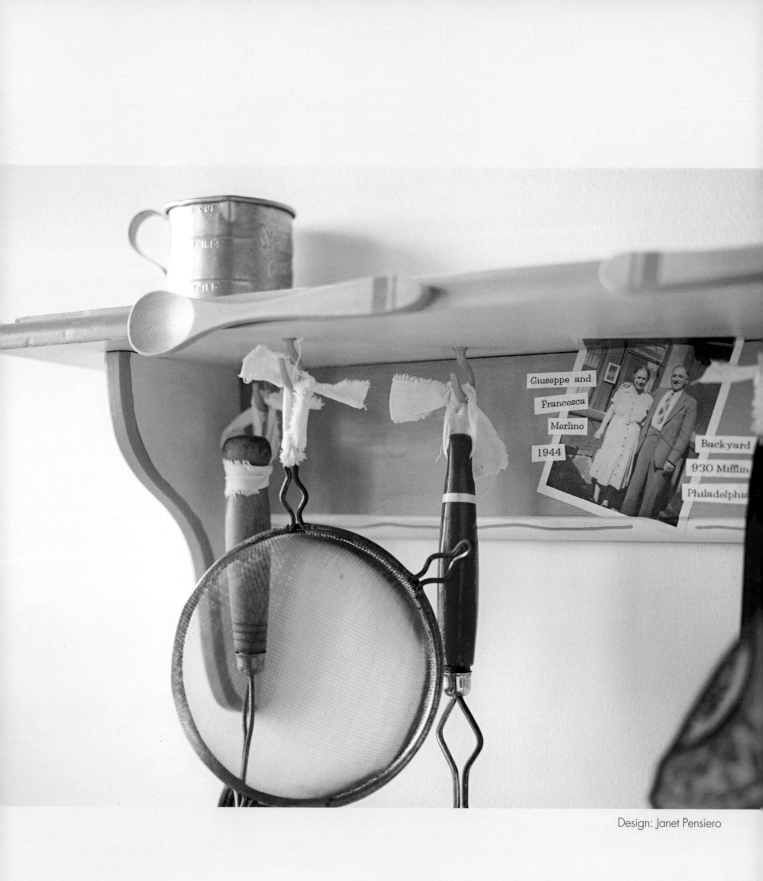

Design: Janet Pensiero

At the American Visionary Art Museum in Baltimore, I saw some wonderful examples of folk art called spirit jars (also called memory jugs), which are containers that have been covered with putty or clay, and have various objects applied to cover their surfaces. These jars are believed to be a part of African-American burial customs, dating back to the time of slavery in this country, with the roots of the custom in African culture. Many cultures have similar rituals, which involve placing cherished objects with the body of the deceased or at the gravesite to ease the transition into the hereafter. These jars were also considered containers for the spirit of the departed and were used to celebrate a life. This twenty-first century spirit jar was made to celebrate a birthday, but other special events, like anniversaries or retirements, could also be celebrated with a jar like this.

Spirit Jar

MATERIALS

- ceramic jug, jar, or earthenware crock
- assorted items belonging to a person or persons to be remembered
- all-purpose, premixed stucco patch (such as DAP; see Keepsake Tip for more information)
- putty knife or flat plastic knife to spread stucco
- latex gloves (optional)

1. Use the putty knife to cover an area of the jug—about 6" (15 cm) square and about ¼" (6 mm) to ⅜" (10 mm) thick—with stucco. The stucco starts to form a skin rather quickly, but takes a while to dry completely.

2. After a minute or two, press the small items into the stucco. Once the stucco has started to harden, you can press out any bumps or lumps with your fingers. Large or heavy items tend to slide down the sides, so keep the items small.

3. After you've covered the first area, let it dry for 30 minutes or so. Repeat this process until the entire jug is covered.

4. Any seams or cracks that appear can be patched with a tiny amount of stucco after it has begun to dry. A cotton swab works well for getting into the small spaces between the objects.

5. After the jug is completely covered, let it dry for several hours until the stucco hardens.

Keepsake Tip

DAP stucco patch works the best of all the materials I tested because it is sticky enough to hold the objects and can be touched up after it has dried. The stucco contains chemicals that may irritate the skin, so you may want to wear latex gloves while working with it.

Design: Janet Pensiero

If your family photos are like mine, they're filled with aunts, cousins, and grandmothers wearing wonderful costume jewelry. It's great to inherit these baubles, especially when you know the ladies who enjoyed wearing them. Making the jewelry into a framed piece of art is a wonderful way to display it and appreciate it—and a terrific way to remember the former owners.

Costume Jewelry Art

MATERIALS

- picture frame (with the glass removed)
- ¼"-thick (12.7 mm) foamcore
- fabric or paper to cover the foamcore
- straight pins and sequin pins
- hot-glue gun and glue sticks
- costume jewelry
- craft knife
- straightedge

1. Use a craft knife and a straightedge to cut a piece of foamcore to fit inside the frame.

2. Choose a piece of fabric or paper to cover the foamcore.

3. Attach the jewelry using the hot-glue gun and pins. The hot glue can be used on anything with a flat back. Use a tiny amount of glue so that it doesn't show.

When attaching jewelry with pins, push in the pins at a slight angle so that the heads hold the piece to the board.

4. Don't forget to acknowledge the former owners on the side or back of the frame and include a photo if you have one.

GRANDMOM'S BROOCH

Design: Janet Pensiero

Sometimes the smallest items—an earring, an old cigar band, a token from an amusement park—can recall happy times with someone who's no longer around. My dad and I had a very special relationship. He was loving, kind, and always made me feel safe and special. I loved his great sense of humor and his sensitivity. At the same time, he was always ready to challenge me on what I thought was right and he thought was wrong. I gave my dad this small box when I was a little girl; now I use it to hold small mementos of him.

Dad's Memory Box

MATERIALS

- wooden box (any size)
- wood stain
- color photocopies of pictures of the person through the years
- archival glue
- Liquid Laminate
- decoupage scissors
- small paintbrush
- fine-line black felt-tip marker
- utility knife
- rubber stamps of words, like *love*, *laughter*, and *friend*
- stamp pad with permanent ink, any color
- self-adhesive cigar and cigar bands (optional)

1. The "Dad" box I had was perfect, but you can purchase any box and stain it with a wood stain of your choice.

2. Plan the arrangement of your color photocopies, and then trim them to your liking. Glue them to the box using the archival glue. Add any decorative touches, such as the self-adhesive cigars and cigar bands, that remind you of your special person.

3. Using the small paintbrush, coat the entire box with Liquid Laminate, and allow it to dry thoroughly.

4. When the laminate is completely dry, carefully trim any of the pictures that overlap the top and bottom of the box with a utility knife.

5. Randomly stamp words on the box that describe your person and your relationship to him or her. You can also add the dates of birth and death with the black felt-tip marker if you'd like.

Keepsake Tip

Glue a favorite picture to the underside of the box's lid for a special surprise. The picture I chose was the earliest one we had of my dad—at age four.

Design: Connie Sheerin

Commemorative *Collage Pillow*

The frame for this photo of my grandfather was made using various ID cards, which tell some of his life story and commemorate his many roles. Ordinary, old documents often have interesting graphic elements, and they confer history and lineage to a project. Approach the design of the pillow as a biographical journey to create an interesting, effective, and highly personal collage. Try using diplomas, birth certificates, passports, awards, or newspaper clippings of special events. Then, focus on the most important parts of each, like names, signatures, or seals, making sure they are highly visible in the collage. Before assembling the collage, adjust the value of the images so that they are similar by using a using a photocopier or a computer. This will create a unified design with a patterned effect.

MATERIALS

- *1 sheet of printer fabric*

- *½ yard (46 cm) of fabric for border and back of pillow*

- *14" x 14" (36 cm x 36 cm) pillow form*

- *straight pins*

- *needle and thread*

- *scissors or rotary cutter*

- *cutting mat*

- *clear ruler*

- *optional: sewing machine*

Starting *Out*

Before beginning the project, be sure to wash the fabric for the border and the back of the pillow to remove any residual chemicals from the manufacturing process.

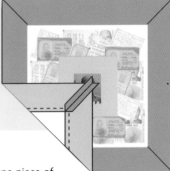

STEP 1

Prepare and print out artwork. Photocopy or scan and print out the photographs and items to be used for the collage. Play with the size and arrangement of the images. Make the final piece of art 8" (20 cm) square, then print it onto or have it copied to the fabric sheet. Trim the fabric so that there is a 1/4" (5 mm) white border around the image.

STEP 2

Assemble the pillowcase. Cut one piece of 14 1/2" x 14 1/2" (37 cm x 37 cm) fabric for the pillow back and four pieces of 3 1/2" x 14 1/2" (9 cm x 37 cm) fabric for the border. Next, center the border strips along each edge of the printer fabric and pin in place. The pieces will overlap at each corner. Stitch each border strip in place, starting and stopping 1/4" (5 mm) from the corners of the printer fabric. Press the seam allowances towards the printer fabric. Then, miter each corner. To do this, bring the outer edges of both border strips together, pin them in place, and mark a 45 degree angle extending from the corner of the printer fabric to the outer edge of the border strips. Sew along this line, then trim 1/4" (5 mm) from the seam. Press the seam allowances open.

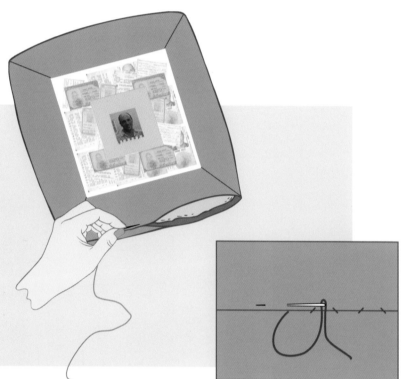

STEP 3

<u>Stuff and close the pillow</u>. Pin the pillow back to the pillow front, right sides together. Stitch 1/4" (5 mm) from the edges of the pillow, leaving an 8" (20 cm) opening at the bottom of the pillow for turning. Then, clip the corners diagonally to reduce bulk. Next, turn the pillow cover right side out and insert the pillow form. Finally, slipstitch the opening closed.

Variation:

Silky satin paired with a central pattern like this illustrated Chinese illustrated lotus, makes an elegant, easy pillow. Most iron-on transfer sheets will work well with 100 percent polyester fabric, such as satin; check the package for specific recommendations. Choose a light or white color that won't obscure the transfer, and be sure to hold the slippery fabric taut and in place while ironing. Then, assemble the pillow as described for the main project, but use two pieces of fabric cut to the same size.

I hoard travel postcards of places seen and unseen. Quite apart from the memories or the dreams they evoke, picture postcards are cheap miniature works of art. At flea markets, great treasures abound for a buck! The beauty of The Postcard Box is the simplicity of its construction: All of the boards are cut out in advance, then glued to a single piece of cloth. There is also a wonderful economy of time and materials. Many of the boards share the same dimensions and are cut with a minimum of measuring. And the scrap fabric is recycled in the finishing. My box is built to hold a 2" (5 cm) stack of postcards.

postcard box...

memories of travels both real and imagined

MATERIALS			
	Binder's board, 60 point	1 button (or more, for	PVA, mixture and paste
	Bookcloth	decorating)	Pressure-sensitive adhesive
	Decorative paper	1 postcard or photograph	
	Elastic cord	Sewing thread	

getting started: gathering the decorations

- Gather the contents of the box: postcards received from friends and family, postcards from your travels or handmade postcards.
- Collect buttons: One will serve as the clasp, so make sure it is sturdy. The others will be for decoration.
- Decide on decorative paper to line the inside of the box.

1

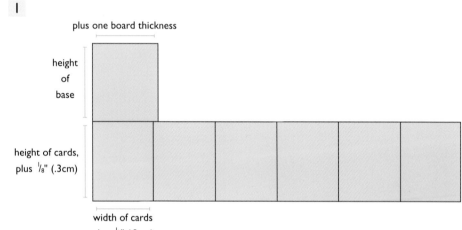

plus one board thickness

height of base

height of cards, plus $^1/_8$" (.3cm)

width of cards plus $^1/_8$" (.3cm)

I CUT OUT ALL OF THE BOARDS

Cut out all of the boards, following the layout above. Cut 6 pieces to:

Height = height of postcards plus $^1/_8$" (.3 cm)
Width = width of postcards plus $^1/_8$" (.3 cm)

Remember: grain must run from head to tail. Label one piece "base," and set it aside. Label one piece "fore-edge flap," and set it aside. Cut one piece in half, crosswise; trim a sliver off each piece, crosswise. Label these boards "head flap" and "tail flap," and set them aside.

Cut two 2" (5 cm) deep strips off one of the remaining boards, crosswise. Label these boards "head wall" and "tail wall." Cut a lengthwise strip, 2" (5 cm) plus one board thickness in width, from one of the remaining boards. Label it "fore-edge wall." From the last remaining board cut a lengthwise strip that measures 2" (5 cm) plus two board thicknesses in width. Label it "spine wall." If you wish to make a shallower or deeper box, adjust the depth of these walls accordingly. You have now used up all six pieces. The final board, the cover board, is cut separately. Cut a board to:
Height = height of base board
Width = width of base board plus one board thickness
Label this piece "cover." From a leftover board, cut a narrow strip a scant two board-thicknesses in width (grain long for ease in cutting). This will be your joint spacer. You need only one spacer; it will be re-used several times.

2   CUT A PIECE OF BOOKCLOTH
large enough to accommodate all of the
boards with a generous margin. This box
requires a piece of cloth approximately
22" (56 cm) square. Trim off the selvage,
or bound edge, of the cloth. Do not trim
any other cloth until the boards have been
glued into place.

GLUE THE BOARDS ONTO THE CLOTH.
Place the cloth, wrong side up, on newsprint.
Arrange the boards on the cloth, making
sure the grain direction of the cloth and the
board is the same. On a separate stack of
newsprint, glue the boards one at a time
and press them onto the cloth. The same
spacer will be used between all of the boards
(see drawing). Start with the cover board
and work your way across the horizontal
plane before gluing the vertical elements.
When all of the boards are in place, turn
the cloth over and rub down with your
folder to make sure no air bubbles remain.

TRIM THE TURN-IN MARGINS. Cut a
scrap board to approximately ³/₄" (2 cm).
Use it to trace around the edges of the
boards, drawing the turn-in allowance. Slide
a cutting mat under the cloth and trim,
using a knife and straight-edge.

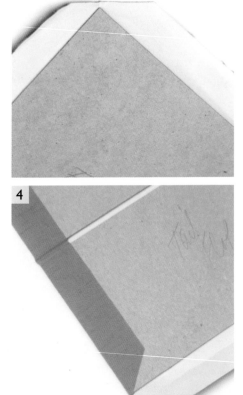

3   CUT THE CLOTH at the four
corners of the base board, slicing diagonally through the turn-in, cutting in as
close as possible to the tip of the board.
Cut off the (8) triangles at the outer corners
of the boards. (See The Basics, page 32.)
Stay 1 ¹/₂ board thicknesses away from the
tip of the boards.

4   GLUE THE TURN-INS.
Start with the eight turn-ins that touch the
walls; finish with the four turn-ins that
land on the flaps. Use your ¹/₂" (1 cm)
brush. Before gluing, slip narrow strips of
newsprint under each turn-in. Glue.
Remove the waste strip and press the cloth
against the board edge. With the edge of
your bone folder, work the cloth into the
two joints, pressing back and forth until
the fabric has stuck. With the broad side of
your bone folder, press the cloth onto the
boards. Work through a waste sheet to
prevent marking the cloth.

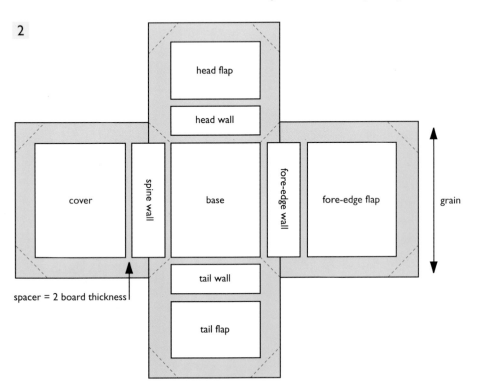

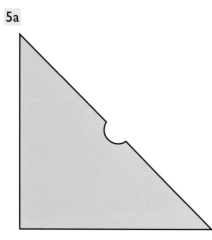

5a   COVER THE TIPS OF THE BASE
BOARD. Cut four triangles from the fabric off-cuts and trim them to fit the corners of the base board. They should match
up with, and complete, the edges of the
turn-ins. Do not overlap the fabric. If necessary, scoop out a slight crescent shape
along the long side of the triangle to keep
the right angle formed by the vertical and
horizontal planes clean and crisp.

5b   Glue out one triangle. Press it lightly onto the base board. Immediately work
the fabric into the two joints, pressing
back and forth with your bone folder.

5c   Mold the cloth around the tip of
the board, patting down any loose threads.
Repeat with the other three triangles.

tip   Allow a ³/₄" (2 cm) margin
of cloth around all board edges.
Reserve the left-over bits of
fabric for finishing details. This
box requires a piece of cloth
approximately 22" (56 cm) square.

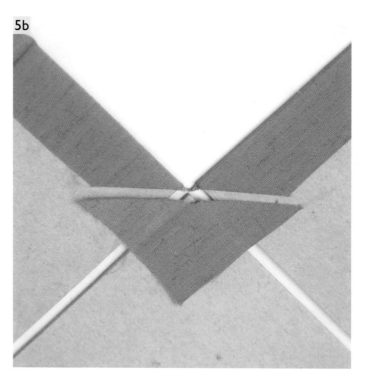

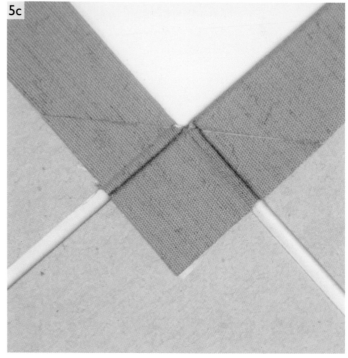

6a

6a DECORATE THE BOX. This is the box's best moment: When you choose a card and a handful of buttons and make your box an object of delight. Design the cover. Include in your design one button that will be the box's closure. If affixing a photograph or a postcard, use a pressure-sensitive adhesive to adhere the artwork to the cover; eventually, the card will be sewn into place. Arrange the button(s) on the cover. Punch holes through the boards to correspond with the button holes. Sew on the button(s).

6b

6b **Note:** If not incorporating buttons into your design, punch holes through the card in strategic places—the corners, for example—and stitch the card in place. The pressure-sensitive adhesive is not secure enough for permanent attachment. Punch two holes in the fore-edge wall for the elastic cord. Thread both ends of the cord through the holes; adjust cord for the proper tension. If desired, thread a button or two onto the cord, to disguise these holes. Cut two shallow channels in the board and tip down the ends of the cord using undiluted PVA. Be persistent: The elastic does not want to stick! Press with your folder to flatten the cord. One or two careful hits with a hammer sometimes does the trick.

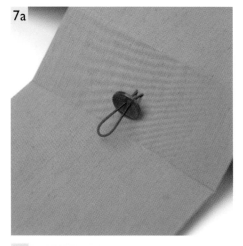

7a

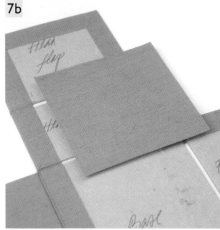

7b

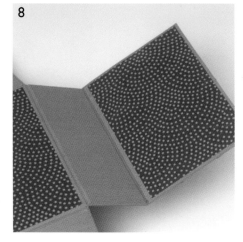

8

7a COVER THE INSIDE WALLS.
Cut four strips of cloth from your leftovers. These strips will extend from the base board to the flaps, covering the walls. They are cut to fit approximately one board thickness away from the outer edges of the box. Cut two strips for the spine and fore-edge walls:
Height = height of walls minus two board thicknesses
Width = depth of walls plus 2" (5 cm)
Cut two strips for the head and tail walls:
Height = depth of wall plus 2" (5 cm)
Width = width of walls minus two board thicknesses

7b Grain should run from head to tail. Glue out the spine wall covering. Position the cloth on the base board, even with the turn-ins and centered heightwise. With the edge of your bone folder, quickly press the cloth into the joint nearest the base; smooth the cloth across the spine wall; press it into the second joint; smooth the cloth onto the cover board. Repeat with the other three wall coverings.

8 LINE THE BOX. Cut five pieces of paper to line all panels of the box. These papers are cut to fit approximately one board thickness away from all four edges of each panel.

This box is a fine container for photographs as well as postcards. To protect the fragile edges of vintage materials, such as this nineteenth-century portrait, frame the artwork prior to sewing it onto the cover. In keeping with the spirit of the photograph, I have used a piece of a handwritten document (also nineteenth century and found in a flea market) to protect and to celebrate this photographic gem.

ROBERT WARNER
Emily Dickinson Box

This box, with its mix of color and pattern, is a quilt-maker's dream. Just reach into your scrap bag, and use whatever bits and pieces come to hand. The box follows the same architectural layout as The Postcard Box but is made in three independent units assembled to form a whole. Because it is built of separate pieces, the design possibilities are vast. I've made my box as exuberant as possible by using different colored cloths to cover the walls and an assortment of decorative papers inside and out. The angling of the head and tail flaps can take many shapes. The cover and the fore-edge panels can be similarly altered.

the patchwork box...
memories of Grandmother's quilts

MATERIALS	Binder's board	Assorted odds and ends	PVA, mixture and paste
	Assorted odds and end	of decorative papers	
	of Bookcloth	Ribbon	

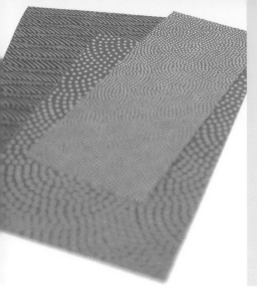

getting started: gathering materials

- Collect the letters and other memorabilia for the box.
- Make sure your collected materials will fit in the box.

I   **CUT THE BOARDS.** Follow the same cutting layout as in The Postcard Box (page 128). Angle the head and tail flaps, as desired.

CUT THE CLOTH. Cloth must be used to cover the walls and the joints of the box where hinging occurs. The amount of cloth that extends beyond the joints is entirely up to you. The measurements below provide for ¹/₂" (1 cm) coverage. Vary them to suit your own sense of design.

Cut two pieces of cloth to cover the spine and fore-edge walls:
Height = height of boards plus 1¹/₂" (4 cm)
Width = depth of wall plus 1³/₄" (4.5 cm)

Cut two pieces of cloth to cover the head and tail walls:
Height = depth of wall plus 2" (5 cm)
Width = width of boards plus 1¹/₂" (4 cm)

I

2a **CONSTRUCT THE CASE.** Locate the center of the spine and fore-edge walls and draw a light pencil line from top to bottom. Repeat with spine and fore-edge cloth. Glue out (with mixture) the spine wall; center the board on the cloth; press. Do not glue the turn-ins. Glue out (with mixture) the fore-edge wall; center the board on the cloth; press. Do not glue the turn-ins.

2b Place the spine wall on a stack of waste papers, larger than the cloth strips by a couple of inches. Glue out the cloth to the left of the wall; remove the waste sheet. Rest the joint spacer against the left-hand side of the wall and push the cover board against the spacer, aligning the height of the boards. Press quickly and pluck out the spacer. Repeat these steps on the right-hand side of the spine wall to attach the base board.

Place the fore-edge wall on the stack of waste sheets. Glue out the cloth to the left of the wall, insert the joint spacer, and push the base board firmly against the spacer. Repeat on right hand side to attach the fore-edge flap.

Glue out the turn-ins and bring the cloth onto the boards, pushing the fabric firmly into the joints of the case.

3 **CONSTRUCT THE HEAD AND TAIL UNITS.** These two units need more generously measured strips of cloth than the spine and fore-edge walls. A 1" (3 cm) extension of cloth will become the hinge attaching the head and tail flaps to the case. Glue out the head wall and position it approximately ³/₄" (2 cm) away from one long edge of cloth, centered left to right. Working on a stack of waste sheets, glue out the ³/₄" (2 cm) extension; remove the upper waste sheet. Gently rest the joint spacer against the wall and push the head flap firmly against the spacer. Press quickly and pluck out the spacer. Repeat with the tail wall and tail flap. Glue out the two short turn-ins on each unit. With the edge of your bone folder, work the cloth crisply into the joint. Pat into place on the boards. Make sure that the turn-ins and the 1" (3 cm) (hinge) extension have been thoroughly pressed together.

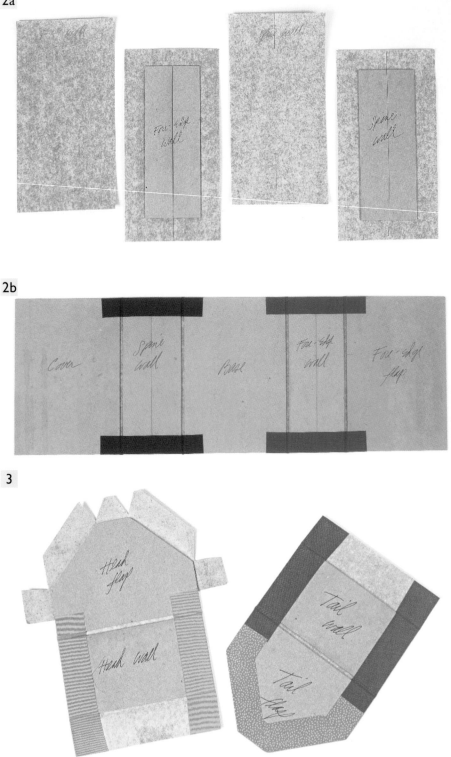

2a

2b

3

5 CUT AND APPLY DECORATIVE PAPERS (head and tail flaps). Cut two pieces of paper:

Height = distance from edge of cloth to board edge plus $^3/_4$" (2 cm)

Width = width of boards plus $1^1/_2$" (3 cm)

Pierce guide marks on cloth; paste out paper; apply paper to board and press (as in Step 6). Fold and unfold the turn-ins a few times, see where there is too much bulk, cut out a few **V**-shaped pieces—staying, always one board thickness away from the board edge. Re-apply paste to the turn-ins and press them onto the board. Put aside, under newsprint, boards, and a weight, to dry.

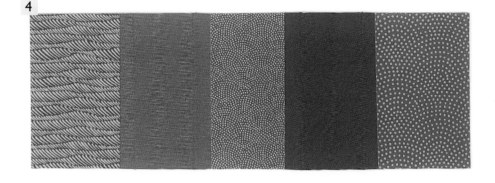

4 CUT AND APPLY THE DECORATIVE PAPERS (case). Cut two pieces of paper for the cover and fore-edge flaps:

Height = height of boards plus $1^1/_2$" (4 cm)

Width = distance from edge of cloth to edge of board plus $^3/_4$" (2 cm)

Cut one piece of paper for the base board:

Height = height of boards plus $1^1/_2$" (4 cm)

Width = distance between both cloth edges plus $^1/_4$" (.5 cm)

Note: These papers will be pasted slightly ($^1/_{16}$"–$^1/_8$" [.15cm–.3 cm]) over the edge of the cloth to prevent the cloth from unraveling and to insure uniform and total coverage of the board. To accurately position your paper, mark both cover and fore-edge flap. Set your spring divider to a measure just short of the distance between the edge of the wall board and the edge of the cloth; pierce the cloth, near the head and tail. Repeat this procedure on the base board, marking only one of the two fabric edges.

Prepare waste sheets. Paste out the cover paper and position it on the case, covering the two guide marks. Make sure the paper is centered. Working through a waste sheet, press first with your hands and then with your folder. Take care not to press too vigorously along the edge overlapping the cloth; paste could seep out and stain the fabric. Flip the case over, cut the corners and finish the edges. (See The Basics, page 32). Repeat with the fore-edge paper.

Note: Do not cut corners off the base paper. Simply bring the turn-ins onto the board and press with your folder. Sandwich case between dry waste sheets, place under a board and a weight, and put it aside.

tip   To find the center of the spine cloth, pinch the cloth lightly at the top and bottom, wrong sides together.

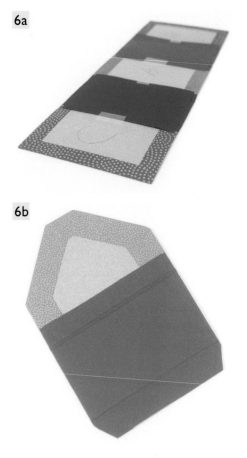

6a

6a COVER THE WALLS (inside). Cut two pieces of cloth for the spine and fore-edge walls:

Height = height of boards minus two board thicknesses

Width = depth of wall plus 2"

Cut two pieces of cloth for the head and tail walls:

Height = depth of walls plus 2"

Width = width of walls minus two board thicknesses

Cover the spine and fore-edge walls. For details on covering these two walls, see The Postcard Box, Step 7 (page 133).

6b

6b To cover the head and tail walls: Glue out the head wall covering and apply it to the flap, approximately $^3/_4$" (2 cm) away from the joint. Push the cloth firmly into the joint, then across the wall, and finally onto the cloth hinge that extends from the wall. Press the hinge firmly so that the two pieces of fabric are thoroughly bonded. Cut a slight wedge off each corner of the cloth hinge. Repeat with the tail flap.

7a ATTACH THE RIBBON TIES. To determine the placement of your ribbons, make a pattern out of a piece of paper cut to the height of the cover board. Place this pattern on the outside of the cover and pierce the cover board with your awl or potter's needle. These pinpricks are your guide marks for chiseling. Before chiseling, protect your table top with scrap board. Select a chisel that is the width of your ribbon. Place the chisel on the guide mark and chisel (from the outside in).

7b Thread the ribbons into the slits (about $^1/_2$" (1 cm)). On the inside, peel away a thin layer of board just deep enough to accommodate each ribbon.

Glue the ribbon (using undiluted PVA) and sink it into the excavated area. Press down and burnish with your folder. Repeat these steps to attach ribbons to the base board.

7a

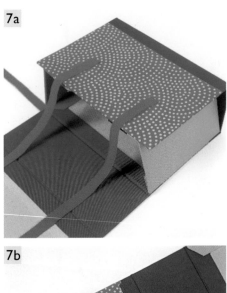

7b

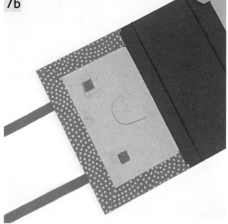

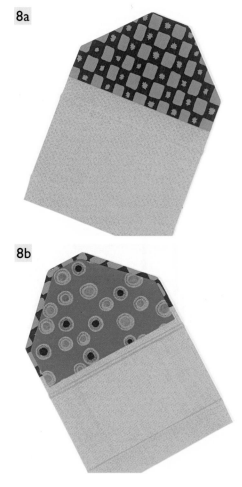

8a LINE THE HEAD AND TAIL FLAPS.
Cut two pieces of paper to line the head and tail flaps:
Height = height of boards minus two board thicknesses
Width = width of boards minus two board thicknesses (adjust if necessary)

8b Before pasting these two papers, fit them to the angled flaps and trim off the excess paper. Paste out these papers (one at a time) and apply them to the appropriate panels. Rub down with your bone folder, through a protective waste sheet. Put the flaps aside to dry between waste sheets, under a board and weight.

9a ATTACH THE HEAD AND TAIL FLAPS TO THE CASE. Sharply crease the hinge against the wall, to form a right angle. Place a flap, right side up, on a waste sheet. With a stiff piece of waste paper, mask the area to be kept glue free. Using undiluted PVA, glue out the hinge. Take care to stay one board thickness away from the wall with your glue brush.

9b Center the hinge on the base board, and press down well. Make sure no glue has squeezed out and stained the wall. Keep your micro-spatula handy, should you need to remove excess glue. Repeat with the other flap.

10 LINE THE CASE. Remember that when pasted, paper will expand in width, anywhere from a hair to a full $1/4$" (.5 cm) depending on the paper and the adhesive. Trim accordingly. The measurements below are approximate.

Cut three pieces of paper, to line the cover, base and fore edge flaps:
Height = height of boards minus two board thicknesses
Width = width of boards minus two board thicknesses (adjust if necessary)

Paste out these papers (one at a time) and apply them to the appropriate panels. Rub down with your bone folder, through a protective waste sheet. Sandwich the box between sheets of dry newsprint; place under boards and a weight, until dry.
Note: Changing the newsprint sheets speeds up the drying process.

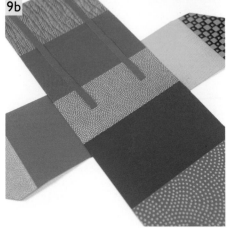

In Loving Memory
Pocket Shrines

When a loved one passes away, the grieving process can be overwhelming. Aside from a multitude of memories, each living being leaves behind a unique imprint—not only in the lives of family and friends but also in the universe itself. These pocket shrines are affectionately created to embrace and elevate the features for which that person is most remembered. The rust depicts the passing of time and healing, and the contents represent the personality. Altogether, the completed mini masterpiece serves as a portable example of a beautiful person and all the hopes and dreams he or she left behind.

Materials

Mint tin

Photo of loved one

Small items that relate to the individual's personality: dried flowers from the funeral, portions of letters, a snippet from a handkerchief, jewelry, a car key, food label, etc.

Miniature decorative items: beads, coins, flowers, pictures, colored pebbles, seashells, stamps, and tinsel

Small angel decorations

Rusting agent

Gold paint

Acrylic paint and/or glitter in assorted colors

Foam board

Basic craft supplies

1) Empty the mints from the tin and wipe clean. Apply the rusting agent to the inside and outside of the tin according to directions on package.

2) Glue the photo of your loved one inside the tin. Arrange items to your liking and then glue them in place. Use small pieces of foam board to elevate objects for a dimensional look.

3) Decorate the front of the box in the same fashion. Add paint and glitter for extra embellishment.

TIPS
• Use glitter glue stick to add color to the objects.
• Let rust additive completely dry before gluing items to it.

VARIATION
Instead of gluing objects, write a poem or letter to your loved one and attach it inside. Add a small music unit so a favorite song will play when a button is pushed.

In Loving Memory

Gregorio Y. Ybarra

Born
March 12, 1909
Sonora, Mexico

Entered into Rest
October 1, 2001
Phoenix, Arizona

Dimensions 4" X 2" X 1" (10 cm X 5 cm X 3 cm)

Artist Kathy Cano-Murillo

Pet Memorial: Multi-page Booklet

ARTIST: SUSAN JAWORSKI STRANC

Although the artist stamped the paw prints directly on the tabs in constructing this booklet, stickers would be an ideal way to avoid risking a misplaced stamp after a page is created. Simply stamp the images and write the names and years on individual round shapes, make them into stickers, and affix them to the pages.

When this booklet page is closed, all the tabs are visible. It is composed of four photo pages, each dedicated to a different pet who shared the lives of the artist and her family at various times. To add more pages, make the spine longer; to subtract pages, make it shorter.

Each page of the booklet is constructed separately with cardstock and art paper joined together, creating a sturdy, double-thick page.

Making the Pages

The small purple pages at right seem very different from the pet pages to the left, but their construction is the same. This technique would make a great journal of the garden, or a terrific recipe book. To make the pages, begin with a rectangle of purple cardstock and a smaller rectangle of green cardstock or paper. The smaller piece should be about one-third the size of the larger one. Glue the green piece flush with one edge of the purple paper and offset slightly from center. To make the pointed tab, use a template to lightly pencil a diamond shape on the green rectangle, positioning it about ½" (1 cm) from the edge. Mark a line across the green strip exactly at the center of the diamond and use the craft knife to cut out the half of the circle that is nearest the edge. Fold the page on the line that bisects the diamond so the cut end sticks up and the cardstock is folded back against itself. Glue the folded part in place and weigh it down with a book until dry, creating a tab. Use a veggie stamp to make a sticker from a separate piece of green paper and stick it to the tab.

Make some more pages, moving subsequent tabs over ½" (1 cm) so they will all be visible when the book is bound. Use different colors for the small rectangles, stamping them with other veggies that grow in your garden.

To Bind the Booklet

Begin with an 8½" × 11" (22 cm × 28 cm) sheet of matte board and a 1½" x 11" (4 cm × 28 cm) strip of the same board. Stamp the board to coordinate with the booklet and to act as a background page. On the left side of the matte board, mark off a margin and use a three-hole punch to create holes so it can be inserted in your scrapbook. Starting at the top third of the matte board, glue the individual pages in place, moving each one down ½" to 1" (1 cm to 3 cm), depending on how many pages you have. When all the pages are in place, use an awl to punch through all the layers—the matte board, the pages, and the binding strip—and lace them with string or cord, tying a bow on the front. Don't pull tightly enough to cause friction on the holes. For viewing, you may want to untie the cord and loosen slightly while the pages are turned.

Kathleen Meyer & *Timothy Peters*

are getting married (to each other)
and we would like you to come to our wedding.

The ceremony will begin at 1:00 p.m. on September 27, 1997

at Corpus Christi Church, Charleston Road, Willingboro, New Jersey.

The reception will follow at St. Mary's Hall, Burlington, New Jersey.

Please respond by August 30, 1997.

Directions, map, and response card enclosed.

Please come!

LOVE AND *FRIENDSHIP, FRIENDS* AND *LOVERS*—any way you say it, they are very special words in all of our vocabularies. The fun part about these two relationships is that, unlike our family relationships, we get to choose them. And often those relationships are as cherished and long-lasting as those with our families.

Love and Friendship

For many of us, our friends are just another type of family. The projects in this chapter range from beautiful and personal wedding keepsakes to fun and informal picture place cards for a dinner party. If your friends are like ours, then they will enjoy these gifts of the heart much more than any store-bought gift.

Special People

When you look through your collections of pictures of friends and lovers, you will surely find some that you have forgotten, but all will certainly bring a story to mind. Although some may have passed in and out of your life over the years, others may still be an important part of it. Many of these pictures and keepsakes can be made into wonderful gifts for those friends who still remain in your life—and you can treasure your memories together.

We have given you a variety of ideas, from the sublime to the fun, each creating a tactile memory of a moment in a shared friendship—from wedding celebrations to special dinners. Think of the gatherings you have with your friends as opportunities to document and preserve the time that you share with these special people in your life. Are you having a wedding shower? Why not invite all the guests to autograph the tablecloth with a special pen, and give the tablecloth to the bride at a later date? Are you hosting a potluck dinner party? Request that everyone send you the recipe from their dish, and begin to create a recipe book from all your parties.

In fact, turn your treasure keeping into a party—get friends together for a creative night called a "swap." Select a project or a theme, and have everyone make multiples, then exchange your creations at the end of the night. The biggest pleasure comes from seeing the individual expressions of the very same idea!

Ivy is traditionally used in bridal bouquets because of its symbolism. It stands for wedded love, fidelity, friendship, and affection. I've been to many weddings over the years—even caught the bouquet once—and I like to make this gift for special friends. Remember to pinch off two or three sprigs of ivy from the bouquet after the ceremony, and wrap them in a damp paper napkin until you get home. The new bride will be thrilled to have a living part of her bouquet come back to her, months after the flowers are gone.

Bridal Bouquet Ivy Pot

MATERIALS

- small terra-cotta flowerpot
- large glass pot or other glass container
- sheet moss
- white or pastel fine-line paint pen
- decorative ribbon or trim
- double-sided tape

1. Line the bottom of the glass pot with moss. Place the small terra-cotta pot centered on the moss. Make sure there is about ¹/₂" (1 cm) of space between the sides of the small pot and the larger one.

2. Gently insert small pieces of moss in the space between the two pots until the cavity is completely filled.

3. With a white or pastel fine-line paint pen, write your message on the outside of the glass pot. You can also write your message for the outside of the pot on a small piece of paper, tape it to the inside of the glass pot, and trace the lettering with the paint pen.

4. Attach a piece of ribbon or trim to the top edge of the pot with double-sided tape.

5. Carefully transplant your rooted ivy into the terra-cotta pot

Keepsake Tip

Rooting ivy is simple. First remove two or three leaves from the cut end of the ivy sprigs. Place the cuttings in water with a small amount of plant food and allow them to sit for several weeks, making sure there is plenty of water, until roots begin to sprout. Then transfer the ivy to a small pot filled with potting soil. Water and feed the cutting until you present it to the bride.

This ivy was rooted from Kathy's bridal bouquet 9·27·97

Design: Janet Pensiero

It's so easy to create an iron-on photo transfer, and the possibilities for using this process are almost limitless. Type, artwork, and photographs can all be transformed into iron-ons with ease at most copy centers. All you need is an iron to complete the process. Most home computer printers are designed to use the iron-on transfer paper as well. Imagine a birth announcement turned into a sweet pillow for the baby's room. Or a real estate ad or flyer enlarged and presented to the new owners of the house as a special housewarming gift. This is a fun way to preserve newspaper clippings, too—the sportsman (or woman) in your house would love to have their winning game stats and photos immortalized on a pillow. And what about those album covers you can't bear to part with? Picture your easy chair filled with your favorite albums in pillow form!

Wedding Invitation Pillow

MATERIALS

- photo iron-on transfer of a wedding invitation
- small piece of solid colored fabric for iron-on
- coordinating fabric for front and back of pillow, approximately $1/2$ yard (46 cm).
- polyester stuffing or pillow form
- trim
- pins
- needle and thread

1. Have an iron-on transfer made at your local copy center, or make one using your home computer. If you're using iron-on paper with your computer printer, be sure to follow package directions carefully. Iron the transfer to a solid piece of fabric, leaving a fabric border of 1" (3 cm) around the edge of the invitation.

2. Cut two pieces of fabric to the size you would like the finished pillow to be.

3. Center the fabric with the iron-on invitation on one piece of the pillow fabric and pin in place. Turn the edge over, and hand-stitch the invitation in place using a blind stitch. Sew or glue decorative trim around the edge of the invitation or in a random pattern.

4. Place the front sides together, and sew around three sides of the pillow shape. Then turn the pillow cover inside out, and fill it with polyester stuffing, or insert a pillow form. Hand-stitch the open side closed using a blind stitch.

Keepsake Tips

- Make a small pocket for the back of the pillow, and fill it with written remembrances of the happy couple.
- Many copy centers have special irons that work better than your home iron at transferring large iron-on images. They will usually iron them for you at no charge.

Kathleen Meyer & Timothy Peters

are getting married (to each other)
and we would like you to come to our wedding.

The ceremony will begin at 1:00 p.m. on September 27, 1997,

at Corpus Christi Church, Charleston Road, Willingboro, New Jersey.

The reception will follow at St. Mary's Hall, Burlington, New Jersey.

Please respond by August 30, 1997.

Directions, map, and response card enclosed.

Please come!

Design: Janet Pensiero

Nothing takes you back to your younger and carefree days more than saved love letters, especially from someone still dear to you. When my mother showed me these letters she had saved from my dad, it made me realize how important handwritten letters are, as opposed to the electronic correspondence we use today. My dad's penmanship reminded me of his artistic, creative, and passionate way of expressing himself through writing, not to mention his great sense of humor.

Love Letters Envelope Wall Hanging

MATERIALS

- rusted metal envelope wall hanging, 7½" (19 cm)
- color photocopies of love letters
- color photocopies of the letter writer and recipient
- acid-free glue
- decoupage scissors
- decaled edge scissors
- lace
- fabric adhesive, such as Fabri-Tac

1. Make color photocopies of the letters, and cut out some of your favorite lines from the letters with the decaled scissors. You can use the decaled or decoupage scissors to cut out the pictures of the featured people.

2. Arrange your pictures and sentences until you like the design. You can trace the position of the pictures and sentences on a piece of paper for a template before actually gluing.

3. Glue some lace on the inside of the metal envelope with some fabric adhesive for a romantic touch.

4. Using the acid-free glue, apply each design, working from the background of your design to the foreground. Allow each layer to dry thoroughly before going to the next layer.

5. Add any additional touches to make the project personal and unique.

Keepsake Tip

Make color copies of both the letters and the envelopes so you can cut out special lines and the postage stamps and date to use as embellishment on the wall hanging.

Design: Connie Sheerin

We all save cards and small mementos from special occasions. But where do we put them? Usually in a drawer with a rubber band around them. This project shows you how to create a decorated keepsake box with your mementos, and you can even store any additional items inside it. I hope this box will be a treasured memory for Karen and Brian, the bride and groom for whom it was designed. Think about how many different occasions a box like this could be used for, from a birth to a special birthday to an anniversary.

Wedding Keepsake Box

MATERIALS

- papier-mâché heart dome box, 10" x 10" x 5" (25 cm x 25 cm x 13 cm)
- one package of decorative tissue paper
- wedding invitation and save-the-date card
- one page of dried flowers and leaves
- tweezers
- 1' (0.3 m) of gold trim
- decoupage medium, such as Mod Podge, in a satin finish
- white glue
- white acrylic paint
- two sponge brushes

1. Using a sponge brush, paint all parts of the box that will be visible with white acrylic paint.

2. Follow the directions that come with the box to assemble the top. Use white glue to attach the pieces together.

3. Cut the invitation to fit under the dome. Glue it in place with the white glue according to directions that come with box.

4. Use the tweezers to pick up the dried leaves and flowers. Dip each piece into the white glue, and place the pieces around the invitation to create a frame. Then glue the dome over the invitation. Measure and cut the gold trim, and glue it around the dome.

5. Tear the tissue paper into fairly large pieces, enough to cover the entire box, inside and out. Glue the pieces onto the box using the decoupage medium and a sponge brush.

6. Glue the save-the-date card and its envelope onto the bottom of the box. Apply a second coat of the decoupage medium.

Keepsake Tip

The save-the-date card's envelope tells the bride and groom whom the gift is from, and the postage stamp and postage mark add more documentation to the gift.

Design: Connie Sheerin

Dinners with family or friends, especially on special occasions, are always the best time for sharing and laughter. These place cards are a fun and memorable idea that are sure to evoke another story or memory. You could make these photo place cards on inexpensive napkin rings for favors to take home and start all over again with new ones for the next gathering.

Fun Photo Placecards

MATERIALS

- assortment of self-adhesive photo cards
- color photocopies of pictures that will fit nicely under the photo cards
- decoupage scissors
- dried flowers for embellishment (optional)
- inexpensive napkin rings
- epoxy glue, such as Glass, Metal & More

1. Trim the color photocopies to fit each photo card. Peel off the protective backing from the photo card, and attach the photocopy. Trim off any excess pieces of the picture.

2. Glue the photo cards onto the napkin rings with epoxy glue. Let dry and decorate with dried flowers, if desired.

3. Avoid writing on these—everyone needs to guess who is who and what the story is behind the pictures.

Keepsake Tip

The self-adhesive photo cards can be found in most craft and stationery stores. You can also use clear acetate cut to size. Attach the photo to the acetate with silver foil tape around the edges.

Design: Connie Sheerin

No glue! No paste! No complicated cuts! This box is, simply, two pieces of paper joined at the base with strips of pressure-sensitive adhesive. Since it is such an austere construction, The Paper Box needs a paper with character and body to give it charm. If the color is vibrant, this spunky box needs very little ornamentation: A button or two and a piece of bright thread are enough. The paper used here is a lustrous handmade. Its linen content gives the paper both strength and tactility. In this project you will use a new technique: scoring paper. This is a simple but important technique (see The Faux Book Box on page 206 for an additional application), and deserves the highlighting starting on page 159.

the paper box...
for the love of paper

MATERIALS

A good-quality hand-made paper	Buttons	Pressure-sensitive adhesive on a roll
Thread	Elastic cord	PVA

getting started:
cutting the first piece of paper

- Cut out the first piece to the following dimensions:
  Height = height of object to be boxed (referred to as "object" hereafter)
  Width = width of object, plus twice the thickness of the object, plus 2"–4" (5–10 cm), depending on the size of the box.
- If you intend to sew through the spine and fore-edge walls (as in the box pictured), increase this width measurement by approximately ¼" (.5 cm) since the stitching on the inside of the box juts into the base, diminishing its overall width.

ONE

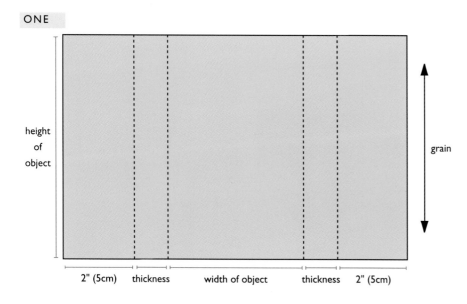

height of object

grain

2" (5cm) thickness width of object thickness 2" (5cm)

HOW TO SCORE A PIECE OF PAPER

Place a sheet of blotter, or a pad of newsprint, on your workbench. To make deep, crisp score marks, you must work on a cushioned surface.

Mark the paper for scoring. To mark, make small pinpricks with a sewing or potter's needle. (If you make pencil markings, you will need to erase them later.)

Place your triangle on the paper. The right angle of the triangle must sit on top of the pinprick. Draw a line with your bone folder, from the marked edge to its opposite edge (head to tail; spine to fore-edge). Keeping the triangle in place, scoot under the paper and run your folder up and down, pressing the paper firmly against the edge of the triangle. Remove the triangle. Fold over the paper and sharpen the crease with your folder.

Note: Steps 2 through 8 and Step 10 are illustrated with scale models of the actual box.

1   SCORE THE PAPER by centering the object on the paper and making two pin-pricks, to the left and right of the object, on the tail edge of the paper. Score and sharply crease the paper. (See How to Score a Piece of Paper on page 159.)

2   FORM THE SPINE AND FORE-EDGE WALLS. Measure the thickness of the object and transfer this measurement to your paper, with pinprick markings, to the outside of the previously scored lines. (To measure for thickness, see The Basics, page 26.) Score and sharply crease the paper. Round the sharp corners, at head only.

3   CUT OUT THE SECOND PIECE:
Height = three times the height of the object plus twice its thickness
Width = width of object enclosed in the first piece
Grain must run from spine to fore-edge.

3

enclosed in piece #1

height
of
object

thickness
of
object

thickness

height

grain

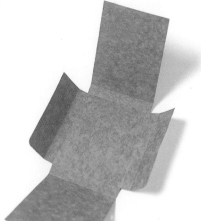

4 **SCORE THE PAPER** by centering the (enclosed) object on the paper and making two pinpricks, to the top and bottom of the object, on the spine edge of the paper. Score and sharply crease the paper.

From the head and tail walls. Measure the thickness of the object to be enclosed and transfer this measurement to your paper, with pinprick markings to the outside of the previously scored lines. Score and sharply crease the paper.

5 **TRIM HEAD AND TAIL FLAPS** to desired shape and depth. Round off all sharp edges on head flap.

6a **SEW ON BUTTON AND APPLY REINFOCEMENT PATCHES.** Decide on the placement of the buttons and elastic cord on the head and tail flaps. Punch holes.

6b Before sewing, cut and glue small patches of paper over punched area, either inside or out. Insert cord and sew on buttons.

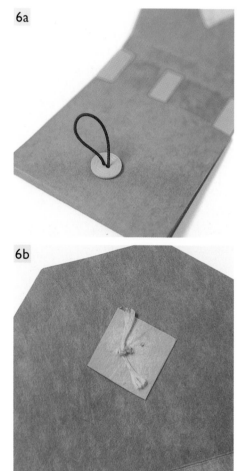

7a

7b

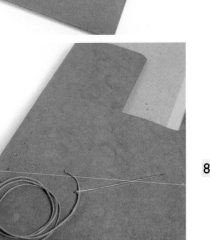

8

8a

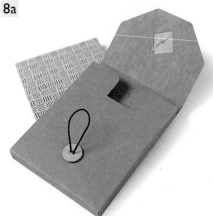

7c

7a, b, c   If sewing the spine and fore-edge walls, punch holes through the tail flap, the flanges under the flap, and through corresponding areas on the spine and fore-edge walls. (See Tip on page 163.) Do not sew.

8   **ATTACH THE TWO UNITS** by applying strips of pressure-sensitive adhesive to the second piece, in the areas illustrated.

8a   Peel off backing paper on the base area only, and stick the two units together. If omitting decorative stitching, peel off backing paper on the tail flap and carefully align this flap with the spine and fore-edge flanges; press down into place.

8b   If sewing, thread two needles. Start on the inside of the tail flap, and sew toward the head in an overcast stitch, sewing up both sides simultaneously. When the sewing is complete, sneak inside and peel off backing paper on tail flap; press the flap onto the flange.

There are many ways to close this box. Apply ribbon ties, as in previous projects. Use adhesive-backed Velcro dots. Or, cut a slit in the tail flap and insert head flap into this slit.

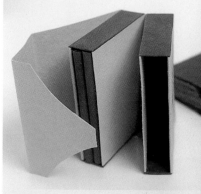

Tip *How to Punch Holes*

Make a punching block by taping scrap boards together, to the depth of your walls and to the appropriate height. To punch holes through the tail flap and the flanges underneath, insert this block into the box, align the papers in the proper position, and punch through both papers simultaneously. I held a ruler $1/4$" (.5 cm) away from the edge of the tail flap and punched holes at $1/2$" (1 cm) intervals. To make sure the holes in the two walls are in the corresponding positions, move the right angle of a triangle from hole to hole, punching holes in the wall as you go from head to tail.

HEDI KYLE *Demosta*
5" x 4$^3/_8$" x 2$^1/_2$"
(13cm x 11cm x 6cm) (closed)

books: Firenze paper soaked in coffee
box: Tim Barrett handmade and Moriki papers

This is indeed a sweet container, and a versatile one as well. It can hold a single piece of chocolate or a ton of St. Valentine's Day cards. The Candy Box, like the prototypical Whitman's Sampler, consists of two nesting trays. Because this is a simple project—the second tray is an exact repeat of the first—it is a good candidate for multiples. To make an edition of three small boxes instead of one requires just a few more minutes in cutting time, an extra hour or two in construction time, and a couple of dollars more in materials. Be brave: produce an edition!

A survey of vintage candy boxes reveals yards of embossed, gilt, and lace papers. For my edition, I likewise selected a textured, brilliant red paper. The boxes are lined with antique tea chest paper—paper used in Japan to wrap bricks of tea.

the candy box...

memories of fudge and friendships

MATERIALS	Binder's board	Decorative paper
	Bristol or museum board for linings	PVA, mixture and paste

getting started:
cutting the boards for the tray

- Cut out the boards for the inside tray, following the layout shown.
- Base:

    Height = desired height of box, plus two paper (covering) thicknesses

    Width = desired width of box, plus two paper (covering) thicknesses

- Head and tail walls:

    Width = desired width of box, plus two paper (covering) thicknesses

    Depth = desired depth of box, plus one board thickness, plus one lining thickness

- Spine and fore-edge walls:

    Height = height of base, plus two board thicknesses

    Depth = desired depth of box, plus one board thickness, plus one lining thickness

1a, b   **CONSTRUCT THE TRAY**
(see The Basics, page 30). Smooth all seams
with a sanding stick.

1a

CUTTING LAYOUT FOR ONE BOX

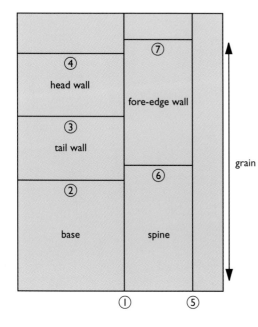

1b

CUTTING LAYOUT FOR THREE BOXES

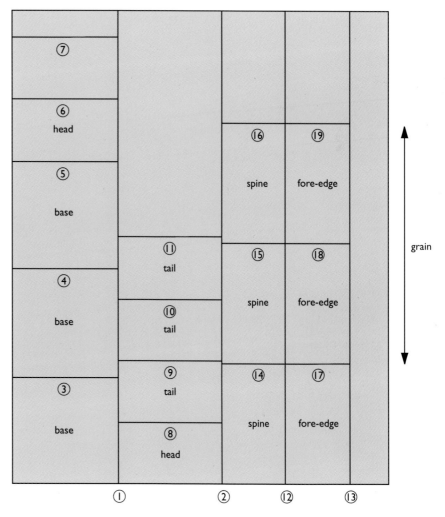

2a, b   COVER THE TRAY. Cut out the covering paper—a strip twice the depth of the tray plus 1 1/2" (4 cm), and long enough to wrap around all four walls plus 1/2" (1 cm). If the paper is too short to wrap around the tray in one continuous strip, piece together two shorter strips, making sure that the seam falls on a corner of the tray. Cover the tray (see The Basics, page 31).

2b

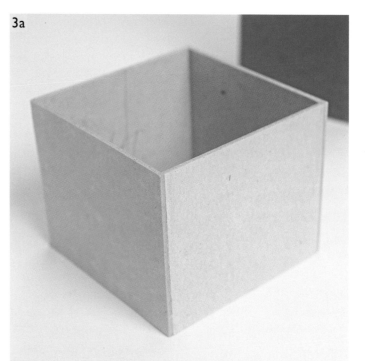

3a

3 CUT OUT THE BOARDS for the outside tray following the layout in Step 1. This tray is slightly larger than your inside tray.

3a To measure for its parts you must use your completed inside tray as a pattern. Place your tray on the squared corner of a piece of board (see page 26).

3b Make sure the grain runs from head to tail on both units, and that the spine and tail of the tray are flush with the squared
corner. Mark for cutting. Cut.
Base:
Height = height of tray plus two paper (covering) thicknesses
Width = width of tray plus two paper (covering) thicknesses
Head and tail walls:
Width = width of tray plus two paper (covering) thicknesses
Depth = depth of tray plus one board thickness
Spine and fore-edge walls:
Height = height of base plus two board thicknesses
Depth = depth of tray plus one board thickness

NEXT **CONSTRUCT AND COVER THE TRAY** (as in Steps 1 and 2).

NEXT **CUT OUT THE TWO PLAT-FORMS.** These boards are identical in size. They extend beyond the parameters of the larger tray by one board thickness in all four directions. Place the larger tray on the squared corner of a piece of board, flush spine and flush tail. Add two board thicknesses to the height and the width of the tray. This will later be redistributed as a one-board-thickness margin around all edges. Mark and cut out two boards.

3b

Head Wall

Spine Wall

Base

Fore-Edge Wall

Tail Wall

4 COVER BOTH PLATFORMS.

Cut out two pieces of decorative paper, larger than the boards by 1 1/2" (4 cm) in both height and width.

4a   Make sure the grain runs from head to tail. Cover the boards, cut the corners and finish the edges (see The Basics, page 32).

4b   Cut two pieces of scrap paper to fill in the remaining exposed board. This filler will balance the board, inducing it to flatten and to adhere more strongly to the tray.

 4a

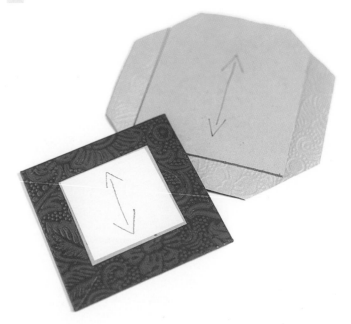

NEXT   GLUE THE TRAYS to the platforms. Brush undiluted PVA onto the bottom of the larger tray; wipe excess glue away from the edges. Center the tray on the wrong side of the lid platform. The other platform becomes the base platform. There should be a uniform small extension of a single board thickness beyond the edges of the tray. Hold these two units together for a few minutes, until the tray stops sliding and begins to stick. Flip the box over and place newsprint, a board, and a weight on top of the lid. Keep weighted until dry. Repeat all of these steps with the inside tray. Remember that this tray is smaller than the outside tray. When you are centering the tray on the base platform, the extension of the platform will be larger than one board thickness.

4b

5a

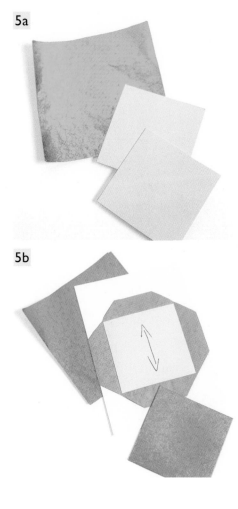

5b

To create a dazzling display of color and pattern, cover the individual parts of the box—trays, platforms, and liners—with a mix of papers.

5 LINE THE TRAYS.

5a   If lining the box with a medium or heavyweight paper, cut out two pieces of paper, one to fit inside of each tray. Don't forget to anticipate the stretch of the paper against the grain, and be sure to cut it a bit narrower in width.

5b   Paste out these papers and stick them down. Press, as usual, with newsprint, a board, and a weight, until dry. (If your box is quite small, there is no need to press it.)

If lining the box with a delicate or lightweight paper (such as the gold paper pictured here), it is first necessary to card the paper around boards. Cut out two pieces of lightweight board (bristol or museum board) to the same dimensions:
Height = height of interior of small tray, minus $1/8$" (.3 cm)
Width = width of interior of small tray, minus $1/8$" (.3 cm)
Cut out 2 pieces of covering paper:
Height = height of boards, plus $1 1/2$" (4 cm)
Width = width of boards, plus $1 1/2$" (4 cm)
Cover the boards, cut the corners, and finish the edges. (see The Basics, page 32.)

Apply undiluted PVA to the backs of these boards, wipe away excess glue, and carefully lower the boards into the trays. Hold for a few minutes until the glue begins to set. Cut a piece of scrap board to fit inside each tray. Drop this board into the tray, place a weight on top, and press until dry.

What is more tender than a ribbon-tied bundle of letters? Pushed to the back of a desk drawer or aban-
doned in a dark closet, they are poignant testimony to friendship and love. They deserve a box of their own.
Here, the letters nestle within a tray; the tray is tucked inside an extended case. The ribbons, besides being
decorative, restrain the letters and also allow their graceful removal from the depths of the tray. The box
closes, seemingly magically, with hidden magnets.

My choice of a textured cloth and a patterned lining paper is not accidental. Because it is difficult
to totally disguise the presence of magnets, lively materials help to distract the eye. The beautiful hand-
painted paste paper, made by Lost Link Design Studio, is based on techniques used in the production of
cover and endpapers in Europe from the late sixteenth through the eighteenth century. A wonderful book
on the subject, originally published in 1942 and still unsurpassed, is Rosamond B. Loring's Decorated
Book Papers *(Harvard University Press).*

the letter box...
memories of lives past and present

MATERIALS	Bookcloth	Bristol or museum board	Magnetic strips
	Binder's board	Lining paper	PVA, mixture and paste
	(100 point)	Ribbon	

getting started:
cutting the boards for the tray

The goal is a snug fit, with just enough breathing room to allow the ribbons to lift the letters out of the box. To determine the height of the tray, find your tallest letter; to determine width, find your widest letter. Follow the formula below:

- Base:

    Height = height of tallest letter plus $\frac{1}{8}$" (.3 cm)

    Width = width of widest letter plus $\frac{1}{8}$" (.3 cm)

- Head and tail walls:

    Width = width of widest letter plus $\frac{1}{8}$" (.3 cm)

    Depth = $1\frac{1}{2}$" (4 cm) or desired depth

- Spine and fore-edge walls:

    Height = height of base board, plus two board thicknesses

    Depth = $1\frac{1}{2}$" or desired depth, matched to head and tail walls

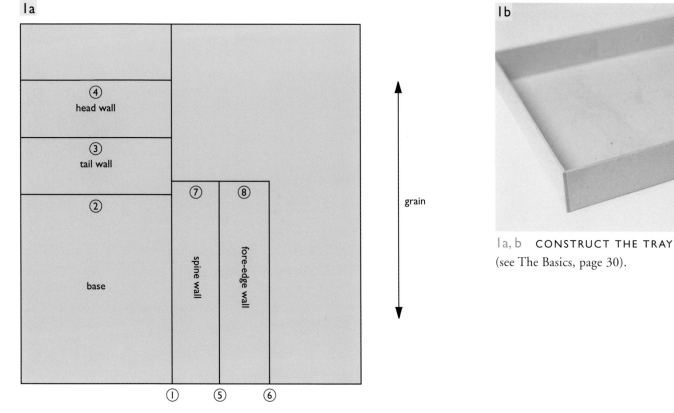

1a, b   CONSTRUCT THE TRAY
(see The Basics, page 30).

2a

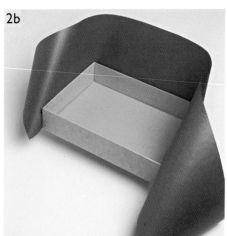

2b

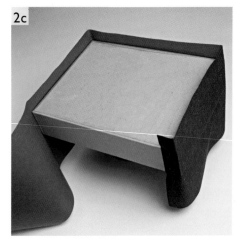

2c

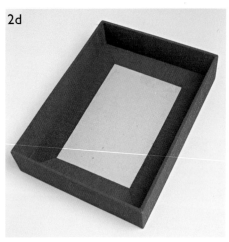

2d

2 COVER THE TRAY.

2a–c   Cut out the covering cloth—a strip twice the depth of the tray plus 1 1/2" (4 cm), and long enough to wrap around all four walls plus 1/2" (1 cm). If the cloth is too short to wrap around the tray in one continuous strip, then piece together two shorter strips, making sure that the seam falls on a corner of the tray.

2d   Cover the tray (see The Basics, page 31).

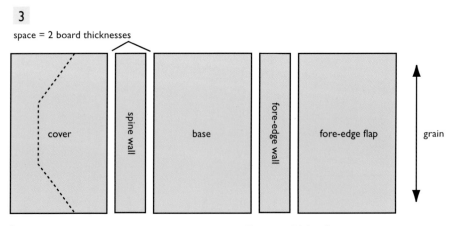

3

space = 2 board thicknesses

cover

spine wall

base

fore-edge wall

fore-edge flap

grain

3   CUT THE BOARDS FOR THE CASE.
Select boards thick enough to accommodate the magnetic strips that will be embedded in the cover and the fore-edge flap (Minimum board thickness: 100 point).

The height is the same for all five case boards:
Height = height of the covered tray, plus two board thicknesses
The width of the boards is the same for the three main panels:

Base = width of tray
Fore-edge flap = width of tray
Cover = width of tray (to be adjusted)
The depth of the walls is as follows:
Fore-edge wall = depth of covered tray, plus a hair
Spine wall = depth of fore-edge wall, plus one board thickness
From your scrap board, cut a slender strip two board thicknesses in width. This will be a joint spacer. See above for a diagram of the board layout.

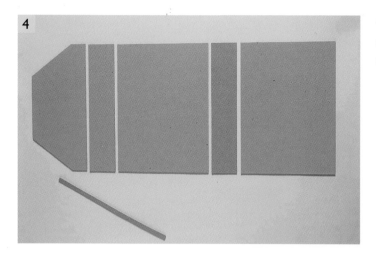

4 TRIM AND ANGLE the cover board, as desired. Smooth all sharp edges and corners with a sanding stick.

5a APPLY THE MAGNETIC STRIPS. Draw a pencil line ³/₄" (2 cm) away from the angled edge of the cover. Draw a parallel line ¹/₂" (1 cm), or the width of your magnet, away from the first line. Cut two magnetic strips to the length of these lines.

5b Cut and peel up a layer of board equal to the thickness of the magnet.

5c Remove the backing paper and sink the magnet into this recessed area. Find the corresponding area on the fore-edge flap for the placement of the second magnet. Be precise because the magnet will not hold unless the two are perfectly aligned.

5d Cut and peel away board. Sink the magnet.

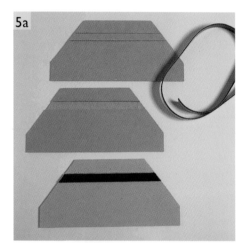

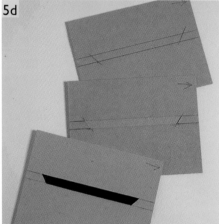

6a

6b

6c

NEXT   CUT THE CLOTH FOR THE
CASE:

Height = height of boards plus 1 1/2" (4 cm)
for turn-ins

Width = width of boards laid out, plus joint
spacing plus 1 1/2" (4 cm) for turn-ins

NEXT   CONSTRUCT THE CASE.
Note: When gluing up the case, the cover
board is glued magnet side *up* on the cloth;
the fore-edge flap is glued magnet side *down.*
Glue the boards and apply them to the
cloth, working from left to right and using
the joint spacer between every two boards.
Flip the case over and press down well,
eliminating any air bubbles.

NEXT   CUT THE CORNERS and
finish the edges (see The Basics, page 30).
As with The Patchwork Box, when dealing
with the angled panel you will need to
invent a pattern of cuts that allows for the
clean coverage of all corners.

6a   COVER THE (INSIDE) WALLS.
Cut two strips of cloth from your leftovers
to cover the walls, fill in the joints, and
extend onto the three main panels:
Height = height of case minus two board
thicknesses
Width = depth of spine wall plus 1 3/4"
(4.5 cm)
Make sure, as always, that the grain runs
from head to tail.

6b, c   Glue out one strip and position it,
centered, on the spine wall. Press it down
quickly and work the cloth into the two
joints with the edge of your bone folder,
moving back and forth between the two
joints until the fabric has stuck. Press the
cloth onto the cover and base panels.
Repeat with the fore-edge wall.

7

7   LINE THE CASE. Cut two pieces of
paper to line the cover and the fore-edge
flap:
Height = height of case minus two board
thicknesses
Width = width of cover and fore-edge
flap, minus two board thicknesses
Remember to anticipate the stretch of the
pasted or glued paper in width, and cut
accordingly. Glue or paste these papers to
adhere them. Put newsprint, boards, and
weights on these two panels, and let dry.

NEXT   GLUE THE TRAY TO THE
CASE. Cut two pieces of scrap cloth, large
enough to fill in (1) the bottom (outside)
of the tray; and (2) the base board of the
case. Glue them out and stick them down.
Using undiluted PVA, paint a thin, consistent layer of glue onto the bottom of the
tray. Wipe excess glue from the edges.
Position the tray on the base of the case,
centered head to tail, and hold until the
glue begins to set. Fill with weights, and
let dry.

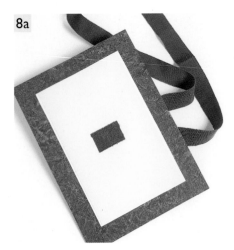

8a

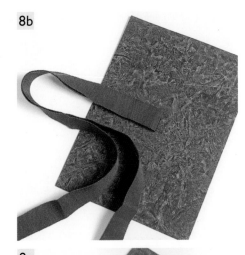

8b

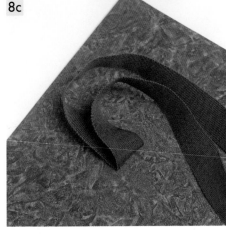

8c

8d

8 ATTACH RIBBONS AND LINE THE TRAY.

8a, b   Cut a piece of lightweight board to fit inside of the tray. Allow ¹/₈" (.3 cm) breathing room in both height and width. To cover this board, cut a piece of either paper or cloth to the following dimensions:

Height = height of board plus 1¹/₂" (4 cm)
Width = width of board plus 1¹/₂" (4 cm)

Adhere the covering material to the board, cut the corners, and finish the edges (see The Basics, page 30). Fill in the back of the board with scrap paper. Select a chisel the width of your ribbons and make a vertical slit through the center of this board.

8c, d   Push the ends of two ribbons through the slit and glue down with undiluted PVA on the back of the board. Paint a thin layer of undiluted PVA on this board, wipe off excess glue from the edges, and carefully lower the board into the tray. Keep the ribbons away from the glue. Put a protective waste sheet on top of this liner, fill the tray with boards and a weight, and let dry.

NEXT   GLUE THE CASE WALLS TO THE TRAY. Brush a thin layer of undiluted PVA onto the spine wall of the tray. Wipe excess glue from the edges. Roll the tray onto its spine wall; fill the tray with weights and press until the spine walls of the tray and case are thoroughly bonded. Repeat with fore-edge wall.

Tip: *To Line the Tray with a Framed Photo*

Remove the letters from the box and discover an image of the writer—or the recipient—framed beneath. Alter the previous instructions in two places: (1) In cutting out the boards for the tray (Step 1), increase the depth of the walls to accommodate the additional thicknesses of the covered mat and the photograph; and (2) replace Step 12 with the following:

1. Cut two pieces of lightweight board to fit inside the tray. Allow $^1/_8$" (.3 cm) breathing room in height and width.

2. Cut a window out of one of the boards. Cut a piece of decorative paper, to cover this mat, to the following dimensions:
Height = height of board plus 1 $^1/_2$" (4 cm)
Width = width of board plus 1 $^1/_2$" (4 cm)

3. Cover the mat, by pasting out the paper and centering the board on the paper. Finish the interior of the mat only (see The Picture Frame Box, Step 2, page 55). Do not cut corners or finish the outer edges.

4. Glue the two ribbons onto the back of the mat.

5. Affix the photo, with pressure-sensitive adhesive, in the proper location on the second (uncut) board.

6. Glue the wrong side of the mat with undiluted PVA to the photo board. Keep the ribbons free of glue. Press.

7. Place the mat, wrong side up, on the workbench. Cut the corners of the paper, staying 1 $^1/_2$ board thicknesses away from the tip of the board. Remember that your "board" consists of the mat, the photo, and the photo board. Re-apply paste to the turn-ins, and adhere them. Fill in the back of the board with scrap paper.

8. Glue the board to the tray by painting a thin layer of undiluted PVA on the board, wiping off excess glue from the edges, and carefully lowering the board into the tray. Put a protective waste sheet on top of the liner, fill the tray with boards and a weight, and let dry.

If you wish to protect the photograph, cut a piece of Plexiglas to the height and width of the two boards, and sandwich it between the mat and the photo board before completing the turn-ins (Step 7).

To Life: Just the Beginning
Wedding Wall Shrine

In the world of weddings, vows are meant to last forever. What better way to relive the once-in-a-lifetime experience than to capture the magical memories in a stunning wall display? Much like weddings, planning is a crucial element for this project. Before the big day, recruit a loved one as the designated memory caretaker—a job that will require them to meticulously collect a variety of personal objects associated with the wedding from beginning to end. Eventually these prized possessions will be assembled into a beautiful wall shrine of eternal bliss—and a constant reminder of those special vows and that unforgettable day.

Materials

Shadow box with 4 shelves or compartments (door is optional)

Bridal shower, wedding, and honeymoon mementos: invitations, photos, flowers, napkins, receipts, maps, love letters, fabric swatches from clothing, table accessories, menus, sand, shells, rocks or leaves from location, and champagne corks/glasses

Basic craft supplies

1) Categorize the mementos into four groups: wedding, honeymoon, bride, and groom.

2) Designate a compartment in the wall shrine for each group.

3) Use a glue stick and card stock or scrapbook borders to add an elegant background to the photos or other paper objects.

4) Spend some time assembling objects in the compartments until a balanced form is achieved, then adhere to the surface. Suspend objects from the top of the compartments with string and small suction cups.

5) If your wall shrine has a door, use it to hang objects such as a garter belt, jewelry, or tie.

TIPS
- Decorate the outside of the wall shrine with beautiful wrapping paper from gifts or lace. To add dimension to photos, apply background layers of colored card stock.
- Use decorative scrapbook borders, die cuts, stickers, or wedding-themed accessories for added embellishments.

Dimensions 30" X 18" X 6" (76 cm X 46 cm X 15 cm)

Forever Friends Photo Box

A golden moment captured on film is what this photo box is all about. Following childhood and preceding adulthood, we develop some of our most cherished relationships that will endure throughout our lives. If we do happen to lose touch with them, this project will preserve the memory just as you left it. Choose one classic image that relays the extraordinary feeling of serendipitously showing off youthful grins, gorgeous figures, and spiffy clothes. Splurge on a fancy frame, glass beads, and floral roses to enhance the beauty of your visual time capsule.

Materials

Old photo of a gathering of friends

6" × 8" × 1½" (15 cm × 20 cm × 4 cm) wood box

10" × 8½" (25 cm × 22 cm) wood frame

3" × 5" (8 cm × 13 cm) wood block with scalloped edge

Bag of glass seed beads

4 medium-sized fabric or dried roses

Bottle of translucent squeeze glitter

Acrylic paints in black, white, and gold

Stencil brush

Picture-hanging attachment

Basic craft supplies

1) Paint the box white and the frame black. When dry, stencil gold on top of both and let dry. Squeeze the translucent glitter on both surfaces and gently sweep it across with the brush to create a shimmery effect.

2) Copy an old photo in color and use a glue stick to adhere it to the wood block. Paint the ridges black and stencil with gold. Working on top of newspaper, line the top edge of the block with industrial-strength craft glue. Sprinkle the seed beads and then pat them with your finger to create an even layer. This will reduce the number of beads that will fall off. Tap the block on the paper to catch loose beads. Let it dry and then attach the block to the center of the wood box.

3) Rest the picture frame over the front of the box and line it up evenly. Hold it firmly and turn it upside down. Run a bead of hot glue along the seams where the frame and box meat to secure it and let dry.

4) Adhere a layer of seed beads around the outer edge of the frame. Glue one rose to each corner of the frame. Add a hanging attachment to the back.

TIP

Take extra care when lining up the frame with the box to ensure the two are sealed in a straight and even manner. Lightly tap box to remove loose seed beads. Gently remove any stragglers by hand or with tweezers.

VARIATION

The color scheme of this box was created for an old black-and-white photo. If using a color photo, change colors to match. Add small keepsakes around the border that are associated with the picture.

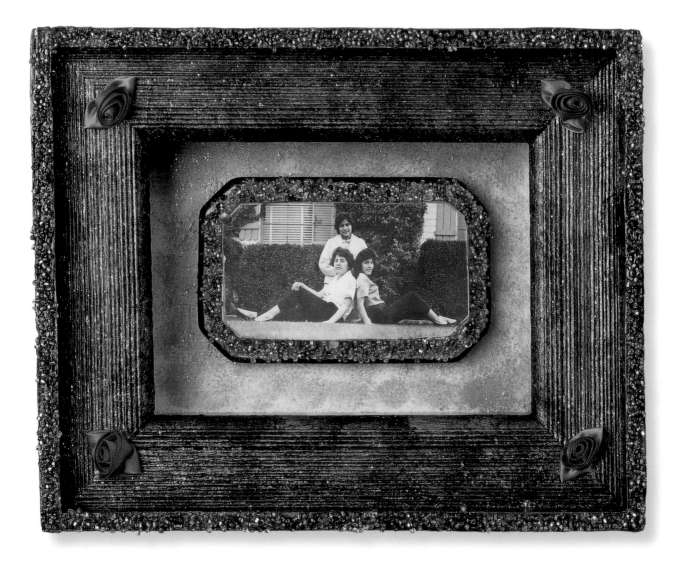

Dimensions 6" X 8" (15 cm X 20 cm)

A Soldier's Prayer Shrine

Throughout history, many American service personnel have brought along spiritual items with which to pray while stationed or fighting overseas. This portable, patriotic prayer shrine is small, quiet, and personalized to offer a soldier sanctuary and comfort. The center panel is tailored to the soldier's particular faith. With camouflage fabric and batting as the foundation, this lightweight piece comes with a family photo and includes two secret pockets to hold a rosary, a letter, or a memento. This inspirational shrine protects the most important ideas contained inside: duty to one's country and family bound by faith in God.

Materials

¼ yard (23 cm) camouflage fabric

¼ yard (23 cm) white cotton fabric

17" × 5" (43 cm × 13 cm) batting

Matching thread

Coordinating embroidery floss

Embroidery needles and hoop

Family photo and iron-on photo-transfer kit

Drawing pencil and white paper

2 small flag patches

3 buttons, ⅞" (2 cm) in diameter

Off-white dimensional squeeze paint for fabric

1) Wash and dry the fabrics. Cut two pieces of camouflage fabric to measure 19" × 7" (48 cm × 18 cm), and two pieces of white cotton to measure 5½" × 7" (14 cm × 18 cm). Cut another to measure 6" × 6¼" (15 cm × 17½ cm). On the center of the largest fabric rectangle, draw a cross in the center and a random camouflage pattern inside.

2) Set an embroidery hoop over the rectangle with the cross and embroider with satin stitch, French knots, or decorative stitching to fill. Fold ½" (1 cm) seam selvages

around the edge of the piece. The fabric should now measure 5" × 5¾" (13 cm × 14½ cm). At the top of the 6" (15 cm) white fabric, finish edge with zigzag stitching. Fold under the ½" (1 cm) seam selvage on all edges. Embroider the outer edge of the fabric to form the border for the photo. Use an iron-on photo transfer, trimmed to fit the center of the panel. After the transfer has cooled, use squeeze paint to add a border around the photo, and let dry.

(continued on page 184)

TIP
Hand stitching and quilting adds a heartfelt element to the piece. Don't worry about getting everything straight and even—it's the thought that really counts in this piece. Iron in between steps to keep fabric flat and crisp.

Dimensions 18" X 6" (46 cm X 15 cm)   **Artist** Anita Y. Mabante Leach

3) Stack and center two flag patches on the remaining 6" (15 cm) white fabric. Fold ¼" (2 cm) selvages on the sides. By hand or machine, tuck and roll the top in by ¼" (2 cm); sew to finish. At the bottom, press a ½" (1 cm) seam selvage. Center the batting on the wrong side of camouflage piece. Baste around the edges to keep the batting in place. Center the embroidered crosspiece in middle of the right side of the batting-backed camouflage. Baste into place, tucking raw edges under. Place the flag piece to the left of the cross piece, placing the fabric ½" (1 cm) away from the center panel. Baste into place, tucking raw edges under. Place the photograph to the right of the cross panel, about ½" (1 cm) away. Baste into place, tucking raw edges under.

4) Sew the side seams, leaving the upper edge of the flag and photo panels free to form pockets. Knot and trim any loose threads. Place the remaining camouflage fabric, right sides together. Stitch ½" (1 cm) seams all around, leaving 6" (15 cm) at bottom. Trim seams and corners. Turn the piece right side out and iron. Hand stitch a 6" (15 cm) hole at the bottom to close. Flip the quilted piece over. On the outer left edge (flags are on the flip side), machine or hand stitch three 1" (3 cm)-wide buttonholes, spaced evenly. Fold the piece in thirds, positioning buttonholes. Mark. Sew buttons, taking care not to sew through the photo on the flip side.

VARIATIONS
- Choose camouflage that matches the solder's uniform.
- Sew on appropriate insignias, if desired.

Forever Yours: Double Wedding Pages

ARTIST: VICKI SCHREINER

To construct these coordinating wedding pages, stamp the roses and words with gold ink on white cardstock, then color the images with art pencils. Cut out the motifs and set aside. Make the frames on the left page by cutting squares, ovals, and rectangles, about ½" (1 cm) larger all around than the photos, from moss green cardstock. Trim the edges of the cardstock with paper edgers and adhere the photos, centered on top of the shapes. Make the large photo frame on the right page by cutting two corner triangles from the lace place mat and fitting them together to form a rectangle. Cut another smaller rectangle of handmade paper and center it on top of the lace one. Center the photograph on top of the handmade paper and add ribbon trim along each edge.

Place the framed photos on the striped pages, leaving room for ribbon garlands at the top of each page. Glue ribbon across the tops of the pages and add embellishments to the ribbon and to the frames.

MATERIALS

- **Stamps**

  Forever Yours

  Small rose engraving

  Romantic rose garland

  Romantic rose corner

- **Ink and Inkpads**

  Metallic gold ink

- **Papers**

  White cardstock

  Moss green cardstock

  White lace paper place mat

  Handmade paper

- **Miscellaneous**

  Art pencils

  Moss green acrylic paint, clear glaze base

  Removable tape

  Sponge

  Victorian paper edgers

  Ribbon

Step 1

Here is an easy and effective way to make a striped background. First, measure and lightly mark the top and bottom edge of the cardstock where the stripes will go. Place the cardstock on a large cardboard work surface, and lay the stripes with removable tape, extending them over the edge of the paper onto the cardboard. Sponge a thinned layer of paint and glaze base over the entire page, including the tape. Dip the sponge in the paint mixture and blot lightly on folded paper towels before applying to the page so the paint won't seep under the edges of the tape.

Step 2

Allow the paint to dry and carefully remove the tape to reveal the striped background. Repeat this background striping on as many pages as you need at one time so the colors on facing pages will match.

Step 3

Randomly stamp over the stripes with the rose stamp and gold ink, retaining a light and airy appearance. Ink the stamp and blot lightly on a folded paper towel to remove some of the ink. Experiment on a separate sheet of cardstock until you achieve the look you want, then re ink and stamp over the striped background.

Friends: Layered Border Pages

ARTIST: SANDRA McCALL

This bright and imaginative border combines several techniques and unifies the page with careful placement of all the elements. At first glance, it seems not to be a border at all. Some of the photos are repeated on the right page in a smaller format, and they form part of the border.

QUICK TRICK

When creating or ordering the photographs for a page, get several copies of the featured photos in small prints, about 1" × 2" (3 cm × 5 cm), depending on the shape of the original. Cut out the smaller photos and repeat them to form a border.

Getting Started

To make a page like those shown at the left, stamp and decorate many sheets of paper and cardstock in a variety of bright colors and patterns. Choose patterns that will look good when cut into strips or other small shapes. Stamp some sheets with allover patterns of the same motifs in a larger size. Coordinate the colors, but don't let them clash or become too repetitive. The technique for making beautiful Faux Batik paper may be found in the Basics section of the book (page 35).

Arranging the Page

Once you have created several sheets of coordinated paper, gather your photos and begin laying all the elements on a sheet of blank cardstock. Look for designs that will complement the features of the photos, and carry out the theme of the page. This one is joyful and light, so the colors accent that feeling of happy and carefree times. The colors and shapes harmonize with the mood of the page but do not fight with the photos for prominence.

Using Photos in a Border

Repeating the photo on the lower portion of the right page creates an illusion of depth, so the larger image almost steps out of the border with lighthearted movement.

Buddy and Friends: Repeating Borders

ARTIST: SANDRA McCALL

The border along the bottom of these pages is made up of several small versions of the cat photo shown elsewhere. The cat has been cut out and applied over the top of a checkerboard strip. This is a very effective treatment because it harmonizes with the other elements, adds depth, and emphasizes the importance of the precious cat.

Notice how the narrow checkerboard carries across from one page to the other, tying them together and repeating the colors and patterns.

MATERIALS

- **Stamps**
  Two or three small flowers
  Background swirls
  Checkerboard border
  Saying with heart flowers
- **Ink and Inkpads**
  White, yellow, and black pigment pads
  Rainbow dye inkpad
  Blue and magenta dye inks
- **Papers**
  Two sheets of black cardstock
  Monoprinted or handmade paper for middle ground
  Two sheets of 20# all-purpose copy paper
- **Miscellaneous**
  Variety of markers
  Deckle paper edgers
  White or silver gel pen

Getting Started

Before beginning to assemble this page, make several color copies of the photographs. Vary the sizes of the photos, and use deckle paper edgers to trim some of them. You will need about ten stamp-sized copies of one photo for the lower border. Choose a small version of one of the photographs used elsewhere on the page.

Making the Background

Use white pigment ink to stamp the swirl pattern over the two sheets of black cardstock for the background. Make two sheets of monoprint paper as described in The Basics section, page 35, or select two coordinating sheets of handmade paper. Make the checkerboard strips by stamping several rows of checks on white copy paper. Rub some yellow pigment ink over the checkers, then spot-color them with markers to coordinate with the monoprint paper. Stamp fifteen to eighteen flowers on copy paper with dye inks and cut them out.

Lay the two black background sheets next to one another on the work surface. Trim two pieces of monoprint or handmade paper to cover about two-thirds of each page and mount them similarly on each black page. Mount a strip of checkerboard across the bottoms of the pages, ½" (1 cm) up from the bottom, and make sure they are even. Cut out eight or more small photos and place them on top of the checkerboard strip, spacing evenly on each page.

STAMPING TRICK

When stamping, save all your scraps and small bits to use later. The bright flowers seen on these two pages are also used in a very different context with the babies on page 64. When you find an image you like, stamp extras and use them throughout your scrapbook pages.

Adding the Photos

Mount the remaining photos on the two pages, over the background and the middle ground. Use the largest photos or the featured photos on the left page, and the smaller ones on the right. Cut more strips of checkerboard and make frames and lines from the left page to the right page, continuing them at an angle across the two pages to tie the composition together. Cut out the small flowers and scatter them over the pages along with the stamped saying. Write some labels on black cardstock and cut them out to make the title blocks, then mount them on the pages.

My Best Friends: Sticker Lettering

ARTIST: VICKI SCHREINER

On these two pages, the lettering continues from the left page across to the right, uniting them and unifying the designs.

STAMPING TRICK

Whenever possible, stamp words and letters on separate sheets of paper instead of stamping directly on the page. That way, you can choose the best stampings and cut them out to add to a completed scrapbook page without risking damage to your artwork.

MATERIALS

- **Stamps**

  Animal paw

  Cool cat

  Doggy Dalmatian

  Play ball

  Purrfect match

- **Ink and Inkpads**

  Black pigment inkpad

- **Paper**

  Two or three sheets each of white and black cardstock

  Two or three sheets of plaid paper

- **Miscellaneous**

  Assorted dye markers

  Fine-point black permanent marker

  Large red alphabet stickers

  Small black alphabet stickers

Getting Started

Stamp the black paw print randomly on white cardstock strips and allow to dry. Adhere the red letters over the paw prints. Use the black marker to outline the letters so they will stand out from the background.

Mounting the Words

Cut two strips of plaid background paper to form an even border behind each paw print strip and adhere the assemblage to the tops of two pages of printed or plain paper.

Finishing the Page

To finish the page, cut mats of plaid paper to form ½" (1 cm) borders all around the photos. Cut black mats the same size, and offset the plaid ones on top of them. Mount the photos in the centers of the plaid mats. Place the mounted photos on the page and add small black letters as desired. Stamp the cats and dogs on white cardstock and color with markers. Cut them out and stick them to the pages.

ARTIST: DAWN HOUSER

ABOVE: This example of lettering identifies the people in the photographs and also sets a whimsical mood for the entire page. Stamp the words on white cardstock and cut them out, then place them over the edges of photos and on the background. The arrangement of the words adds to the visual interest and variety of the page while keeping its light and playful tone.

Love and Marriage: Mesh Lettered Pages

ARTIST: SUSAN JAWORSKI STRANC

These pages introduce a unique method for adding letters to your scrapbook. The artwork begins with a piece of wire grid with ⅜" mesh, but you may want to experiment with smaller and larger openings as well. Use wire cutters to snip the grid down to a workable size, about 3" × 4" (8 cm × 10 cm). Be sure to clip off all sharp, protruding wire points and flatten it completely. A 3" × 4" (8 cm × 10 cm) piece of fine, dense foam may be used with the grid to make the textured background.

NOTE: Various sizes and styles of mesh, available at stamping stores and from online merchants, may be used for this technique. If unavailable, you can use wire screening from the hardware store. Stamp stores also have heatable foam blocks which will accept the mesh pattern and which may be reheated to change the pattern as desired.

QUICK TRICK

For a rich, muted look in the photographs, experiment with your computer's photo program and try different screens as well as different colors. Color copiers can also print photos in a single color.

MATERIALS

- **Stamps**
  Small flower on a wooden dowel
  Tiny ivy garland
- **Ink and Inkpads**
  Gold metallic
  Black pigment
  Deep red pigment
- **Papers**
  Burgundy cardstock
  Gold metallic paper
  Burgundy textured art paper
- **Miscellaneous**
  3/8" (1 cm) mesh wire grid made for stamping
  Fine, dense heat-sensitive foam pad
  Wire cutters
  Heat tool

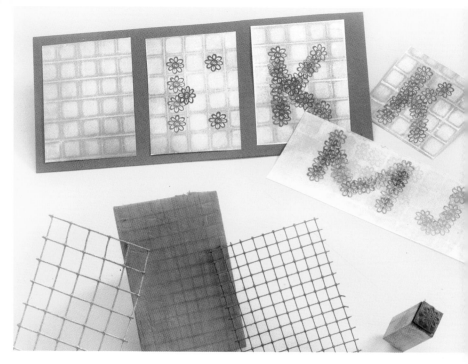

Getting Started

Method 1

Ink a block of heay-sensitive foam with gold metallic ink and lay it, inked side up, on the work surface. Place a piece of wire screen or mesh on top of the inked foam and lay a sheet of art paper or handmade paper on top of the screen. Gently press down on the paper with your fingertips, covering the entire surface and pressing it down into the ink beneath. Take care not to tear the paper by pressing too hard. For a variation, remove the paper and the mesh and stamp the foam onto a fresh piece of paper. Reink and repeat, to cover the page.

Method 2

Warm a block of heat-sensitive foam with a heat tool and press it onto the mesh to create a grid of raised squares on the foam. The impressions will remain until you reheat the foam. Ink the foam pad with gold metallic pigment ink and use it to stamp the page.

Stamping the Page

When the page has been covered with a grid of color, randomly stamp the tiny ivy garland pattern over the surface with red ink and then with black. Decide where your photos will go, then use the tiny flower to stamp the word "love" several times. You can form the letters by staying within the colored squares, or by stamping on the lines between the squares. To tie the pages together, let the word travel from the left page over onto the right side.

Finishing the Page

To finish the page, mount the photos on successively larger pieces of gold paper, burgundy textured paper, and gold paper again. Mount the photos at an angle on each page, noticing how they relate to one another when the pages are side by side.

Fun with Mom: A Mother/Daughter Page

ARTIST: DAWN HOUSER

Although this page is shown as a left-hand scrapbook page, it could also be mounted on the right and become a dividing page for the section to follow.

Evan and Haley:
Illuminated Letters

MATERIALS FOR MOTHER/DAUGHTER PAGE

- **Stamps**
  Background block with metro theme
  Butterfly with zebra wings
  Alphabet
  Shoes
  Party dress
- **Ink and Inkpads**
  Black, charcoal, pink, magenta, blue-violet, and red pigment inks
  Charcoal, black, and sparkle embossing powders
- **Papers**
  Two sheets of turquoise cardstock
  Scraps of white, pink, and lavender cardstock
- **Miscellaneous**
  Stippling brush

To Make the Mother/Daughter Page

Stamp an entire sheet of turquoise cardstock with the metro stamp and charcoal pigment ink. Stamp the individual letters for the words with black or clear pigment ink on various pastel colors of cardstock and emboss with charcoal powder. Do only two or three letters at a time so they won't dry out before the embossing powder is added. Cut out the letters and set aside. Stamp the four butterflies, the dresses, and the shoes on white or pastel cardstock, then emboss as you choose. Cut them out. Cut pieces of black or pastel cardstock slightly larger than the photos and mount the photos on the pieces of cardstock to create slender frames. Mount the photos on the page, then add the other elements.

MATERIALS FOR BABY PAGE

- **Stamps**
  Bollio with flower theme
  Illuminated alphabet blocks
- **Ink and Inkpads**
  Pine green dye ink
  Scarlet and forest green pigment ink
  Pastel embossing powder
- **Papers**
  Three sheets of ivory cardstock
- **Miscellaneous**
  Transparent ruler for placing letters
  Oval cutter (optional)
  Pastel markers

ARTIST: pj DUTTON

To Make the Baby Page

Using pine green ink, stamp the flower Bollio along the top and bottom of a sheet of ivory cardstock. Color the leaves and flowers with markers. Trim the photograph into an oval and mount it in the center of the page.

Stamping the Names

On a separate sheet of ivory cardstock, stamp the individual illuminated letters for the names, using scarlet for the girl and forest green for the boy. Doing one or two at a time, emboss the letters with pastel embossing powder before the ink has dried. Color the letters and embellish with markers—this will make them pink and blue. Cut out each letter and use the transparent ruler to help in gluing them evenly around the photo. Note that the letters in the boy's name are just touching each other, while the girl's are overlapping because there are more letters in hers.

Events, Trips, and Favorite Things

The first scrapboard I ever saw was in a wonderful painting by the American trompe l'oeil master John Frederick Peto (1854–1907). A simple board crisscrossed with ribbons, it held letters and other ephemera and was an enchanting precursor to the modern bulletin board. My desk-sized version, encased in a portfolio, is a celebration of Victorian design. The bookcloth is embossed with a floral pattern, the ribbon is extravagant, and the tiers of pockets are cut from sheets of hand-marbled papers.

the victorian scrapboard...

organize your memories

MATERIALS

Binder's board
Bristol board (10 point)
Decorative paper; one
sheet 19" by 25"

(48 cm by 64 cm) is suffi-
cient for the scrapboard
pictured here
Bookcloth

Ribbon
PVA and mixture
Pressure-sensitive
adhesive (roll)

getting started:

- Collect the memorabilia for your scrapboard: letters, birth announcements, cards.
- Gather the decorative materials for your box. These can include decorative paper, ribbon, or swatches of fabric for pockets.

1a

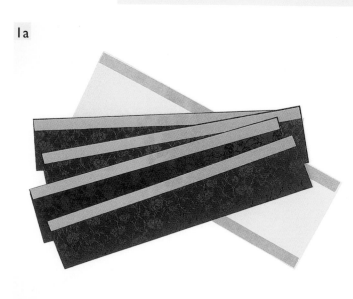

1a CONSTRUCT THE SCRAPBOARDS.
Cut two pieces of binder's board to the desired height and width. My boards are 12" by 10 ¹/₂" (30 cm by 27 cm).

Cut decorative paper into eight strips:
Height = 4" (10 cm) (adjust this measurement to accommodate pockets of different depths)
Width = width of boards plus 2" (5 cm)

Cut bookcloth into six strips:
Height = 2¹/₂" (6 cm)
Width = width of boards plus 2" (5 cm)

Apply strips of pressure-sensitive adhesive to the right side of the bookcloth, along one long edge. Do not peel up the paper backing. Apply strips of pressure-sensitive adhesive to the wrong side of the decorative paper, along both long edges. Do not peel up paper backing. Apply a strip of pressure-sensitive adhesive to the entire width of the lower (tail) edge of each board. Do not peel up paper backing.

1b

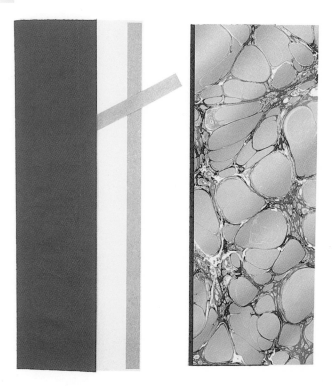

1b Adhere the decorative papers to the bookcloth strips. Peel off the backing paper from one edge of the decorative paper. Press the paper onto the cloth, approximately ¹/₈" (.3 cm) away from the edge of the cloth without adhesive on it. Roll back the paper, peel off the backing strip from the cloth, and press the paper onto the cloth. Repeat with the other five strips. If your cloth tends to unravel, dip a finger into the PVA and run it along the exposed edge of cloth, sealing it. **Note:** The photos illustrating Step 2 are of small scale models of the actual scrapboards.

2a

2b

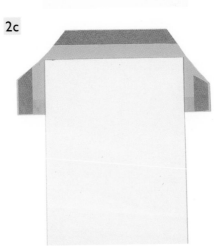

2c

2d

2e

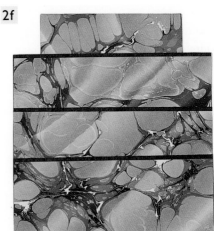

2f

2a ASSEMBLE THE SCRAPBOARDS.
Place one of the two reserved decorative papers face down on the workbench. Remove the adhesive backing from the lower edge. Position the right side of the board (the side with the adhesive strip along its tail edge) on the paper, centered left to right and approximately 1" (3 cm) down from the head. Press.

2b Cut the corners, staying 1 1/2 board thicknesses away from the tip of the board.

2c Apply adhesive to the two side (spine and fore-edge) turn-ins.

2d Bring the head turn-in onto the board and pinch in the corners.

2e Press the two side turn-ins onto the board.

2f To attach the first pocket, mark the board for its placement. Peel off the backing strip and stick down the pocket. Repeat with the second pocket. To adhere the third pocket, mark for its placement, remove the backing strip from the lower board edge, and stick down the pocket.

2g Turn the board over and complete the turn-ins. Starting with the upper pocket, apply strips of adhesive to the two side turn-ins; press them onto the board. Repeat with the second pocket. At the third pocket, first cut the corners and then bring in the long (tail) turn-ins before the two side ones.

2h–i Repeat Step 2 to complete the second scrapboard.

NEXT CUT OUT THE CASE UNITS.
The case is composed of three parts: front
and back, made of binder's board; and
spine, cut from the flexible (bristol) board.
There is no joint spacer. Pay attention to
the grain direction which runs, as always,
from head to tail.

CUT THE FRONT AND BACK CASE BOARD:

Height = height of scrapboards plus $1/4$"
(.5 cm)

Width = width of scrapboards plus $1/4$"
(.5 cm)

CUT THE SPINE PIECE:

Height = height of scrapboards plus $1/4$"
(.5 cm)

Width = thickness of the two scrapboards
plus two (case) board thicknesses plus two
cloth thicknesses, plus $1/8$" (.3 cm)

CUT THE BOOKCLOTH:

Height = height of case boards plus $1 1/2$"
(4 cm)

Width = width of case boards, laid out,
plus $1 1/2$" (4 cm)

Make a pattern to determine the placement of the ties. Place the case, right side up, on a protected work surface. Transfer your placement mark to the case, and chisel. Repeat on the back board.

4b Push the ribbons, with the help of your micro-spatula, through the slits and glue them into place.

3 **CONSTRUCT THE CASE** by gluing out the boards and adhering them to the cloth (see drawing). Cut the corners and complete the turn-ins (see The Basics, page 32).

Cut a hinge strip from the bookcloth:
Height = height of scrapboards
Width = width of spine piece plus 2" (5 cm)
Apply mixture to the cloth, center it on the spine, and press it firmly into place. Use your bone folder to sharply impress the edges of the case boards through the cloth.

Fill in the case. Cut two pieces of scrap paper large enough to fill in the area of exposed board on the inside of the case. Apply mixture to these papers and adhere them. This will counterbalance the pull of the boards toward the outside of the case. Put the finished case aside to dry, between newsprint sheets, under pressing boards and a weight.

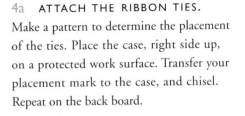

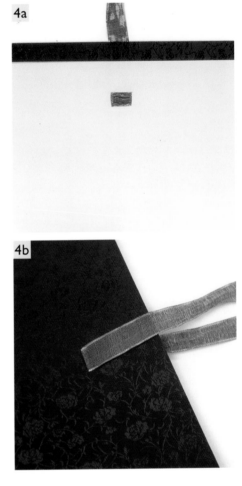

3

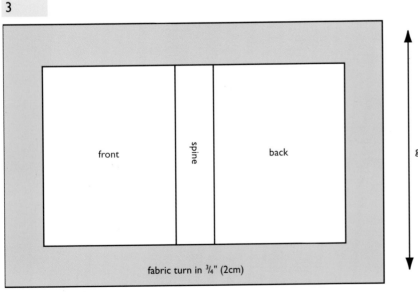

front

spine

back

grain

fabric turn in 3/4" (2cm)

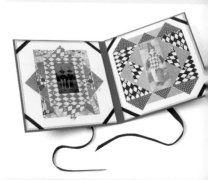

5

Ribbons can be used as fairly minimal corner restraints. They could also be glued diagonally, from side to side, across the entire surface of the board, creating the pineapple pattern in Peto's depictions.

5   GLUE THE SCRAPBOARDS TO THE CASE. Apply undiluted PVA to the wrong side of a scrapboard. Remove excess glue from the edges. Center the board on the case board and press it into position. Hold it for a minute or two, until the glue begins to set. Put newsprint, a pressing board, and a weight on top. Repeat these steps to attach the second scrapboard, making sure the pockets on both boards are facing in the same direction.

LEAVE THE FINISHED CASE under weights for several hours.

The inspiration for this box is a poignant object from centuries ago. Made when the possession and reading of Tarot cards was a dangerous pursuit, this box was built to deceive. The titling on the spine is a clue to the contents, but the craftsmanship of this small beauty manages to hide its secrets. My box holds a collection of cards of another sort. In France, April Fool's Day is celebrated with fish: chocolate fish, pastry fish, paper fish. "Poissons d'Avril" fill this box.

The Faux Book Box is composed of two units: An inner scored paper container and an outer case. If you intend to make the spine of your box resemble an old book, choose the covering material carefully. Select a strong but flexible handmade paper, and paint or stain it to look like leather. Accept the crinkles that will inevitably develop as the paper is molded over the fake raised bands. They are suggestive of a well-used, much-loved object.

the faux book box...
memories of second-hand bookshops

MATERIALS

For the scored container:	A good-quality medium-weight paper	Decorative paper	Pressure-sensitive adhesive on a roll
		Paste	
For the case:	Binder's board	Decorative paper	Cord
	Strong, flexible handmade paper (spine)	Bristol board, 10 point	PVA, mixture and paste
		Headbands (optional)	

getting started:
select the paper for the laminate

- Cut one piece of medium-weight paper and two pieces of decorative paper to the same dimensions:
  Height = height of object to be boxed, plus two thicknesses of object, plus 1" (3 cm)
  Width = twice the width of the object, plus one thickness of object, plus 1" (3 cm)
- Make sure the grain runs from head to tail on all three papers.

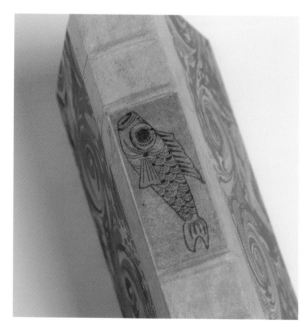

I PREPARE THE LAMINATE
to become the scored-paper container. Dampen the plain paper with a wet sponge. Paste out the decorative papers (one at a time) and apply one to each side of the dampened paper. Press out air bubbles with your hands. Place this laminate between dry newsprint sheets, sandwich it between pressing boards, and leave it under weights for half an hour.

Cut the laminate to the following dimensions.

Height = height of object plus a hair, plus two thicknesses of object.
Width = twice the width of object, plus one thickness of object.

2a

2b

2c

2d

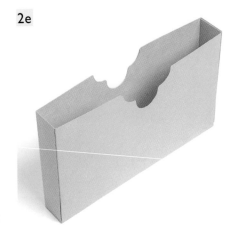

2e

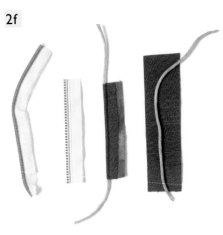

2f

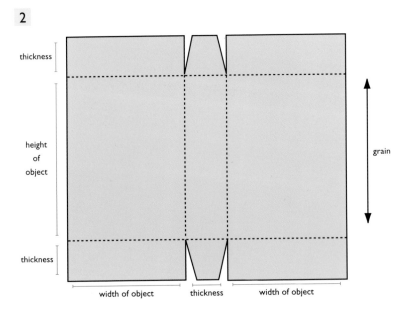

2 CONSTRUCT THE PAPER CON-
TAINER. The laminate *must* be scored
while it is still damp. If it is dry, the
against-the-grain folds are cracked and
flaky. When using expensive materials,
make a prototype out of cheap paper then
transfer the measurements to the laminate.

2a   Following the procedure for scoring
paper described in The Paper Box (page
159); score the laminate.

2b   Cut away triangular wedges.

2c   On the left-hand panel (inside),
apply strips of pressure-sensitive adhesive
close to the outer edges of the head and
tail turn-ins. Repeat on the right-hand
panel, applying the adhesive to the reverse
(outside) of the laminate.

2d   Make thumb cuts on the fore-edges,
of desired size and design.

2e   Fold up the box and stick the turn-
ins together, tucking the spine tab
in between the two long turn-ins.

2

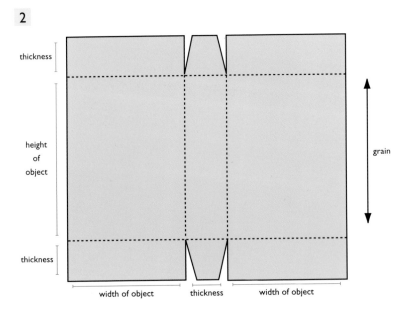

thickness

height
of
object

thickness

grain

width of object   thickness   width of object

2f   **Optional:** Glue endbands (available
from bookbinding suppliers, or made by
gluing fabric around a piece of cord) to
head and tail, at spine. The bands are cut to
the exact thickness of the box spine.

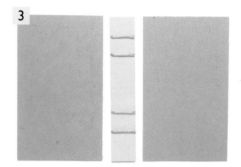

3 CUT OUT THE CASE BOARDS.
The front and back boards are cut from binder's board:

Height = height of box, plus two board thicknesses

Width = width of box, plus one board thickness

The spine is cut from 10 point bristol board:

Height = height of box, plus two board thicknesses

Width = thickness of box, plus two (case) board thicknesses, plus slightly more than two spine paper thicknesses

Optional: To make fake raised bands, glue strips of cord across the spine board, at desired intervals. If you plan to label your box, space these bands accordingly.

4 CUT OUT THE COVERING MATERIALS. Cut one piece of strong but thin and resilient handmade paper to cover the spine:

Height = height of boards, plus 1 ½" (4 cm)

Width = desired width—from front board, across spine, to back board

Cut two pieces of decorative paper to cover the boards:

Height = height of boards, plus 1 ½" (4 cm)

Width = distance from edge of spine paper to fore-edge of board plus 1" (3 cm)

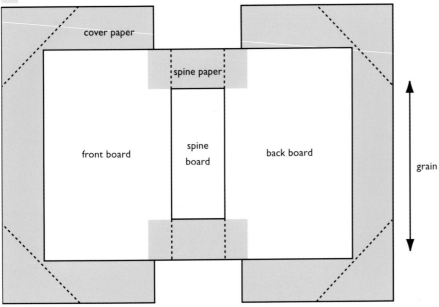

5a

cover paper

spine paper

front board

spine board

back board

grain

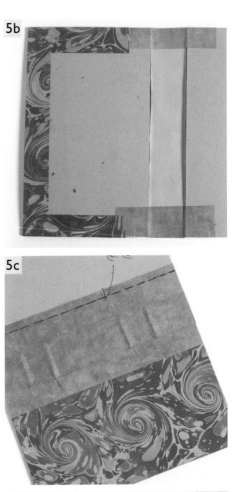

5b

5c

5d

5 ASSEMBLE THE CASE
(see diagram.)

5a Paste out the spine paper. Center the spine piece (cord side down) on the paper. Flip the spine over onto a piece of wax paper. Mold the paper around the cords, sliding the paper down from the head and tail to provide ample material to stretch around the cords. Moisten the paper with a sponge and continue to work it around the cords with your bone folder, until the hubs are well-defined. Turn the spine over, onto a piece of newsprint, and re-apply paste to the head, tail, and spine extensions. Place the front and back boards on the paper, snugly abutting the spine board. Bring in the head and tail turn-ins. Turn the case over and carefully try to smooth out the wrinkles. Don't be too obsessive: They are inevitable and they contribute to the old-book look.

5b–d Paste out the decorative papers and apply them to the boards. These papers should overlap the spine paper by a small margin. Cut the corners and finish the edges (see The Basics, page 32).

Cut the inner hinge strip from the spine covering paper:
Height = height of paper box
Width = width of case spine board, plus 2" (5 cm)

Do not paste this strip to the case.

6 ATTACH THE BOX TO THE CASE.
Glue the spine of the box with undiluted PVA, taking care not to stain the end-bands. With your finger, remove any excess glue. Stick the right side of the hinge strip onto the spine, centering it head to tail and left to right.

6a, b   Rub it down well. Paste out the entire back of the hinge strip and center the box on the spine of the case. Use your bone folder to force the hinge sharply against the spine edges of the case boards. Press the paper onto the boards. Keeping the box in an upright position, fill it with scrap boards cut to fit. This will help press the box to the case.

NEXT   **LINE THE CASE.** Cut two pieces of decorative paper:
Height = height of paper box
Width = width of case boards, minus two board thicknesses
(Remember to anticipate the stretch of the paper in width, and trim it a bit narrower if necessary.)

Paste out these papers and apply them. With the case remaining in this open position, stack newsprint, pressing boards and weights on top of each board, and let dry.

7   LABEL THE BOX. Using a pen, paintbrush, rubber stamp or computer, generate artwork for the label. Draw or print it on a contrasting paper. Paste the label to the spine, between the bands.

6a

6b

7

VARIATION

The marbled paper used on this box is a contemporary Italian marble based on a traditional pattern. Old book papers can also be retrieved and reused on new book and box projects. Scavenge around second-hand bookstores for discarded covers. Take them home and let them soak in a bathtub filled with warm water. As the adhesive dissolves, the papers will loosen and peel away from the boards. If this doesn't happen, keep adding hot water to the bath, and gently pull the papers away from the boards. Remove the papers and blot them with paper towels. Place them right side up on wax paper (in case of a sticky residue). Sandwich the papers between blotters, pressing boards, and weights until dry.
If the papers seem too fragile for re-use, paste them onto sheets of Japanese tissue while still damp, and press as above.
Sometimes, the best surprises are the unexpected ones. As the marbled papers float off the boards, printed "waste sheets"—magazine pages, handwritten account-book pages, a sheet of music—appear below. Used as board liners, these sheets can also be retrieved with additional soaking time.

Creative ideas—whether watercolor paintings or sketches for a new craft project—deserve a special home. You won't find a more wonderful home for your work than The Artist's Portfolio.

And just as the artwork deserves a special place, so does your portfolio deserve a label. Labels enliven objects, identify their contents, and help to distinguish the fronts from the backs. In this case, the artist is a wonderful calligrapher, Anna Pinto. To protect the paper label, cut away several layers of the cover board, creating a well into which the label can be dropped. The cutaway area is slightly larger than Anna's artwork. The result is a shadow that frames the artwork.

The Artist's Portfolio consists of a case with three separately constructed flaps. Keep the outside plain, to highlight the unique contents. But there is a surprise when you open this box: Here is one portfolio that will never be mistaken for a standard art-supply-store item.

the artist's portfolio...

preserve your memories

MATERIALS	Binder's board (case)	Bookcloth	PVA, mixture and paste
	Museum board, two or four ply (flaps)	Decorative paper	Artwork for cover
		Ribbon	

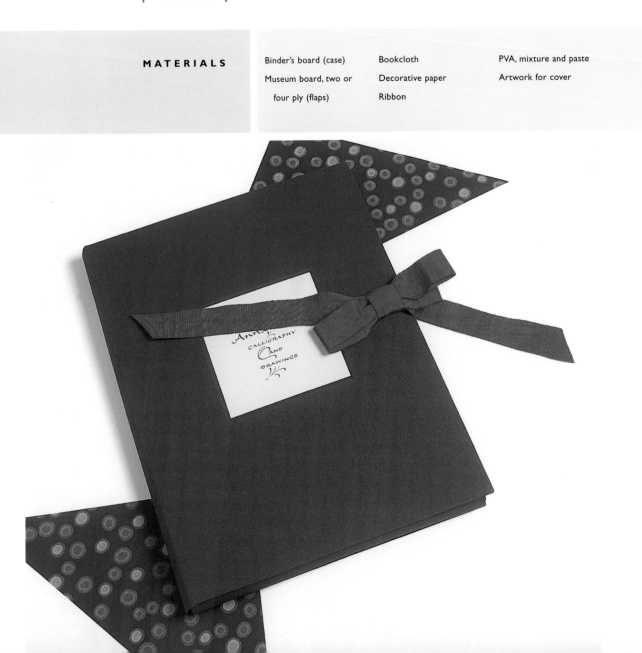

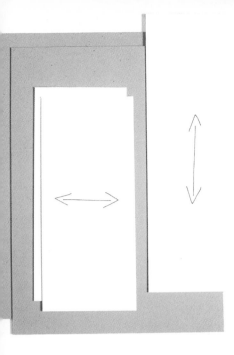

getting started:
cutting the boards

- Cut out the front and back case boards:
  Height = height of material to be boxed, plus $^1/_2$" (1 cm)
  Width = width of material to be boxed, plus $^1/_4$" (.5 cm)
- Cut out the boards for the flaps:
  Head and tail flaps: cut two
  Height = 4" (10 cm), or desired height
  Width = width of material to be boxed, plus $^1/_8$" (.3 cm)
  Fore-edge flap: cut one
  Height = height of material to be boxed, plus $^1/_4$" (.5 cm)
  Width = 4" (10 cm), or desired width, matched to height of
  head and tail flaps
- Grain should run from head to tail on all boards.

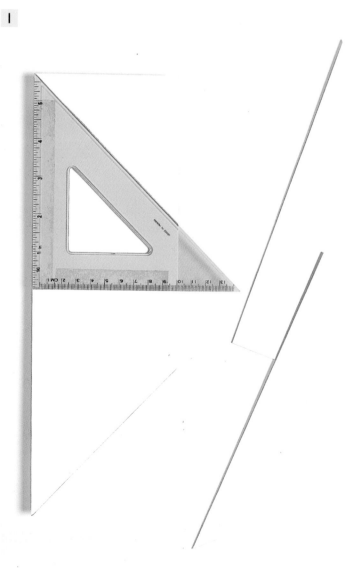

I   **MITER THE CORNERS** of the flaps. Using a 45-degree triangle, draw and cut off one wedge from each head and tail flap, and two wedges from the fore-edge flap.

2a–f   **CONSTRUCT THE FLAPS.**
For the head and tail flaps, cut two pieces of cloth:
Height = height of board, plus the thickness of the material to be boxed, plus 1 $^3/_4$" (4.5 cm)
Width = width of board, plus 1 $^1/_2$" (4 cm)
For the fore-edge flap, cut one piece of cloth:
Height = height of board, plus 1 $^1/_2$" (4 cm)
Width = width of flap, plus the thickness of the material to be boxed, plus 1 $^3/_4$" (4.5 cm)
Glue out the boards using mixture and stick them onto the cloth. *Pay attention: The head and tail flaps are mirror images and must be glued in opposite orientations.* Note that the untrimmed long edge of each board sits near a generous cloth extension. This cloth—the thickness of the material to be boxed, plus 1" (3 cm)—will eventually become the walls of the portfolio and the hinge attachment of the flaps to the case.

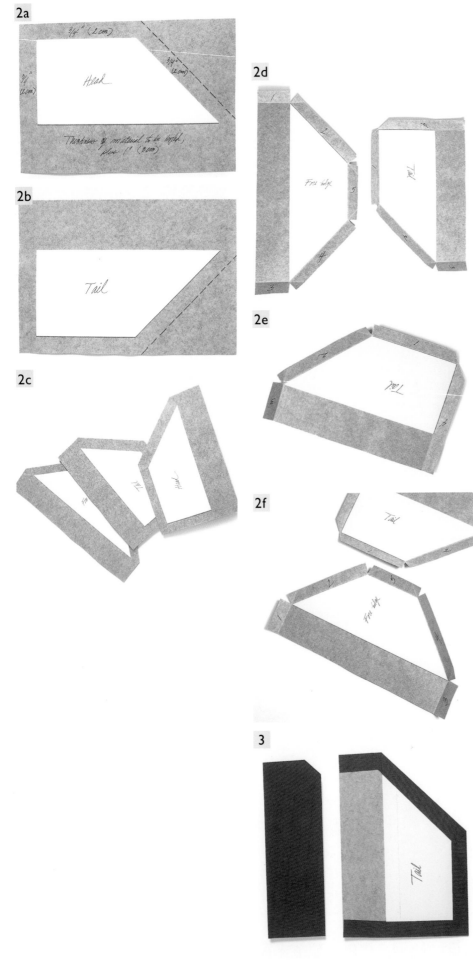

Trim cloth near the angled edges of the boards, as illustrated, to create the usual ³/₄" (2 cm) turn-in. Cut corners and finish all edges except the long edge, which will become the hinge attachment to the case. To cleanly cover the angled edges of the flaps, remove triangular bits of cloth. Crease and re-crease the turn-ins in all possible sequences to determine which bits to cut. When cutting, end cuts 1 ¹/₂" board thicknesses away from the boards. Glue the turn-ins in the labeled sequence.

3 CUT THE INNER HINGE STRIPS for all three flaps. For the head and tail flaps, cut two strips of cloth:
Height = thickness of the material to be boxed, plus 1³/₄" (4.5 cm)
Width = width of flap, minus two board thicknesses
For the fore-edge flap, cut one strip of cloth:
Height = height of flap, minus two board thicknesses
Width = thickness of the material to be boxed, plus 1³/₄" (4.5 cm)
Before gluing, place the hinge strips in the proper position on the flaps, and cut off the corners that extend beyond the angled edges. With pencil, mark each flap approximately ³/₄" (2 cm) away from its long edge. Apply mixture to the hinge strips (one at a time). Starting on the ³/₄" (2 cm) markings, press the cloth onto the board. Push the cloth sharply against the board edge with your folder. Press the extending cloth onto the fabric below. Don't stop pressing until the two are well bonded. Sandwich this hinge between newsprint, pressing boards, and weights until dry. To even out the raw edges of this hinge extension, trim a uniform amount of cloth off each of the three flaps.

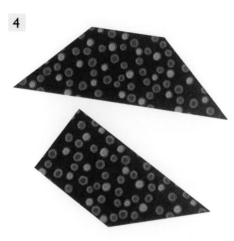

4 LINE THE FLAPS. Cut two pieces of paper to line the head and tail flaps:

Height = height of board, minus two board thicknesses

Width = width of board, minus two board thicknesses

Cut one piece of paper to line the fore-edge flap:

Height = height of board, minus two board thicknesses

Width = width of board, minus two board thicknesses

Before gluing, place the lining papers in the proper position on the flaps and cut off the corners that extend beyond the angled edges. Apply adhesive to the papers and stick them down. Put flaps aside to dry, between newsprint sheets and under boards and a weight.

5 FORM THE FLAP WALLS. From your scrap board, cut a strip equal to the thickness of the material to be boxed; this is your wall spacer (Spacer 1). To form the head, tail, and fore-edge walls, push this spacer firmly against the long edge of each flap and crease the fabric hinge to form a right angle. On the head and tail flaps only, trim a wedge off the cloth hinge near the spine edge. Put the flaps aside.

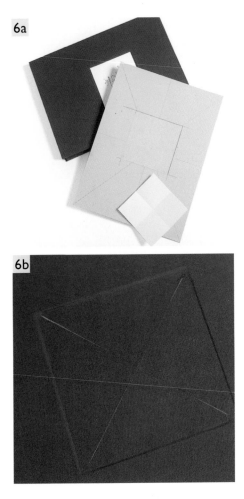

6a CONSTRUCT THE CASE. Decide on the placement of the cover artwork. Cut and peel away layers of board equal to the thickness of the artwork (See Tip on page 218). Cut the spine spacer from a strip of scrap board. The width of this spacer is the thickness of the flap spacer, plus two (case) board thicknesses, plus the thickness of one flap, plus two cloth thicknesses. Cut a piece of bookcloth to cover case:
Height = height of boards, plus 1 ¹/₂" (4 cm)
Width = width of boards laid out with spacer in place, plus 1 ¹/₂" (4 cm)
Glue out the front board. Draw away excess glue with your brush from around the edges of the label recess. Make sure that no small bits of cardboard are stuck to the surface. Place this board on the left-hand side of the cloth, centered on height and with a ³/₄" (2 cm) margin on your left. Press the board down. Turn the cloth over immediately and, working through a sheet of scrap paper, press out all air bubbles with your folder. Find the edges |of the cut-away area and shape the cloth sharply against these edges.

6b If your cloth is stubborn and refuses to stretch, cut an X in the middle of the recessed area; start and end the cuts approximately ¹/₄" (.5 cm) away from the corners. As you shape the cloth against the edges, be careful not to smear the glue. Once shaped, flip the case over, place the spine spacer next to the cover board, glue out the back board, and put it down. Press, then remove the spacer and turn the case over. Press the cloth down well, working first with your hands and then with your folder. Flip the case back to its original position, cut the corners, and finish the edges (see The Basics, page 32).

7 CUT AND APPLY THE SPINE HINGE STRIP.

7a Cut a piece of cloth:
Height = height of case minus ¹/₄" (.5 cm)
Width = width of spine spacer plus 2" (5 cm)
Apply mixture to this hinge and center it on the spine.

7b Rub vigorously, forcing the fabric against the board edges. Trim a hair off the spine spacer in width, and re-position it in the spine area. With a weight on top, it will press both cloths together. Let sit for half an hour to one hour.

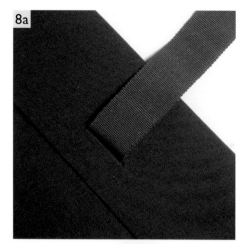

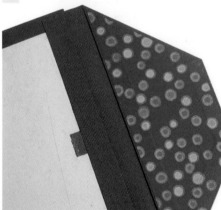

NEXT LINE THE CASE.
Cut two pieces of paper:

Height = height of case, minus two board thicknesses

Width = width of case, minus two board thicknesses

The lining for the back board might need to be trimmed; check the fit before gluing. Apply adhesive to these papers and stick them down. Place newsprint, boards, and weights on the case, and let sit until dry.

NEXT APPLY ARTWORK TO COVER.
Apply appropriate adhesive to artwork, and stick down into cover recess. Remember to anticipate the expansion of wet paper, and trim accordingly. When setting in a photograph or artwork involving water-based inks, use a moisture-free (pressure-sensitive) adhesive.

8a ATTACH THE RIBBON TIES.
Decide on the placement of the ties. (If you wish to center them, cut a scrap of paper to the height of the case and fold it in half. Voila! The center.) Mark this area with a pinprick. Select a chisel the width of your ribbon. Chisel, vertically, from the outside of the case. Be sure to protect your tabletop before chiseling. Repeat on the back board.

8b Insert the ribbons into these slits and pull them to the inside of the case. Cut and peel up a shallow layer of board and glue the ribbon ends with undiluted PVA, sinking them into the recess.

9 GLUE THE FLAPS TO THE BACK OF THE CASE. Use undiluted PVA, and start with the fore-edge flap. Masking the walls with a piece of scrap paper, glue out the hinge. Remove excess glue, taking care not to smear glue onto the wall area. Center the flap by height on the case; it should sit just inside the board edge of the case. Press down well with your folder. Repeat with the head and tail flaps, positioning the flaps flush with the spine edge of the case. To reduce bulk at the outer corners where the head and tail flaps overlap the fore-edge flap, miter the corners after gluing. To miter, make a diagonal cut through both hinges simultaneously, drawing the knife from the right angle formed at the outer overlapping area to the right angle formed at the inner overlapping area. You will need to peel up the head and tail flaps slightly, to remove the triangular wedge from the fore-edge flap underneath. Re-apply a dot of adhesive, if necessary, and stick back down.

Tip: How to Prepare a Cover Board for a Label

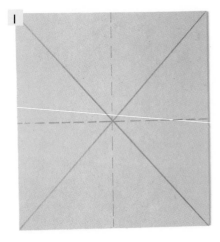

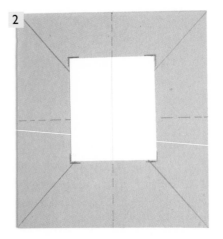

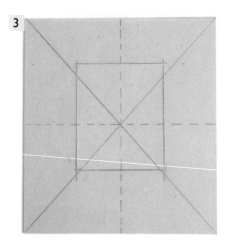

1. Cut a paper pattern:

Height = height of artwork, plus $1/8$" (.3 cm)

Width = width of artwork, plus $1/8$" (.3 cm)

(The pattern is larger than the artwork to allow for a shadow around it once it is glued into place.) Crease this pattern in half, both vertically and horizontally, to find the center.

NEXT Draw diagonal lines, from corner to corner, on your cover board. Using your triangle to maintain right angles, draw a line from head to tail, through the bisecting point. Draw a second line, from spine to fore-edge, through the bisecting point.

2. Place the paper pattern on the board, aligning its creased lines with the drawn lines. Slide the pattern up and down and side to side to decide on the placement of your artwork. Or keep it right where it is at dead center.

NEXT Trace the outline of the pattern on the board.

3. Using your triangle and a knife with a sharp blade, cut through the pattern's lines. Make several cuts over the same area before proceeding from one line to the next.

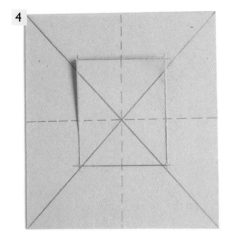

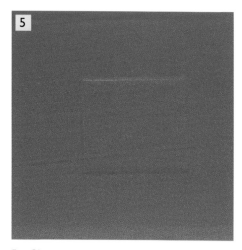

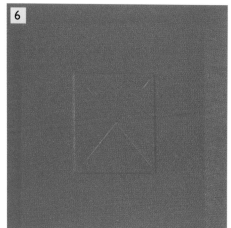

4. Use the tip of the blade to dig under and lift up the board in one corner. Grab this corner and peel up several layers of board with the help of the knife. Peel and lift in the direction of the grain. Clean up the corners by scraping with your knife. Make sure the edges are crisp.

NEXT Smooth the cut-away surface by rubbing vigorously with your folder. Also smooth down the roughed-up outer edges of the cut-away.

5. Glue out the board and position it on the cloth. Flip the board over and immediately find the edge of the recess with your hands. (Work through a newsprint sheet to protect the surface of the cloth.) Work out all air bubbles, puncturing the cloth with a sewing needle, if necessary. Shape the cloth sharply against the edges of the recess with a tapered bone folder.

6. If the cloth is stubborn and refuses to mold itself against the edges of the cut-away, make two diagonal slits through the cloth, starting and ending the slits at least $1/8$" (.3 cm) away from the corners.

Its charm is in its size (2¹/₂" [6 cm] square), as well as in its materials. Several small boxes, stacked or scattered, have more presence than one large and lonely box. So make lots of boxes—and let them become your jewels!

The Jewelry Box consists of two units: a four-walled tray and a case. The case extends slightly beyond the edges of the tray, creating a small lip. Once assembled, the front of the case becomes the hinged lid of the box.

Keep in mind the rules of boxmaking: Wherever hinging occurs, use cloth instead of paper. The one exception is in the use of Momi papers (please see my note in The Picture Frame Box on page 55). If not using these resilient Japanese papers, I use bookcloth for the case construction. In the directions, the case material is referred to as cloth.

the jewelry box...
memories of treasures and trinkets

MATERIALS	Binder's board	Cloth or paper (tray)	Ribbon
	Museum board, two ply (liners)	Cloth or Momi paper (case)	PVA, mixture and paste
		Bone clasp	

getting started: cutting the boards

- Cut out the boards for the tray following the layout shown.
- Pay attention to the logic of the cuts, which ensures that all parts sharing the same measurements are cut in sequence, and with a minimum of marking.
- Base:

  Height = desired height of tray, plus two covering thicknesses

  Width = desired width of tray, plus two covering thicknesses
- Head and tail walls:

  Height = desired depth of tray, plus one board thickness

  Width = desired width of tray, plus two covering thicknesses
- Spine and fore-edge walls:

  Height = height of base board, plus two board thicknesses

  Width = desired depth of tray, plus one board thickness

1a

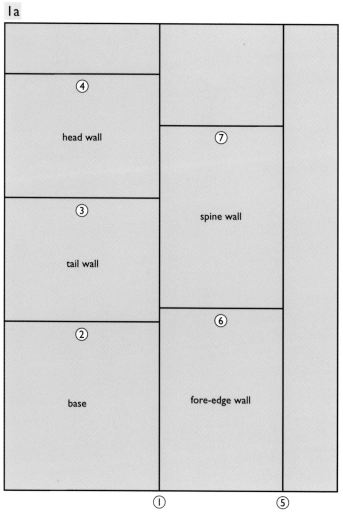

head wall ④

tail wall ③

base ②

spine wall ⑦

fore-edge wall ⑥

① ⑤

grain

1b

1c

1a–c CONSTRUCT THE TRAY
(see The Basics, page 30.) Glue the walls in the proper sequence: head, fore-edge, tail, spine.

2a

2b

3

2a COVER THE TRAY. Cut out the covering material, a strip twice the depth of the tray plus 1 1/2" (4 cm), and long enough to wrap around all four walls plus 1/2" (1 cm). If the material is too short to wrap around the tray in one continuous strip, piece together two shorter strips, making sure that the seam falls on a corner of the tray.

2b Cover the tray (see The Basics, page 30).

3 CUT OUT THE THREE CASE BOARDS to the following dimensions. Remember that the grain must run from head to tail on all boards.
Front and Back:
Height = height of tray, plus two board thicknesses
Width = width of tray, plus one board thickness
Spine:
Height = height of tray, plus two board thicknesses
Width = depth of tray (Here's an easy and accurate way to get this measurement: Sharply crease a small piece of scrap paper to form a right angle; place the tray on top of this paper and push the tray snugly into the right angle; make a second, parallel crease, over the top of the tray. The distance between these two crease marks is the exact depth of your tray.)

From your scrap board, cut a slender strip a scant two board thicknesses in width. This will be used as a spacer when gluing up the case.

NEXT CUT OUT THE CASE CLOTH or Momi paper:
Height = height of boards, plus 1 1/2" (4 cm)
Width = width of boards, laid out with joint spacer plus 1 1/2" (4 cm)

4 CONSTRUCT THE CASE. Glue out the front board and place it on the cloth, approximately 3/4" (2 cm) away from all three edges. Press into place. Position the spacer against the spine edge of the board, glue the spine piece, position the spine on the cloth, and push it firmly against the spacer. Remove the spacer and place it on the other side of the spine. Glue the back board, position it on the cloth pushed firmly against the spacer, and press into place.

5 CUT THE CORNERS and finish the edges (See The Basics, page 22). Cut the inner hinge cloth:
Height = height of the tray
Width = width of case spine, plus 2" (5 cm)
Grain, as always, runs from head to tail.
Cut shallow triangular wedges off all four corners of this cloth.

4

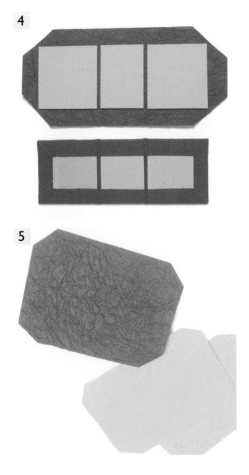

5

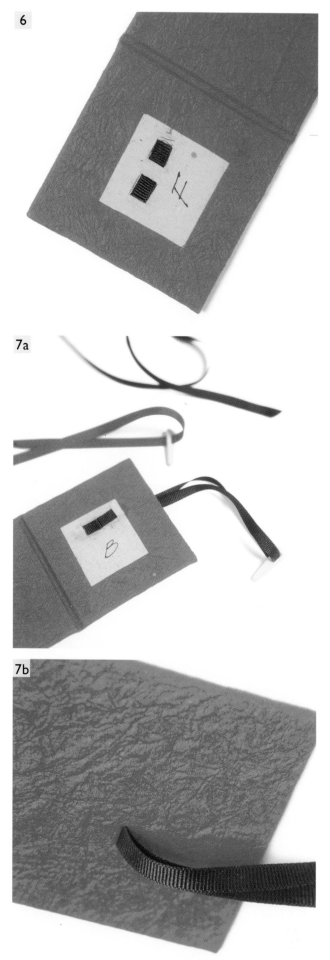

6 GLUE OUT THE HINGE CLOTH, center it on the spine, press the cloth firmly into the joints of the case with your bone folder, then onto the front and back case boards. Rub down well.

7a ATTACH THE BONE CLASP. Feed the ribbon through the slit in the bone clasp. Place the tray in the case, close it, and position the bone clasp on the front of the case, in its desired location. (If making more than one box, prepare patterns for the placement of the ribbons on both front and back.) Mark the front of the case with two pinpricks, one on each side of the clasp directly below its slit. Remove the tray and arrange the case right side up on a piece of scrap board. Select a chisel to match the width of your ribbon. Holding the chisel vertically make two parallel chisel cuts, starting at the pinpricks and chiseling downward.

7b Angle the ends of a short piece of ribbon and push the ribbon down through the cuts to form a receiving loop for the clasp. Slide the clasp into the loop. Pull the ribbon ends snugly on the inside of the case. Guide the main ribbon to the back of the case; mark for its insertion and make one vertical slit. Feed both ends of the ribbon into this slit, and make the ribbon taut. On the inside of the case, spread the ribbon ends in opposite directions. With your knife trace the outlines of the ribbons, cutting and peeling up a shallow layer of board. Glue the ribbons into these recesses using undiluted PVA. Bone down this area well to make it as smooth as possible.

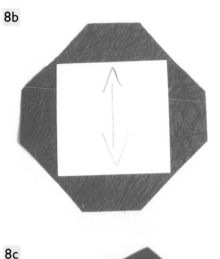

8a

8b

8c

NEXT **ATTACH THE TRAY TO THE CASE.** Spread undiluted PVA onto the bottom of the tray; wipe away excess glue. Place the tray on the back case board. The spine edge of the case should be flush with the spine edge of the tray. Center the tray by height. This placement allows a small lip around the head, fore-edge, and tail. Hold the tray in position for a few minutes, until the glue begins to set. (Take care to keep the tray centered—it's quite a slippery creature at first!) Invert the case, place a board and hefty weight on top, and press for at least a half hour.

Spread undiluted PVA onto the spine wall of the tray; wipe away excess glue. Roll the tray onto the case, spine walls touching; slide a board and a weight into the tray, and press until dry.

8 LINE THE BOX.

8a   If lining with a medium or heavy-weight paper, cut two pieces of paper to the same dimensions. (Remember to anticipate the stretch of the paper across the grain, and to cut it a bit narrower in width.)
Height = height of interior of tray, minus two paper thicknesses
Width = width of interior of tray, minus two paper thicknesses
Paste the papers and apply them to the bottom of the tray and the inside of the box lid. Press until dry.

8b   If lining with a thin or fragile paper or with cloth, first "card" the material around lightweight boards, following the procedure below.
Cut out two pieces of museum board:
Height = height of interior of tray, minus $^1/_{16}$" (0.15 cm)
Width = width of interior of tray, minus $^1/_{16}$" (0.15 cm)

8c   Cut out two pieces of covering paper:
Height = height of boards, plus 1$^1/_2$" (4 cm)
Width = width of boards, plus 1$^1/_2$" (4 cm)
Paste the papers, center the board on the papers, cut the corners and finish the edges (see The Basics, page 22).

Glue out one board with undiluted PVA and carefully lower it into the tray. Press until it takes hold. If your box is large, place newsprint, a board and a weight on top, and let sit for half an hour. Glue out the second board, and center it on the box lid. Press until it takes hold. Weight and let sit for one half to one hour.

224 memory keepsakes

Tip: *How to Make a Ribbon from Bookcloth*

1. Cut a piece of bookcloth a scant $^3/_4$" (2 cm) in width and twice the desired length, plus 2" (5 cm). Grain must run lengthwise. Use your spring divider to divide this strip into $^1/_4$" (.5 cm) increments (lengthwise).

2. Score the fabric into thirds. To score, position the cloth wrong side up on a piece of blotter. Working against a metal straight-edge with a tapered bone folder, "draw" two parallel lines $^1/_4$" (.5 cm) apart from head to tail. Crease the fabric firmly along these score lines.

3. With your small brush, apply mixture to the cloth, starting in the middle of the fabric and working the adhesive toward the ends. Do not over glue. Turn the edges of the strip in toward the center of the fabric—first one, then the other—pressing with your fingers as you go. Place the strip between two waste sheets and press well with your bone folder. Let sit, between pressing boards and under weights until ready to use.

To close this little brocade box, make a ribbon from book cloth. This is an elegant alternative to store-bought ribbon when using bone clasps as closures on an all-cloth project.

My mother's button "box" was actually a large glass jar filled to the brim with a glorious mixture of buttons. When we were sick we sorted the buttons by color and size. When well, and playing pirates, we poured buttons over the carpet and reveled in our "pieces of eight." In homage to that jar, The Button Box is a true treasure chest full of plastic bounty. It even depends on buttons for its finial and feet embellishments. The Button Box is composed of a four-walled tray mounted on a platform, and a removable lid.

the button box...
memories of once-treasured garments

MATERIALS

Binder's board	Ribbon	PVA, mixture and paste
Museum board, two-ply	Buttons	Epoxy or wood glue
Assorted decorative	Thread	(optional)
papers		

getting started:
cutting the boards

- Cut out the boards for the tray, following the layout below.
- Base:

    Height = desired height of tray, plus two covering thicknesses

    Width = desired width of tray, plus two covering thicknesses

- Head and tail walls:

    Height = desired depth of tray, plus one board thickness

    Width = desired width of tray, plus two covering thicknesses

    (same as width of base board)

- Spine and fore-edge walls:

    Height = height of base board, plus two board thicknesses

    Width = desired depth of tray, plus one board thickness

    (same as height of head and tail walls)

la–c **CONSTRUCT THE TRAY**
(see The Basics, page 30). Glue the walls
in the proper sequence: head, fore-edge,
tail, spine.

la

lb

lc

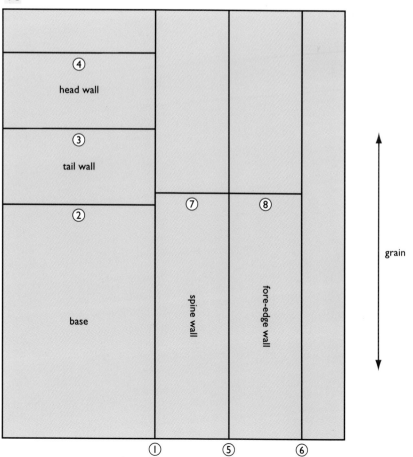

④ head wall

③ tail wall

② base

⑦

⑧

spine wall

fore-edge wall

① ⑤ ⑥

grain

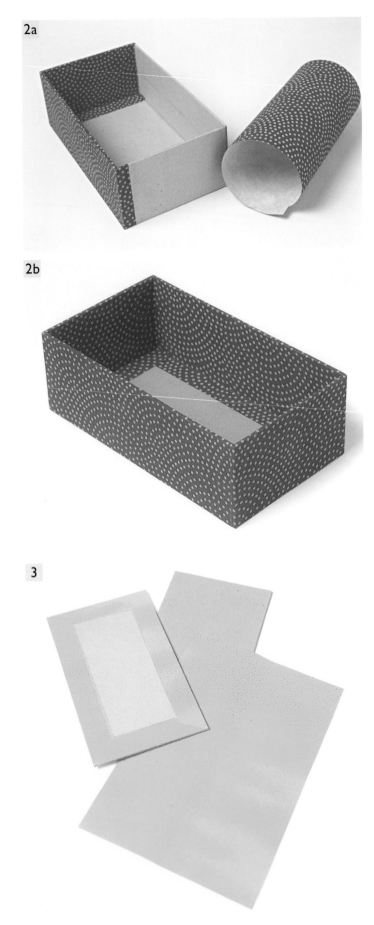

2a

2b

3

2 COVER THE TRAY.

2a   Cut out the covering paper, a strip twice the depth of the tray plus 1 ^{1}/$_2$" (4 cm), and long enough to wrap around all four walls plus ^{1}/$_2$" (1 cm). If the paper is too short to wrap around the tray in one continuous strip, piece together two papers, making sure that the seam falls on a corner of the tray.

2b   Cover the tray (see The Basics, page 31).

3 CONSTRUCT THE LID AND THE BASE PLATFORM. Cut out two boards to the same measurements:
Height = height of tray, plus two board thicknesses
Width = width of tray, plus two board thicknesses
Cut two pieces of decorative paper to the same measurements:
Height = height of boards, plus 1 ^{1}/$_2$" (4 cm)
Width = width of boards, plus 1 ^{1}/$_2$" (4 cm)
Cover the boards by pasting the papers and centering the boards on them. Cut the corners and finish the edges (see The Basics, page 32). Fill in the exposed area of the board with scrap paper. Put the boards aside to dry between newsprint sheets and pressing boards, and under weights.

4

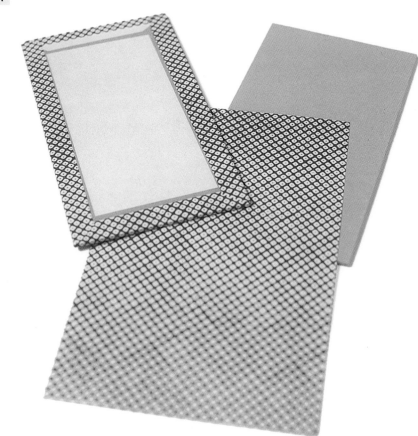

4 CONSTRUCT THE LID LINER. This board, glued to the inside of the lid, keeps the lid anchored to the tray. Cut one board:

Height = height of interior of tray, minus two paper thicknesses

Width = width of interior of tray, minus two paper thicknesses

Cut one piece of decorative paper:

Height = height of board, plus 1 1/2" (4 cm)

Width = width of board, plus 1 1/2" (4 cm)

Cover and fill in this board, following the procedure described above. Put it aside to dry.

5

5 DECORATE THE TRAY. Cut two lengths of ribbon, long enough to wrap around the tray plus 2" (5 cm). Starting 1" (3 cm) in from one end, sew on buttons. Avoid placing buttons where the ribbon folds around the corners. Glue the ribbon with undiluted PVA—one wall length at a time—and stretch it around the tray, pressing with your bone folder as each wall is covered. Hide the raw ends of the ribbons by overlapping and tucking under the leftover bits.

6a

6b

6 FINISH THE LID.

6a Cut, cover and glue together small pieces of board to create an interesting lid. Thread several buttons together to form a finial. Punch holes through all lid layers except for the liner, and sew on the finial. To protect the finial as the liner is being pressed onto the lid, arrange two stacks of small boards, side-by-side with a gap in between the size of the finial and its anchor boards. Invert the lid over this setup. Glue the lid liner with undiluted PVA, wipe off excess glue from the edges, and center this board on the lid. Hold this liner in place for a few minutes, until it stops sliding and begins to set. Place a pressing board and weights on top, and let sit for a half hour to one hour.

6b Glue the tray to the base platform. Apply undiluted PVA to the bottom of the tray. Wipe off excess glue from the edges. Center the tray on the platform and hold in place for a few minutes, until it begins to set. Invert the tray and place a pressing board and a heavy weight on top. Let sit for a half hour to one hour.

7 LINE THE BOX and attach the feet. If sewing buttons (feet) to the base platform, punch holes and sew on buttons before lining the box. If gluing buttons with either epoxy or wood glue, attach buttons after lining the box. Cut a piece of two-ply museum board just large enough to fit inside the tray, with a little breathing room. Cut a piece of covering paper:

Height = height of board, plus $1^1/_2$" (4 cm)

Width = width of board, plus $1^1/_2$" (4 cm)

Paste out the paper and center the board on it. Cut the corners and finish the edges (see The Basics, page 32). Press briefly. Glue the wrong side of this board with undiluted PVA, wipe away excess glue from its edges, and drop the liner into the tray. Hold for a few minutes until the glue begins to set. Put a scrap board (cut to fit) and weights in the tray, and let sit a half hour to one hour.

Ornaments are everywhere! This box, with its flip-top lid and many compartments, can hold collections of all sorts—pens and pen nibs, marbles, costume jewelry, sea shells, special holiday decorations. The Ornament Box is a wonderful vehicle for papers (such as gift wrap papers) too fragile to wrap around the walls of a tray. Cloth does all of the hard work here; decorative papers are pasted on top of the cloth in the final step to give the box its visual punch. I have used an inexpensive Italian Bertini paper because I like its geometric pattern and simple one-color printing. Some of the papers are more typically Florentine, with flourishes and highlights of gold.

The Ornament Box consists of a four-walled tray with partitions and a hinged lid. The lid is actually an upside-down three-walled tray.

the ornament box...
memories of a collector's passions

MATERIALS

Binder's board

Bookcloth

Decorative paper

PVA, mixture and paste

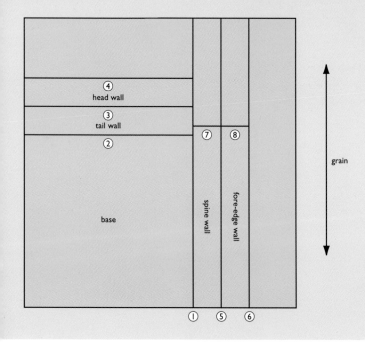

- Cut out the boards for the tray, following the layout.
- Base:

  Height = desired height of tray, plus two cloth thicknesses

  Width = desired width of tray, plus two cloth thicknesses
- Head and tail walls:

  Height = desired depth of tray, plus one board thickness

  Width = desired width of tray, plus two cloth thicknesses

  (same as width of base board)
- Spine and fore-edge walls:

  Height = height of base board, plus two board thicknesses

  Width = desired depth of tray, plus one board thickness

  (same as height of head and tail walls)

1a, b   **CONSTRUCT THE TRAY**
(see The Basics, page 30). Glue the walls in the proper sequence: head, fore-edge, tail, then spine.

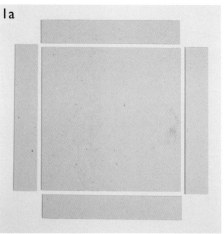

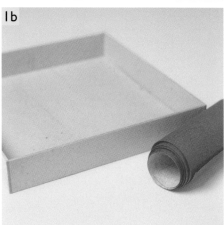

2a

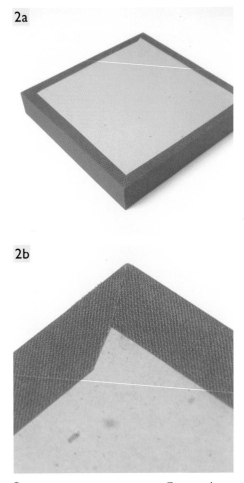

2c

2b

2a–c **COVER THE TRAY.** Cut a strip of bookcloth to a measurement of twice the depth of the tray plus 1 1/2" (4 cm), and long enough to wrap around all four walls plus 1/2" (1 cm).

2d   Cover the tray (see The Basics, page 31).

2d

3a

3b

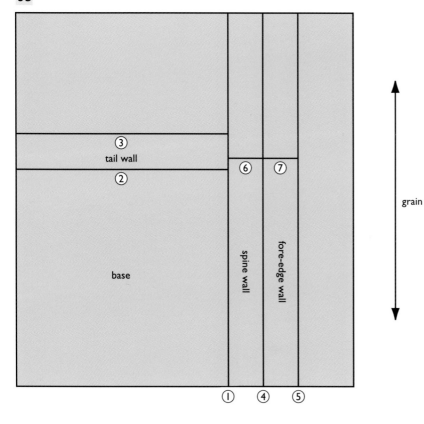

grain

base

tail wall ③

②

⑥ ⑦

spine wall

fore-edge wall

① ④ ⑤

3a, b CUT OUT THE BOARDS for the lid, following the lay-out below. The lid is a three-walled tray, inverted over the lower tray and hinged to it at the back (head) wall. There is no head wall to the lid. Because the lid takes its measurements from the covered tray, start by squaring a piece of board (see The Basics, page 30), and placing the tray on the squared corner. Mark the board, and cut:

Base:

Height = height of tray plus two cloth thicknesses

Width = width of tray plus two cloth thicknesses

Tail wall:

Height = desired depth of lid plus one board thickness

Width = width of tray plus two cloth thicknesses (same as width of base)

Spine and fore-edge walls:

Height = height of base plus two board thicknesses

Width = desired depth of lid plus one board thickness (same as height of tail wall)

NEXT CONSTRUCT THE LID. Angle the ends of the spine and fore-edge walls. Glue up the tray (see The Basics, page 30), starting with the tail wall and proceeding to the spine and fore-edge walls.

4a   **COVER THE LID.**

4b   Cut a strip of bookcloth to a measurement of twice the depth of the tray plus 1 $^1/_2$" (4 cm), and long enough to wrap around all three walls plus 1 $^1/_2$" (4 cm).

4c, d   Cover the tray, following the same procedure as for covering a four-walled tray (see The Basics, page 31). Allow a $^3/_4$" (2 cm) turn-in at the angled edges of the spine and fore-edge walls.

4e, f   Do not glue these turn-ins onto the board until the tray has been wrapped and the appropriate cuts have been made (see diagram).

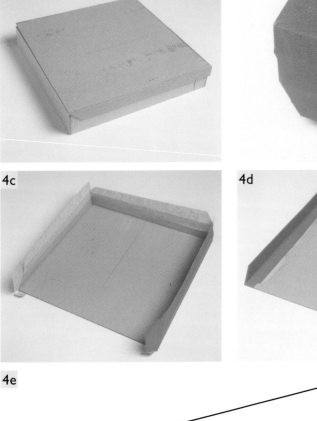

4a

4b

4c

4d

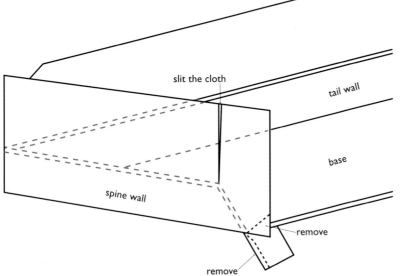

4e

slit the cloth

tail wall

base

spine wall

remove

remove

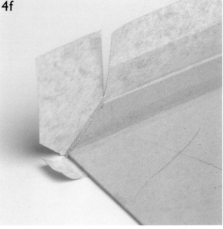

4f

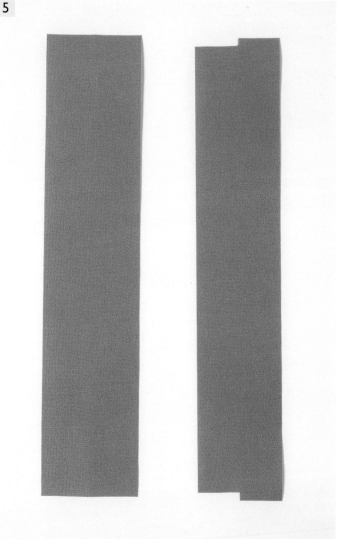

5 **ATTACH THE LID TO THE TRAY.**
Cut two hinge strips from the bookcloth, both to the same dimensions:
Height = 1 $^1/_2$" (4 cm)
Width = width of tray (outside)
One hinge connects the lid to the tray on the outside, at the head wall. The second hinge covers the lid-to-tray attachment on the inside.

Place the lid on the tray. Glue out one hinge. Stick it down, $^3/_4$" (2 cm) onto the lid and centered. Press with your bone folder. Shape the cloth against the right angle formed by the lid and the head wall of the tray, and press the cloth down well, against the wall. Let the box sit closed, for 10 to 15 minutes.

Open the lid and roll the box onto its head wall. Place the second hinge (unglued) in the box, centered over the joint space between the lid and the tray. Trim slivers of cloth off each end so that the cloth fits perfectly inside the tray. Glue out this strip and stick it down. Immediately force the cloth into the joint with a bone folder. Rub vigorously until the cloth is well-adhered to all surfaces. Let the box sit open, for a few minutes, then close the box and let it sit under weights for $^1/_2$ hour.

6a

6b

6c **6d**

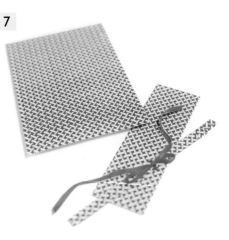

7

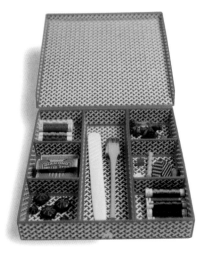

6a-d MAKE AND ADHERE THE PAR-TITION WALLS. (See the Tip on the next page)

Mark the base of the tray for their placement.

Glue out the bottom flanges of each partition and adhere the partition to the base. When the glue has begun to set, apply glue to the side flanges and press them onto the tray walls.

Note: It is easier to line the partition walls with decorative paper before gluing them into the box. In my box, the two long partitions must be lined after all of the partitions are attached in order to hide the flanges from the short partitions. All of the short partitions, however, can be covered before attaching them—and that is what I did. Depending on the configuration of your walls, you must make your own decision.

7 LINE THE BOX. Cut strips of decorative paper to line the lid and tray walls (inside and out). Apply adhesive and stick them down. Cut pieces of decorative paper to cover the floors of all the compartments. Apply adhesive and stick them down. Cut one piece of either paper or bookcloth to line the bottom of the box (outside). Apply adhesive and stick it down. Cut two pieces of paper to cover and line the lid. Apply adhesive to these papers and stick them down. With the box open and sitting on its head wall, press the lid by filling it with newsprint and weights. Leave for several hours, until dry.

Tip: How to Make Partition Boards

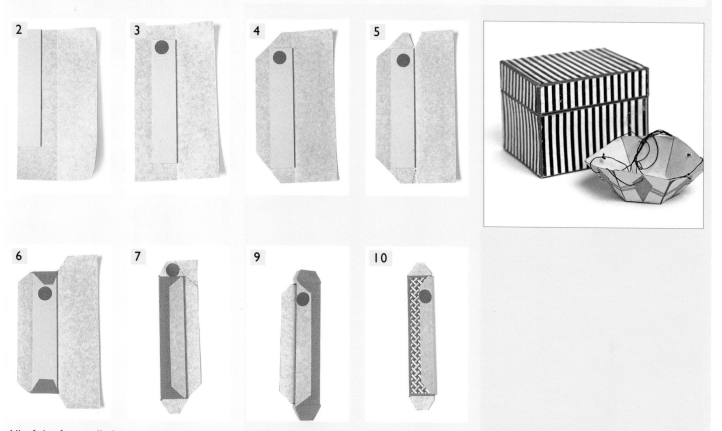

All of the four-walled projects described in this book can have partition walls built into them. Just remember that the flanges attaching the partitions to the tray should be disguised somehow. You can cover the walls with strips of decorative paper to hide the construction details. If the tray and walls are covered in a patterned paper—the busier the better—this protective coloration will help the flanges disappear into the walls. The models above illustrate the ten steps in making partitions.

1. Cut out the partitions. The boards should fit from wall to wall with a little breathing room. In depth, they should be shallower than the interior depth of the tray by one board thickness.

2. Cut out the cloth or covering paper:
Height = height of board plus 1 1/2" (4 cm)
Width = twice the width of the board plus 1 1/2" (4 cm)
Crease the cloth in half lengthwise.

3. Glue out the board and position it on the cloth against the crease mark; center it heightwise. Press.

4. Cut corners off the cloth, at the head and tail near the 3/4" (2 cm) turn-ins only. Keep cuts one-and-a-half board thicknesses away from the tips of the board.

5. Remove triangular wedges of cloth from the head and tail turn-ins, at the creased center of the bookcloth. Cut in close to the board.

6. Glue the head and tail turn-ins, bringing them onto the board and pinching in the cloth at the corners.

7. Glue out the board and roll it onto the right-hand half of the creased cloth. Press it down well.

8. Cut corners off the cloth at the head and tail.

9. Sharply fold the four cloth extensions backward, onto themselves, to form the flanges.

10. If desired, line the partitions with decorative paper. (See the Note in Step 6 of the main project.)

This house of cards will never come tumbling down! Architecturally, it's a simple saltbox. Structurally, it's a handful of postcards laced together with linen thread. The charming and eccentric model for The Buttonhole Stitched Box was found by my friend Robert Warner at the famous 26th Street Flea Market in New York City. I only wish we knew who—thirty, forty, fifty years ago—gathered fourteen postcards, threaded a needle, sat down, and built a house.

the buttonhole stitched box...

memories of special flea market finds

MATERIALS

Graph paper

Card stock

Fourteen postcards—
ten horizontal views
and four vertical views

Pressure-sensitive adhesive

Linen thread

Ribbon

getting started:
preparing the postcards

Trim all postcards to the same size.

Divide the postcards into pairs—five horizontal and two vertical.

Apply a strip of pressure-sensitive adhesive to the center of one card of each pair, sticking the two cards together.

I

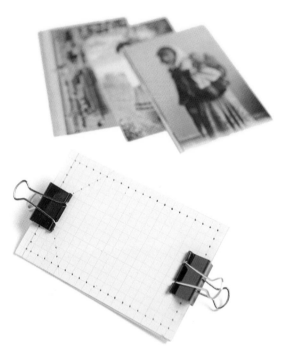

I CUT A SHEET OF GRAPH PAPER and a piece of card stock to the same height and width as the postcards. Stick the two together with strips of pressure-sensitive adhesive.

2

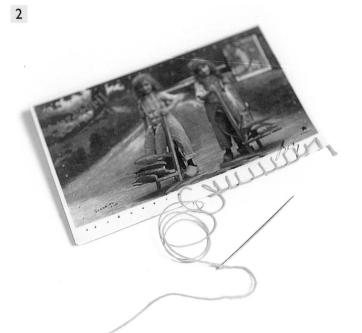

3a

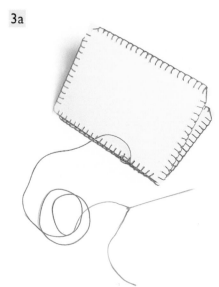

3b

4a

4b

NEXT   ANGLE THE TWO VERTICAL
WALLS by cutting off triangular wedges
to create a roof line.

NEXT   MAKE A PATTERN for punching holes. Using the grid on the graph
paper, punch holes at $1/4$" (0.5 cm) intervals around all four edges of this card.
Clamp the pattern to the postcards and
transfer the holes to all seven cards.

2   EMBROIDER THE EDGES of all the
cards with a buttonhole stitch.
This is a simple overcast stitch in which
the needle is slipped under the thread
and pulled up tautly as the stitch is being
completed. Move from right to left. It
doesn't matter if you start at the top of the
card or its underside. Just be consistent.

3a   LINK THE CARDS TOGETHER
with a running overcast stitch.

3b   To start, pick any two adjacent panels and hold them face-to-face. Slide a
threaded needle under the two links that
sit on the outer edges of the cards. Bring
the thread up and over the tops of the
cards, then back under the next pair of
links. Continue in this way until you have
reached the ends of the cards. Tie off
with a knot. Repeat to join all panels.
Note: Only one of the roof panels is
stitched to the vertical walls. The other is
left free and flips up to provide access to
the box.

4a, b   DECORATE THE BOX with small
ribbon bows tacked on where desired.

Assemblage Trinket Box

Once you've incorporated all your personal mementos into a fabulous work of art, it's only a matter of time before a new collection of keepsakes turns up again. While you're waiting to tackle a new masterpiece, why not create a small trinket box to hold all your tiny treasures for safekeeping? This shadow box within a box concept puts the fun in functional. Use a variety of papers and fabric to add a quaint yet classy element to the decorative contents.

Materials

Small recipe box with removable glass casing on lid

Small found objects with a variety of textures: figures, paint chips, recycled papers, buttons, fabric scraps, pins, or toys

Coordinating acrylic paint

Sandpaper

Basic craft supplies

1) Remove the glass from the box lid and set aside. Apply a base coat of paint to all areas of the box. Sand and then add another layer of paint.

2) Arrange and assemble the collage: Move the paper, fabric, and objects around to experiment with dimensional relationships and composition before applying the glue.

3) Add a light dab of industrial-strength craft glue to the box surface and begin to apply the objects one by

one. If there is a heavier object, such as a toy or button, apply pressure for several minutes until it adheres properly.

4) Smooth out any air bubbles after gluing paper items. Use a cloth or cotton swab to remove excess glue.

5) As you are gluing, continue to alter the composition from your original idea—let one application inspire another. Reattach the glass to the lid and secure with glue.

TIP
If you are unable to locate a box with a glass lid, use a regular wood box and glue a matching-sized Plexiglas photo frame to the lid to create a covered shadow box look. Varnish the box if desired.

Dimensions 6" X 4" X 4" (15 cm X 10 cm X 10 cm)

Artists Cynthia Atkins (assemblage) and Phillip Welch (woodwork)

London Calling Suitcase Shrine

All of us have our guilty pleasures on this planet. It could be by absorbing endless hours of a travel-themed cable channel or repeated cross-Atlantic excursions to the same city. In this case, it's jolly old London, England. It's the ultimate bow of adoration for this legendary metropolis that's rich with royal history, haunting tales, and the best of pop culture. The maniacal way in which this suitcase was layered translates the extreme elation that emerged from three separate visits that spanned a period of nineteen years. For the ultimate suitcase shrine, collect as many odds and ends as you can. They will eventually add the most perfect definition to your British brouhaha. That is, except for the steamy cup of Earl Grey. That's better left in the United Kingdom.

Materials

Suitcase with rigid sides

London stickers, postcards, magnets, small souvenirs, personal photos

Newspaper, magazine, or tour brochure clippings

Trading cards

Small toys

Red, blue, and clear jewels

Scarf

Toy tiara

Punk Rock music buttons

English currency

Strings of beads

Magnetic poetry (London edition)

Squeeze glitter

Basic craft supplies

1) Thoroughly clean the surface of the suitcase with a damp cloth to remove dust or debris.

2) Sort the items by size, and choose one or two pieces that will be the focal points. Using white craft glue, first adhere all of the flat items such as postcards, clippings, and photos. Apply them in a balanced and random fashion.

3) Fill in the empty spaces with dimensional toys on the top and front of the suitcase. Use industrial-strength craft glue for heavier items. Line the borders with strings of beads.

4) There will be small, leftover spaces. Fill these in with squeeze glitter, coins, and magnetic poetry.

5) When the suitcase is completely dry, tie the scarf on the handle, and glue the tiara on the top.

TIP
Look for inexpensive vintage suitcases at thrift stores or yard sales. If you don't have enough souvenirs from your trips, they may be purchased through online shops or auctions. Find a sturdy stand in which to showcase your finished piece.

VARIATION
For a less cluttered look, use large images from an outdated London calendar as the focal point of your suitcase shrine. For a smaller piece, use a small vanity suitcase. This project can be altered to fit any vacation or favorite location.

Dimensions 13" X 20" (33 cm X 51 cm)

Artist Kathy Cano-Murillo

Seaside Vacation Box

Life is a beach, and here's the proof. This box recalls a seaside vacation with shells, glass, and driftwood encapsulating a relaxing holiday. The map-covered divider creates the illusion of a water line, so the objects below appear to be in an underwater cave. The round metal containers, normally used for fishing tackle, play off the theme of the box.

Materials

Cigar box

Beach glass

Shells

Sand

Driftwood

Map of the ocean

Postcard fragment

Newspaper

Piece of glass to cover the box

3 containers or fishing tackle tins,
1½" (4 cm) in diameter

Rusted metal

1" × ⅜" (3 cm × 1 cm) balsa wood strips

Spackle

Spackle tape

Acrylic paint

Acrylic medium

Putty knife

Sandpaper

Two-part epoxy

Basic craft supplies

Basic tools

1) Mark out a rectangle on the lid of a cigar box so there is a border of ¼" (2 cm) around the edge. Wear safety goggles and clamp the box securely to your work surface. Cut a hole in the lid with a jigsaw, following the drawn lines and using an edge guide.

2) Sand the rough edges of the window. Sand the box to remove paint or varnish on its surface. Wipe the box with a damp cloth and apply the spackle tape to the inside. Apply spackle with a putty knife to all surfaces of the box, then smooth the surface with a damp cloth. Let dry about one hour and then sand the spackle until smooth. Attach a hanging device to the back of the box.

3) Stain the inside of the box with watered-down acrylic paints in burnt umber, red sienna, and yellow ochre. Let dry and then lightly sand to create an aged effect. Cut two pieces of 1" (3 cm)-wide balsa to the right length for your box (this one is 6½" [17 cm]). Paint one piece white, and make a collage with fragments of torn map on the other piece, using acrylic medium. Measure ¼" (5 mm) in from the edge of the wood pieces, and with a craft knife, cut a groove in each piece for the piece of glass.

4) Glue the white piece of balsa wood with the groove facing down to the inside top of the box. Arrange the beach glass and then slide the piece of glass, measuring 6½" × 1½" (17 cm × 4 cm) into the groove. Put craft glue on the bottom and ends of the collaged piece of balsa wood and fix in place, making sure that the groove holds the piece of glass securely and the beach glass is contained.

5) Assemble the beach-combed objects inside the box and attach them with epoxy glue. Paint craft glue to the inside of the round metal containers and sprinkle with sand. Place the shells and fragments inside with some loose sand. Then glue the lids shut. For a finishing touch, paint craft glue on some areas inside the box and sprinkle with sand.

TIP

To create cracks in the spackle, apply thickly and dry with a hair dryer.

VARIATIONS
• Create small compartments inside the box with pieces of painted balsa.
• Create a mosaic of shells and pebbles inside the box.

Dimensions 10½" X 7¼" X 1¾" (27 cm X 18½ cm X 4½ cm)

Artist Paula Grasdal

World Series Collectibles Box

Batter up! The year was 2001, and the Arizona Diamondbacks were considered the rookies of American baseball. After all, the bat-happy desert dwellers had been unified as a team for only four years. Enter the World Series. Decked out in purple and teal, the D-Backs found themselves brim to brim with longtime champs, the New York Yankees. Across the country, little respect was given to the new kids on the block. But by the time the edge-of-your-seat series rolled around to game seven, a new sense of credibility and pride radiated from the Phoenix dugout—especially when the Diamondbacks won the championship! Those fans lucky enough to get tickets have now enshrined their famous stubs as a priceless memory that will be cherished forever.

Materials

Shadow box with removable back panel

Ticket stub

Foam board

Cutouts of sports players

Small mementos from game

Mat frame

Sawtooth picture hanger

Acrylic paints

Stencil brush

Basic craft supplies

1) Remove the back panel from the box. Create a faux finish on the surface with a stencil brush and paints to match the team's colors. Cut a small piece of foam board about the size of a stick of gum and use a glue stick to attach it to the back of the ticket stub. Add a small accent item if desired.

2) Using the glue stick, add pictures of team players to the matt frame. Do not use any dimensional items, as the mat will not rest flat against the glass.

3) Lay the box flat on a table with the front facing down. Gently place glass inside box and then the mat frame. Run a bead of hot-glue around the edges to seal them.

4) Replace the back panel and repeat the sealing process. Add a sawtooth picture hanger to the back.

TIP

Do not use glue gun on the back of the ticket stub, as it will burn through to the other side.

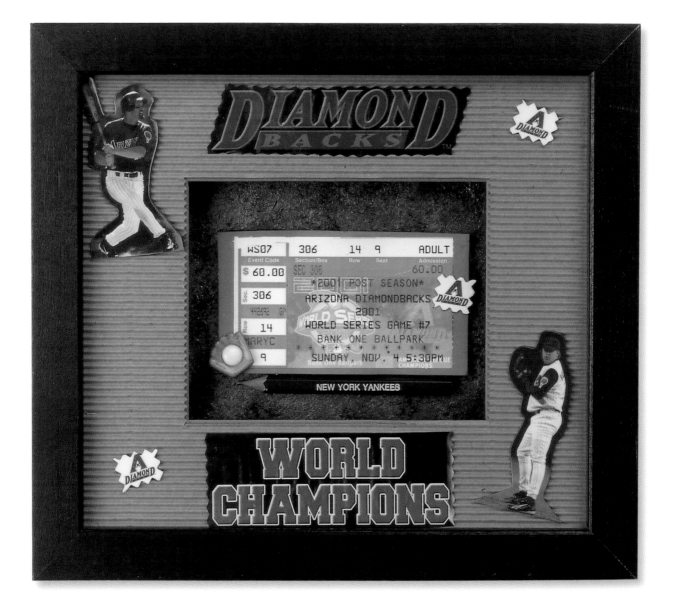

Dimensions 9" X 8" X 2½" (23 cm X 20 cm X 6 cm)

Artist Kathy Cano-Murillo

Anniversary Box

Roses, chocolates, and champagne may be a traditional method for honoring a wedding anniversary, but an artsy alternative is just as meaningful. Large, colorful leaves and pieces of textured birch bark were gathered during a nature walk to create the concept's foundation. Delicate, gold paper decoupage lines the box inside to accentuate the vibrant leaves. Nestled inside is another box that contains a silver heart and a loving message written on a fragment of birch bark. The dictionary pages on the lid display specially selected words such as astronomy, a passion of the artist's husband.

Materials

Box with lid

Old dictionary or photocopied dictionary pages

Pressed leaves

Birch bark

Moss

Matchbox

Heart charm

Gold paper

Acrylic matte medium

Acrylic paint in burnt umber

Staples and staple gun

White gel pen

Basic craft supplies

1) Create a decoupage effect to the box's lid by applying the gold paper and dictionary pages with acrylic medium. Age the papers with an antiquing glaze made from burnt umber acrylic paint and acrylic medium. Attach a pressed leaf to the center of the lid with craft glue and brush a protective coat of acrylic medium over the entire surface. Line the inside of the box with gold paper using the same method.

2) With acrylic medium layer the gold paper onto the inner and outer areas of the matchbox. Attach a tiny, pressed leaf to the lid with craft glue and arrange moss around the inside edge of the box. With epoxy, glue the heart milagro into the box so it is framed by the moss.

3) Write a message with a white gel pen on a tiny strip of birch bark and place it in the matchbox. Write the anniversary date on another piece of birch bark and glue it inside the box.

4) Arrange birch bark on the inside of the lid and attach with craft glue. Weigh the bark down as the glue sets. Add a few staples along one edge of the birch bark composition.

5) Fill the box with pressed autumn leaves. Add the tiny matchbox to complete.

TIPS
- Press the leaves between sheets of newsprint and layers of cardboard weighted with plywood. Change the newsprint every day for two weeks until the leaves are dry.
- To speed up the drying process, iron the leaves between sheets of newsprint.

VARIATION
This box could work for any season; try pressing flowers in the spring or summer as an alternative to the leaves or try making a winter box with silver paper and painted white twigs.

Dimensions 1 ¼" X 8" X 8" (4 cm X 20 cm X 20 cm)

Artist Paula Grasdal

Snow Day: Corners Made with Stamps

ARTIST: SANDRA McCALL

Corners and embellishment for the large photo at the bottom of this wintry scene are made with a combination of techniques, all easy to do. The snowflakes clustered around the photographs add to the crisp, cold feeling of the snow scenes, enhancing the frosty mood of the page.

Making the Corners

Step 1
On a piece of blue cardstock, pencil in a dot where each corner of the trimmed large photo will be. Stamp and emboss a white snowflake over each dot.

Step 2
Cluster more embossed snowflakes around the first one, allowing some to overlap the rectangle where the photograph will go. Cut around the inside edge of the snowflakes at each corner of the stamping and slip the trimmed photograph corners through the slits.

Step 3
The corners of the photo actually slide through to the back of the blue cardstock, holding it in place. Finally, trim around the entire assemblage and adhere it to the page.

MATERIALS
- **Stamps**
  Snowflakes
  Tiny snowflakes
  Background block
- **Ink and Inkpads**
  White pigment
  White embossing powder
- **Papers**
  Paper for faux batik or decorative paper
  Blue cardstock

Getting Started

Size the photos so they fit on the blue cardstock page and leave plenty of room for the snowflake accents and corners. Trim the photographs with deckle paper edgers, leaving some of the white margin around each one. Make the faux batik middle ground paper using the technique on page 35 of the Basics chapter or on page 65, or select a sheet of decorative paper and cut a piece about half the size of an 8 ½" × 11" (22 cm × 28 cm) page. Stamp a sheet of blue cardstock with the tiny snowflake background block and white pigment ink. Set these aside while making the corners.

STAMPING TRICKS

Begin with a selection of photographs that convey the spirit of friends enjoying a good time together in a wintry scene, or choose several frosty white views of a pristine, snowy landscape. Add blue paper and white, embossed snowflakes to increase the chilly atmosphere.

Emboss the most important elements on a page so they will stand out, and stamp, without embossing, coordinating images on the rest of the page in the same color. This will create a unified look and highlight the areas you wish to emphasize.

Garden Beauties: Folded Origami Corners

These gorgeous pages incorporate origami folding into the construction of the corners. The artist is an avid gardener, and has made dramatic pages to enclose some of her most stunning blooms. Why not make art scrapbooks to display photos of your own favorite hobbies? Change the papers and colors to suit a number of themes from model airplanes to butterfly collections.

To practice origami, begin with a 4" × 4" (10 cm × 10 cm) or a 6" × 6" (15 cm × 15 cm) square of paper. Once you have perfected the technique, move down to a 2" × 2" (5 cm × 5 cm) square for the actual corners.

ARTIST: SUSAN JAWORSKI STRANC

STAMPING TRICK

Origami papers are often very shiny, but the metallics are dazzling when they are stamped and embossed. Use a large, open stamped image so the folding won't interfere with the details in the embossing and cause it to crack.

Folding the Corners

Fold a square as you read the steps, always looking one or two steps ahead. Dashed lines indicate folds.

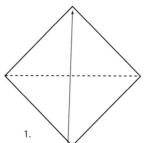

Step 1
Lay a square of origami paper diagonally on the work surface, right side down, and fold the lower point up to form a triangle.

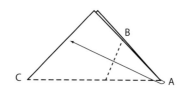

Step 2
With the folded edge at the bottom, fold point A to the center of the left side of the triangle, making the top of the folded corner parallel to the base of the triangle.

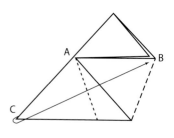

Step 3
Fold point C to point B.

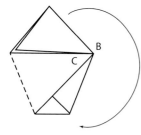

Step 4
Rotate the piece 180 degrees.

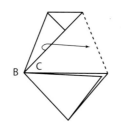

Step 5
Unfold the right corner.

Step 6
Slip your finger inside the corner to open it.

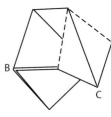

Step 7
Flatten the corner, aligning the front and back creases. Unfold the left corner and repeat steps 6 and 7.

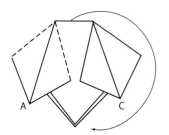

Step 8
Rotate the piece 180 degrees and turn it over.

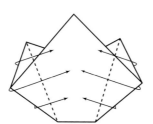

Step 9
Fold both corners in toward the center, following the original crease lines.

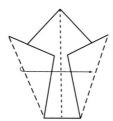

Step 10
Fold the piece in half from left to right.

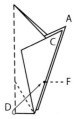

Step 11
To make creases in the base, fold the bottom of the piece up, matching point D to point F.

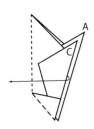

Step 12
Unfold the base and open the piece back to the way it was in Step 10.

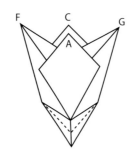

Step 13
Insert a finger into the center of the piece to open it.

Step 14
Make a half turn from left to right and push the triangular base section up inside the piece.

Step 15
The finished piece, ready to accept the corner of your artwork or photo.

Summertime Fun: Cut Outs and Die Cuts

ARTIST: DAWN HOUSER

Two different die cut ideas are shown on this page. The red shapes at the bottom of the page resemble summertime surfboards and help carry out the theme of the page. The green Hawaiian-style shirt is made from a stamp and it has been cut along one side to lay over the edge of the photograph. The inside of the shirt is covered with a piece of turquoise paper, cut to fit, and glued in place.

No photo on this page has its borders completely intact. Interrupt the regularity and sameness of rectangular shapes by overlapping with die cuts and by angling the photos to extend beyond the edges of the page.

QUICK TRICK

Place part of a handmade or purchased die cut over the edge of a photograph to accent the photo or to hide an unwanted element within it.

Another Way to Use Cut Outs

Create a cutout shape from a bow or other stamped image, then select a portion of the cutout to lap over the edge of the photograph. This works best if you choose a stamp composed of solid shapes and stamp it on cardstock.

If using a bow, try placing one streamer over the corner of a photo, or use the entire bow at the top or bottom of the photo. Placement of any cutout will depend on the arrangement of all the elements on the page, and on the subject within the photo.

ARTIST: BETTY AUTH

A Sailing Trip: Pop-up Cut Outs

Die cuts and cutouts can change the pages of a scrapbook from flat to fabulous. In this case, the artist used a single sailboat stamp as the inspiration for a faux booklet. For the reader, it's an adventure of discovery as each new page is lifted and the sailing trip is revealed.

ARTIST: SUSAN JAWORSKI STRANC

QUICK TRICK

To produce sharp cutouts, use a new knife blade each time you start a page. Blades are inexpensive, and should be changed often. Work on a self-healing cutting mat with a standard or swivel knife and turn the paper as you go. Use medium-weight cardstock or art paper and test it with the knife before starting a complicated page. Be patient.

MATERIALS

- **Stamps**
  Small sailboat
- **Ink and Inkpads**
  Medium blue pigment
- **Paper**
  Blue charcoal art paper
- **Miscellaneous**
  Craft knife with extra blades
  Cutting mat

Step 1

Draw a wavy pencil line across the paper for a guide. Stamp the sailboat several times along the wavy line with the hull on the line. Use blue ink that is just dark enough to see, but not dark enough to show after the page is complete. Some of the papers are turned to the front and some to the back when the sailboats move across the page to the left. Stamp so the sails are barely touching one another.

Step 2

With the craft knife, cut out the areas between the sailboats across the paper. This will help hold the row together when cutting small parts.

Step 3

Cut out the sails and the rest of the outline, leaving the joins between the sails intact so the page does not fall apart. As the pages of the booklet are opened, more photographs of the sailing trip are revealed.

School Days and Birthdays: Sticker Pages

ARTIST: VICKI SCHREINER

These two pages illustrate the variety of looks and themes you can achieve with the addition of handmade stickers. The page at the left features ice cream cones that make a statement because of their size. Two stamps were combined to create the cute little ducks floating down on bunches of balloons.

On the right page, stamps with a school theme perk up the page and help balance the strong colors and lettering used throughout.

MATERIALS FOR BIRTHDAY PAGE

- Stamps

  Assorted small to medium stamps

- Ink and Inkpads

  Pinecone and baby blue pigment

  Clear embossing ink and sparkle powder

- Papers

  One sheet each of periwinkle dots, periwinkle strings, solid periwinkle

  One sheet light yellow cardstock

  Two sheets white cardstock

- Miscellaneous

  Laminating machine with sticker-making capabilities

  Pastel alphabet stickers

  Embossing tool

  Victorian paper edgers

  Assorted markers

MATERIALS FOR SCHOOL DAYS PAGE

- Stamps

  Assorted school stamps

- Ink and Inkpads

  Black pigment inkpad

- Papers

  One sheet alphabet paper

  One sheet each red, green, and yellow corrugated

  One sheet each red and green cardstock

  Two sheets white cardstock

- Miscellaneous

  Laminating machine with sticker-making capabilities

  Easel die cut

  Assorted markers

  Removable tape

Making the Pages

These two pages are made in a similar way. Stamp the images onto white cardstock, emboss with sparkle powder for the birthday page, and stamp with black pigment ink for the school page. Color the images with markers and cut them out.

Run the cutouts through a laminating/sticker-making machine and set aside. Construct the pages, leaving plenty of white space, and add the stickers.

STAMPING TRICKS

When making your own stickers, stamp more images than you will need. Color with markers and choose only the best ones to convert into stickers. This will free your creativity and encourage you to experiment with the materials. In most cases, the stickers will look best on the page if they overlap the edges of the photos or other elements. The little floating ducks on the birthday page are an exception because they are used as space fillers while also adding accents and whimsy to the page. On the school page, some of the stickers are placed in an overlapping position while others are not. Notice how the school buses touch and slightly overlap the schoolhouse to provide unity and create a border. More school buses could be added in front of and behind the two shown, lengthening the border.

Paris Dream Trip: Rebus Story Pages

A trip to Paris presented this artist with the chance of a lifetime. She turned the trip into a rebus story on two stamped pages of words and images. A rebus story is created when you substitute symbols, pictures, and graphics for some of the words in a narrative.

To document your own trip, collect postcards, regional and other representative stamps, tickets, photographs, and other memorabilia that symbolize the place, its mood and theme.

ARTIST: pj DUTTON

- **Stamps**

  Travel Bollio

  Baggage

  Compass

  French postcards

  DeGaulle

  Corner script, C. Leroux

  France block

  Flight instrument

  St. Louis skyline

  "Dream"

  "Paris"

  "Visit to Paris"

  Stamp cancel

  Eiffel tower

  Small Eiffel tower

  Maps and visas

- **Ink and Inkpads**

  Lavender, neptune, and stone gray pigment

  Permanent black

- **Papers**

  Two or three sheets each of black, white, and pearl gray cardstock

  One sheet of lightweight clear vellum

- **Miscellaneous**

  Stipple brushes

  Art pencils

  Laminating machine with adhesive cartridge (optional)

  Purple gel pen or fine tip marker

Getting Started

Stamp the gray cardstock with the smaller stamps, overlapping and turning them at various angles. Use stone gray ink to create a shadow effect over both backgrounds. With the stipple brushes, shade and stipple neptune and lavender over the stamped backgrounds. Cut the photos into interesting shapes and attach them to the white cardstock and mount on the page. Stamp the larger images on white cardstock, color with the art pencils, cut out, and attach to the page. Arrange the photos, the stampings, and other elements so that words may be interspersed between and around them, and add words with a purple gel pen.

To Make the Luggage

Stamp the bag on a square of vellum using black ink and let dry. Color with art pencils from the back side. Trim with paper edgers and adhere to the page.

To Make the Corner Pocket

In the lower left corner, stamp the corner script image then cut along the inner edge with a craft knife to form a place for tickets, photos, and other loose memorabilia to be tucked in. Trim ¼" (5 mm) from each edge of the completed pages and mount on black cardstock. This will frame the pages and create a backing for the corner pocket so items won't fall through.

STAMPING TRICK

Before you begin stamping a rebus page, collect photos, memorabilia, maps, postcards, and other elements to express the theme. Lay them out on a sheet of paper and move them around to jump-start a story. Next, look for stamps that will add to the story line and liven up the page. Choose word stamps, letter stamps, and images in a variety of sizes and styles. Make a test page by stamping the words and images around the photos before gluing them down.

Mountain Cabin Retreat: A Journaling Booklet

ARTIST: SUSAN JAWORSKI STRANC

This two-page booklet is a prime example of journaling. The artist and friends spent several days at a mountain cabin, not only enjoying their time and the atmosphere, but also writing about the experience.

Constructing this booklet is much simpler than it first appears. A double sheet (17" × 11" [43 cm × 28 cm]) of art paper is the starting point.

- **Stamps**

  All the stamps are handmade from air-dry
  modeling clay and fine sponges, or are hand
  carved as described in the Basics section (page 36)

- **Ink and Inkpads**

  Dye ink in a full range of colors

- **Papers**

  Light charcoal gray art paper, 11" × 17" (28 cm × 43 cm)

  White charcoal or watercolor paper, 11" × 17" (28 cm × 43 cm)

  Beige or tan paper ribbon

- **Miscellaneous**

  Air-dry modeling clay

  Fine sponges, about 1/2" (1 cm) thick

  Cookie cutters

  Rolling pin, glass quart jar, or other roller for clay

  Black permanent writing pen with very fine point

To make the people stamps, roll out some air-dry modeling compound and cut it with cookie cutters. Let dry overnight and use as stamps. For trees, cut some fine sponge into triangles and gouge out the lines with stamp carving tools.

Getting Started

Begin by creating simple leaf stamps from stamp carving supplies as described in the Basics section, page 36. Make some air-dry clay stamps, also described in the Basics section. Stamp the large sheet or gray paper randomly with carved leaf stamps, adding a few small rubber-stamped leaves in rust or burgundy.

Making the Pages

For each journaling page, cut or tear a strip of white paper about 4" (10 cm) wide by 17" (43 cm) long. At the top of each strip, create a scene to go with your story using handmade clay or sponge stamps. Below that, attach a photograph or two, keeping in mind where the strip will fold back into the page. Stamp a few impressions on the back of the strip. Over the stamping, write a journal entry about the scene and the photos, including what the day was like and what you did. To make the pages even more interesting, don't write in a straight line. Curve the lines, make squares with them, write in circles, and create other interesting patterns with the words.

ABOVE: Photos and journaling are applied to smaller sheets as foldout pages and are attached to the large basic page.

Putting the Booklet Together

Score the back of each strip about 1" (3 cm) from the top and glue to the large page only along the top 1" (3 cm) of the strip so it will fold. When all the strip pages are mounted, fold the large page in half like a book. Punch holes for inserting the closed page into a three-ring binder, cut slits near each hole, and run a flattened strip of tan paper ribbon through each one to fan out on the inside surface of the pages.

Paris Journal: Mica Chip Cover

Here is a way to embellish the cover of a purchased blank journal so it is as beautiful and as important as the words within.

ARTIST: pj DUTTON

MATERIALS

- **Stamps**

  "Paris 1920"

  "Travel Journal"

  Postage and travel stamps

- **Ink and Inkpads**

  Black pigment ink

- **Papers**

  Cream or neutral handmade paper, 11" × 17" (28 cm × 43 cm)

  One sheet of cream cardstock

- **Miscellaneous**

  Large mica chips (embossing tiles)

  Fine gold or copper wire

  Wire cutters

  Round-nose pliers

  Drill with ¹⁄₁₆-inch (1.5 mm) drill bit

  Paper adhesive

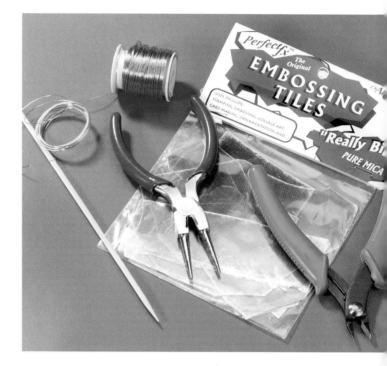

When curling wire, use round nose pliers, not needle nose, and either curl the wire around the pliers themselves or around a knitting needle or wooden skewer.

Getting Started

Stamp the large sheet of handmade paper randomly with black ink, using all of the stamps except the words "Travel Journal." Cover a purchased blank journal with the stamped paper. Stamp the travel images onto cardstock and cut them out, forming 3"–4" (8 cm–10 cm) rectangles and squares. Stamp the words "Travel Journal" on cardstock and cut them out. Glue the words and the images onto the paper cover as shown in the photograph.

Making the Mica Embellishments

Cut the large mica chips into pieces that will cover the cardstock stampings. Lay the mica pieces on a flat surface and stamp them, leaving the centers of the mica chips clear so you can see the images underneath. Open the cover of the journal and lay it on a piece of scrap wood with the mica pieces in places. Drill a few holes through the mica and the journal cover.

Finishing the Cover

To wire the mica chips on the cover, coil about ½" (1 cm) of wire in one end of an 8" (20 cm) length of wire. Push the straight end through the cover, the handmade paper, and the mica from the inside. Trim to 1" (3 cm) and coil that end on the front of the journal. Bend and mash the coils so they lay flat against the surface.

STAMPING TRICK

When planning a vacation or other trip, buy a couple of blank journals to take along and record your thoughts and memories as you go. Leave plenty of space on the pages and tuck your favorite memorabilia into the journal with your words. When you come home, finish up the journal with rubber stamps, handmade stamps, and other techniques found throughout this book. Make a rebus page. Stamp a cover. Stamp some frames, borders, and background papers to add, then tie it together with a ribbon.

By the Shore: Beaded Album Cover

A layered and embellished cover such as this one promises marvelous surprises within and it honors the time that these friends spent together on their seaside vacation.

ARTIST: SANDRA McCALL

MATERIALS

- **Stamps**

  Leaves

  Hearts

  Textures and other elements

- **Ink and Inkpads**

  Reinkers in purple, green, blue, fuchsia and

  turquoise

- **Papers**

  Matte board

  Three sheets of monoprint, faux batik or

  handmade paper (Refer to the Basics section, page

  35, for instructions on making these papers)

- **Miscellaneous**

  Metallic bead strings and flower strings

  Gold metallic cord

  Seaside trinkets and leaf sprays

  Frosted sea glass

  Permanent bonding adhesive or thick white craft glue

  Glue stick

  Craft scissors or clippers

QUICK TRICK

To create pages like these, you will need scraps and partial pages of decorative paper. Leaf through this book and try some of the techniques, then save the papers you create in a folder, a box, or a book for later use.

Step 1

Cut an 8 ½" × 11" (22 cm × 28 cm) piece of matte board and cover it with a sheet of decorative paper to provide a sturdy background. Either wrap the paper around the edges of the board to the back and cover the back with another piece of paper, or cut the paper the same size as the matte board, mount it, and color the edges of the board with markers.

Step 2

Cut an additional piece of matte board about 2" (5 cm) larger all around than the photographs and cover it with a coordinating piece of decorative paper.

Step 3

Cut a frame for the photos from matte board and cover it with handmade or decorative paper. Make the frame windows about ½" (1 cm) larger all around than the photographs.

Step 4

Cut small matte boards the same size as the photos. Mount the photos on the small matte boards and color the edges with markers to coordinate with the background.

Step 5

Assemble the pieces in the same order in which they were made, referring to the project photo at left for placement.

Step 6

Embellish the layers with bead strings, gold cord, and flower strings. Use the permanent bonding adhesive to glue the beads and trinkets in the center of the cover. Hint: Be sure to cut the bead and flower strings accurately so they will fit where they meet at the corners and hold them in the glue until it sets.

THAT FAMILIAR SAYING "when all is said and done" never seems
to hold true for me. As soon as you think that you have things all
wrapped up, the creative juices start to flow and you always come up
with more ideas. We couldn't close the book without including a few
of the pieces that created themselves along the way. It is our pleasure
to offer you these projects, and if not for the deadline, they would

extend for a hundred more pages. Just remember, these types of projects bring forth stories, love, treasures, and memories—there is no limit
of where you will travel into your own gallery of treasures forever.

Family Linens Pillows

When you inherit the odds and ends of a linen closet, what do you do with all the mismatched pieces? Making them into pillows is a great way to display pieces that would normally be hidden in the linen chest. Two linen or damask napkins form the fronts and backs of these pillows. The crocheted pieces and buttons are sewn on by hand. Then a pillow form is inserted, and the open side is sewn shut. Don't limit yourself to napkins, either—you can use favorite old dresses, your grandmother's curtains, or even dish towels.

Design: Janet Pensiero

Vintage Chenille Baby Quilt

Old bedspreads, even if they're not handmade quilts, can trigger memories of childhood rooms or houses. If you have an old bedspread that is worn or stained, or even has a few holes, you can give it a new life in a baby's room as a quilt or a wall hanging. Cut a large piece of the bedspread—36" x 45" (91 cm x 114 cm) is the standard baby quilt size, but a 40" (102 cm) square works well, too. Cut a piece of coordinating fabric the same size and sew around three sides. Place a layer of quilt batting inside, and stitch up the open side. Tack the three layers together with embroidery floss every few inches or so. You can add vintage buttons or other bits of vintage crochet or embroidery. If there's a family story attached to the bedspread, you can write it on the back of the quilt with a permanent fabric marker. Then present the lucky baby with a little piece of family history.

Design: Janet Pensiero

Our House Guest Book

Memories of good times with visitors—family and friends alike—can be even more special in a personalized guest book. For the cover, enlarge a photo of your house on a black-and-white photocopier. Then, enlarge the enlargement to fit comfortably on your cover. Print the second enlargement onto four pieces of different colored paper—most copy centers have 11" x 17" (28 cm x 43 cm) paper in a range of colors. Cut the copies of the colored paper into quarters, making sure they align to create the original photo. Mount two pieces of cardstock together with double-sided mounting adhesive to make both the front and back covers. Then mount the quarter pictures onto the front cover, and cover them with plastic laminating film. Print out a title on your computer, or hand-letter it. For the inside of the book you can use any good quality paper, such as heavy-weight sketchbook paper. Bind the covers to the inside pages with the punch and ring binding system.

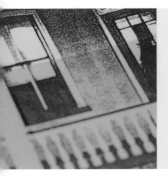

Keepsake Tip

Enlarging a photo twice on a photocopier creates the high contrast black-and-white photo effect used here. It's best to start with a lighter photograph to keep more detail in the photo.

Design: Janet Pensiero

Aunt Mary's Closet *Evening Bag*

Collecting the labels from favorite clothes is a great way to remember not only the clothes, but also the person who owned them. Aunt Mary's closet was an endless source of fascination for me as a kid, because she loved clothes and always had glamorous cocktail dresses for me to try on. I hand-stitched these labels onto a sandwich of two pieces of lightweight polyester-cotton fabric with a layer of polyester batting in between. To make a bag 7" (18 cm) square, cover an area roughly 7" x 14" (18 cm x 36 cm) with labels, and fold it in half. Blind stitching around the edge of each label creates the raised quilted effect. The handles are steel memory wire strung with vintage pearl beads. Use a vintage button and a loop of silk cord for the closure. For a simpler project, glue or stitch the labels onto a small purchased canvas bag.

Keepsake Tip

For a more elegant look, stitch pearls all around the edge of the bag.

Design: Janet Pensiero

License Plate Trip Journal

Two old license plates—cleaned, flattened out, and backed with felt—make the covers of this trip journal. After gluing a strip of folded flocked paper to the long edge of each license plate for the spine, back each plate with coordinating felt using iron-on fusible web. The inside of the book is up to you. You can use the versatile punch and ring binding system and fill it with blank pages for notes, maps, menus, or plastic sleeves for collecting mementos. For a finishing touch, glue two silver shank buttons in the holes of the license plates to simulate screw heads.

Keepsake Tips

- Wash and dry the license plates before you use them. It's important that they be as flat as possible, so straighten out any kinks and bumps as well.
- If you only have one license plate, use it for the front cover, and use a piece of mat board cut to size for the back cover.

Design: Janet Pensiero

Swimsuit Dress Form

This piece came about when I saw the dress form in my favorite rubber stamp store. I thought about the pictures of my grandparents in their old-fashioned bathing suits—and, compared to today's bathing suits, about how hot my grandparents must have been. It's amazing how quickly fashion became more comfortable in less than 20 years. Add some images of seashore-related items, like fish and seashells, among the pictures, and embellish the form with some seashore charms.

Keepsake Tip

The dress form shapes have become very popular for home decorating pieces. You can choose any clothing theme, such as the '70s or prom night.

Design: Connie Sheerin

Translucent Envelope Book

You can purchase large plastic document envelopes in a range of colors at office supply stores. By binding several envelopes together with large rings, you can create a childhood souvenir book in which to keep special things like tiny socks and T-shirts, finger paintings, and report cards.

Design: Janet Pensiero

Decoupaged Makeup Case

I have always loved this little makeup case. It belonged to my Aunt Fran, but you can find one in second-hand stores and at garage sales. I really enjoyed choosing some paint to give it new life. Then I decoupaged it with cosmetic-themed prints. For a finishing touch, I used a rubber stamp and some polymer clay to make a nameplate. The case houses my scarves and goes with me on special road trips. It's perfect when I want just a little more attention—which it certainly does attract!

Keepsake Tip

You can also collect paper items from trips and decoupage a memory suitcase as a decorative piece.

Design: Connie Sheerin

Aunt Rose's Handkerchief Sachets

I used my Aunt Rose' handkerchiefs for this project, but you can use your grandmother's monogrammed linen napkins or a piece from your mother's old kitchen curtains to create a beautiful and aromatic sachet. Wash and iron the handkerchief, then lay it flat, right side down, with the four corners making a diamond shape. Using the diagram on page 295 as a guide, fold the left and right sides to the center, overlapping the points to achieve the desired width. Fold the bottom point up and under. Hand-stitch along the left and right edges of the folded handkerchief. Fold a piece of polyester batting in half to create a pocket that will hold the potpourri inside the handkerchief envelope. Insert the batting pocket into the folded handkerchief, and fill with potpourri or scented dried botanicals. Fold the top flap over and secure it with buttons or beads.

Keepsake Tip

You can also place a small amount of potpourri in the center of a square handkerchief, pull the four corners up, and tie it with a ribbon for a simple sachet.

Design: Janet Pensiero

Patterns

GRANDFATHER'S TIE PILLOW

pages 70-71

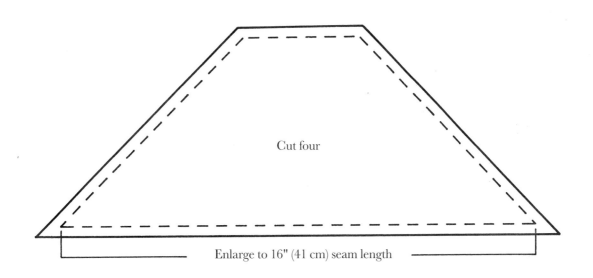

Cut four

Enlarge to 16" (41 cm) seam length

BUTTON BOX CHARM BRACELETS

pages 114-115

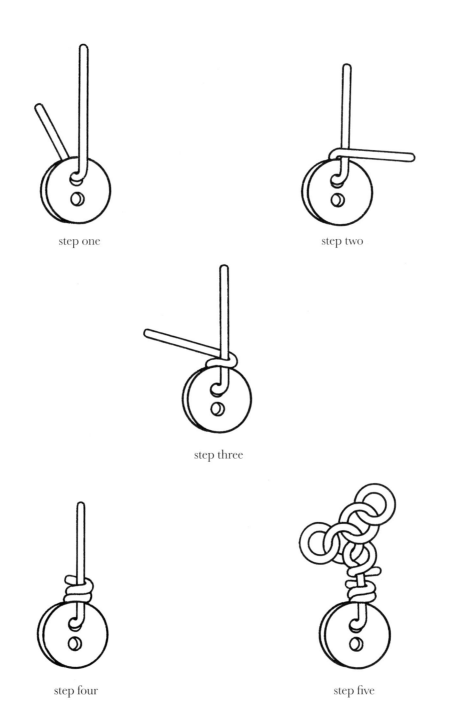

step one

step two

step three

step four

step five

AUNT ROSE'S HANDKERCHIEF SACHETS

pages 290-291

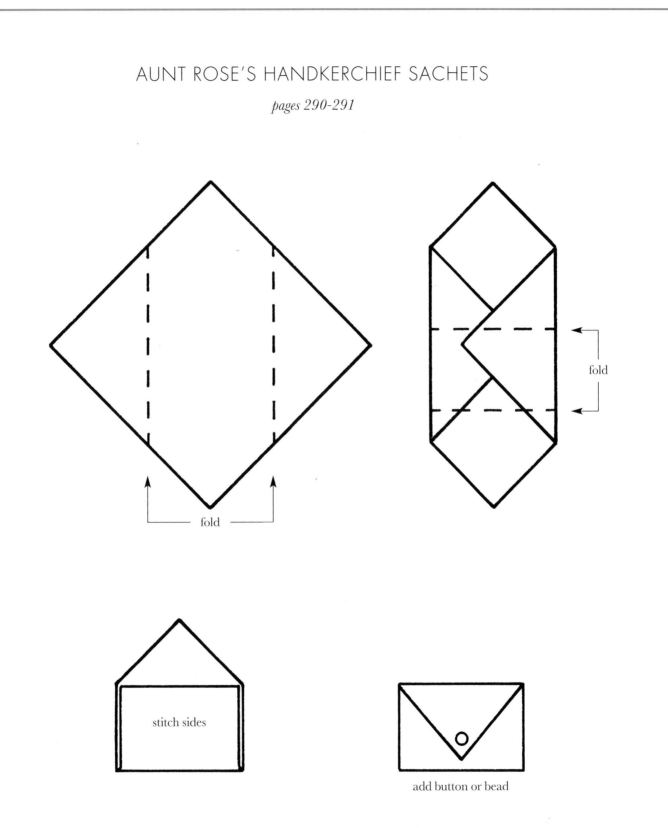

fold

fold

stitch sides

add button or bead

Supplies and Resources

ADAMS MAGNETIC PRODUCTS
2081 North 15th Avenue
Melrose Park, IL 60160
1-800- 222-6686
Fax: (708) 681-1879
Magnetic strips and sheets

AIKO'S ART MATERIAL IMPORT, INC.
3347 North Clark Street
Chicago, IL
(312) 404-5600
Fax: (312) 404-5919
Japanese paper; bookcloth; tools; books
on bookbinding; general art materials

AMERICAN GRAPHIC ARTS, INC.
150 Broadway
Elizabeth, NJ 07206
(908) 351-6906
Fax: (909) 351-7156
Reconditioned bookbinding equipment,
such as board shears, presses, stamping
equipment

ANGELWINGS ENTERPRISES
3065 North Sunnyside #101
Fresno, CA 93727
www.radiantpearls.com
Radiant Pearls translucent, pearlized paint

ARISTA SURGICAL SUPPLY CO., INC.
67 Lexington Avenue
New York, NY 10010
(212) 679-3694
Fax: (212) 696-9046
Knives, handles and blades; micro-spatulas

ART DIRECTION BOOK CO., INC.
456 Glenbrook Road
Glenbrook, CT 06906
(203) 353-1441
The Art Direction Book Co. publishes
books on graphic design and the Scan
This Book clip art series.

THE ART STORE
4004 Hillsboro Pike
Nashville, TN 37215
1-800-999-4601
www.artstoreplus.com
Canvases, varnish, and basic craft tools

ARTISTIC WIRE
752 North Larch Avenue
Elmhurst, IL 60126
www.artisticwire.com
Colored copper wire, tools & accessories

B&C WOODWORKS
gentleben2010@msn.com
Altar stands

BEACON ADHESIVES
125 South MacQuesten Parkway
Mount Vernon, NY 10550
www.beaconcreates.com
Adhesive products

BINNEY & SMITH
1100 Church Lane
Easton, PA 18044
www.binney-smith.com
Distributors of Crayola and Liquitex products,
Model Magic modeling compound

BOOK MAKERS INTERNATIONAL LTD.
6701B Lafayette Avenue
Riverdale, MD 20737
(301) 927-7787
Fax: (301) 927-7715
Bookbinding supplies, equipment and tools;
books on bookbinding

CAMPBELL-LOGAN BINDERY, INC.
212 Second Street, North
Minneapolis, MN 55401-1433
(800) 942-6224
Fax: (612) 332-1313
Japanese bookcloth

CHARTPAK
One River Road
Leeds, MA 01053
www.chartpak.com
Craft pens

CLAY ALLEY
http://clayalley.freeservers.com/tins.htm
Hinged tins

CLEARSNAP, INC.
P.O. Box 98
Anacortes, WA 98221
www.clearsnap.com
Pens, inks, stamps, accessories

COOMER'S CRAFT MALL
Store locations throughout the United States.
www.coomers.com
Wood shadow boxes, art findings

CONNIE SHEERIN ENTERPRISES
P.O. Box 246
Lansdowne, PA 19050
www.mosaicmania.com
concraft@aol.com
General craft supplies

COST PLUS WORLD MARKET
Store locations throughout the United States.
www.costplus.com
Exotic trinkets

CRACKER BARREL OLD COUNTRY STORE
Store locations throughout the United States.
www.crackerbarrel.com
Die-cast cars

CRAFTS ALA CART
1612 Union Valley Road
West Milford, NJ 07480
www.craftsalacart.com

CREATE AN IMPRESSION
A Rubber Stamp Store and so Much More!
56 E. Lancaster Avenue
Ardmore, PA 19003
(610) 645-6500

CREATIVE PAPERCLAY
79 Daily Drive, Suite 101
Camarillo, CA 93010
www.creativepaperclay.com
Air-dry clay

D. BROOKER & ASSOCIATES
Rt. 1, Box 12A
Derby, IA 50068
(641) 533-2103
Fax: (641) 533-2104
dbrooker@dbrooker.com
www.dbrooker.com
Unique wood products

DC&C
Decorator & Craft Corporation
428 S. Zelta
Wichita, KS 67207
1-800-835-3013
Rusty tin-tiques & papier-mâché

DECOART
P.O. Box 386
Stanford, KY 40484
(606) 365-3193
www.decoart.com
Fabric paint and adhesives

DELTA CRAFTS
www.deltacrafts.com
1-800-423-4135

DIEU DONNE PAPERMILL, INC.
433 Broome Street
New York, NY 10013-2622
(212) 226-0573
Fax: (212) 226-6088
Handmade paper; books

DMD INDUSTRIES
2300 South Old Missouri Road
Springdale, AR 72764
www.dmdind.com
Paper, journals, albums

DOS MUJERES MEXICAN FOLK ART
www.mexicanfolkart.com
Mexican postcards

DOVER PUBLICATIONS
Customer Care Department
31 East 2nd Street
Mineola, NY 11501-3852
Fax: (516) 742-6953
http://store.doverpublications.com
Large array of clip art books; request
a free catalog of clip-art titles by visiting
the Web site

EBAY
www.ebay.com
Hard-to-find collectables

FAUSTO'S ART GALLERY
Chihuahua, Mexico
(011) 521-453-0505
www.ojinga.com
Milagros, Day of the Dead items,
Mexican novelties

FIRE MOUNTAIN GEMS
28195 Redwood Highway
Cave Junction, OR 97523-9304
1-800-423-2319
questions@firemtn.com
www.firemountaingems.com
Semi-precious beads, handmade glass
beads, silver and copper beads, wire,
findings, and tools

FISKARS, INC.
7811 W. Stewart Avenue
Wausau, WI 54401
1-800-950-0203
www.fiskars.com
Cutting tools, paper edgers, accessories

FRIDGE DOOR
www.FridgeDoor.com
Decorative magnets

HANKO DESIGNS
875-A Island Drive #286
Alameda, CA 94502
www.hankodesigns.com
Envelope templates

HARCOURT BINDERY
51 Melcher Street
Boston, MA 02210
(617) 542-5893
Fax: (617) 451-9058
Bookbinding supplies, equipment and tools

HERO ARTS
1343 Powell Street
Emeryville, CA 94608
www.heroarts.com
Rubber stamps, sets, and accessories

HILO HATTIE
700 North Nimitz Highway
Honolulu, HI 96817
Other locations throughout the United States
(808) 535-6500
Fax: (808) 533-6809
www.hilohattie.com
Hawaiian novelties

THE HOMIES STORE
3656 South 16th Avenue
Tucson, AZ 85713
(800) 884-5326
http://shop.store.yahoo.com/homiesstore/
Homies dolls

INKADINKADO
61 Holton Street
Woburn, MA 01801
www.inkadinkado.com
sales@inkadinkado.com
Rubber stamps, ink, and embossing supplies

IRIS NEVINS DECORATIVE PAPERS
P.O. Box 429
Johnsonburg, NJ 07846
(908) 813-8617
Fax: (909) 813-3431
Marbling supplies, tools; marbled paper.
Reproduces historical patterns.

JO-ANN FABRIC AND CRAFTS
841 Apollo Street, Suite 350
El Segundo, CA 90245
Store locations throughout the United States
www.joann.com
Fabric and art materials

JUDI-KINS
17803 S. Harvard Boulevard
Gardena, CA 90248
www.judi-kins.com
Cube stamps, Bollios, Diamond Glaze,
crackle stamp, other rubber stamps

JUNE TAILOR
P.O. Box 208/2861 Highway 175
Richfield, WI 53076
(262) 644-5288; 1-800-844-5400
Fax: (262) 644-5061; 1-800-246-1573
customerservice@junetailor.com
www.junetailor.com
Transfer papers and washable, colorfast
printer fabric

JUTENHOOPS
2103 E. Camelback Road
Phoenix, AZ 85106
(602) 957-8006
info@jutenhoops.com
Retro-inspired memorabilia

KATO POLYCLAY
Donna Kato, The Art of Polymer Clay
www.donnakato.com
www.prairiecraft.com
Polymer clay

KINKO'S
Stores throughout the United States
www.kinkos.com
Color copies and transfers

LOEW-CORNELL
563 Chestnut Avenue
Teaneck, NJ 07666-2490
www.loew-cornell.com
Paintbrushes

LOOSE ENDS
P.O. Box 20310
Keizer, OR 97307
www.looseends.com
info@loosends.com
Handmade paper

LOUIE'S JUKE JOINT MUSIC SHOP
P.O. Box 770380
New Orleans, LA 70177-0380
504-944-7536
www.thejukejoint.com
Blank and decorated sugar skulls

MABLES.COM
7071 Warner Avenue #F613
Huntington Beach, CA 92647
www.mables.com
Tiki and other pop-culture items

MAD CHICKEN TOWN
(602) 277-5329
www.madchickentown.com
Mexican novelties, Day of the Dead
items, toys

MAGENTA RUBBER STAMPS
351 Rue Blain
Mont Saint Hilaire
Quebec J3H 3B4
Canada
www.magentarubberstamps.com
Art stamps, papers, cards, scrapbooks
and more

MARVY-UCHIDA
3535 Del Amo Boulevard
Torrance, CA 90503
www.uchida.com
Markers

MICHAELS ARTS AND CRAFTS
850 North Lake Drive, Suite 500
Coppell, TX 75019
Store locations throughout the United States.
www.michaels.com
Basic art materials

NATURE'S PRESSED
P.O. Box 212
Orem, UT 84059
1-800-850-2499
www.naturespressed.com
Dried flowers

NEW YORK CENTRAL ART SUPPLY, INC.
62 Third Avenue
New York, NY 10003
(212) 473-7705; (800) 950-6111
Fax: (212) 475-2513
Paper of all kinds; bookcloth; books;
general art materials

PAPER ADVENTURES
P.O. Box 04393
Milwaukee, WI 53204
www.paperadventures.com
Art and scrapbooking papers

PAPERCONNECTION INTERNATIONAL
208 Pawtucket Avenue
Cranston, RI 02905
(401) 461-2135
Fax: (401) 461-2135
Papers, mostly Japanese handmades

PAPERS BY CATHERINE
11328 South Post Oak Road #108
Houston, TX 77035
www.papersbycatherine.com
Vellum, handmade and art papers

PARTY CITY DISCOUNT PARTY STORE
400 Commons Way
Rockaway, NJ 07866
Store locations throughout the United States
www.partycity.com
Toys, stickers, craft items

PEARL PAINT
308 Canal Street
New York, NY 10013
for domestic mail order,
1-800-221-6845 x2297;
for international mail order,
212-431-7932 x2297
http://pearlpaint.com
General art and craft supplies, including
metal leaf in several colors, spray adhesive,
and tools

PERSONAL STAMP EXCHANGE
360 Sutton Place
Santa Rosa, CA 95407
www.psxstamps.com
Rubber stamps, stickers, accessories

PLAID ENTERPRISES, INC
P.O. Box 2835
Norcross, GA 30091-7600
www.plaidonline.com
Faster Plaster, a quick-drying craft plaster,
molds for creating a variety of plaster objects
perfect for transfer projects

POLYFORM PRODUCTS CO.
1901 Estes Avenue
Elk Grove Village, IL 60007
(847) 427-0020
www.sculpey.com
Sculpey polymer clay, and Liquid Sculpey,
a liquid polymer transfer medium

RANGER INDUSTRIES
15 Park Road
Tinton Falls, NJ 07724
www.rangerink.com
Ink, inkpads, stamping accessories

ROLLABIND INC.
3117 NW 25th Avenue
Pompano Beach, FL 33069
www.rollabind.com
Punch and ring binding system

RUBBER STAMPEDE
Delta Technical Coatings
2550 Pellissier Place
Whittier, CA 90601
www.rubberstampede.com
Stamps, inkpads, Curve Décor stamping
systems, accessories

SHRINE ON!
P.O. Box 781
Bisbee, AZ 85603
(520) 432-2509
Shrine kits

STAMPERS ANONYMOUS
20613 Center Ridge Road
Rocky River, OH 44116
www.stampersanonymous.com
Stamps, papers, inks and accessories

STAMPINGTON & COMPANY
22992 Mill Creek Drive,
Suite B
Laguna Hills, CA 92647
www.stampington.com
Art stamps, books, magazines (Somerset
Studio), accessories

SUNDAY INTERNATIONAL
5672 Buckingham Drive
Huntington Beach, CA 92649
www.sundayint.com
Rubber stamps and accessories

TALAS
568 Broadway
New York, NY 10002-1996
(212) 219-0770
Fax: (212) 219-0735
Paper; bookbinding supplies, equipment
and tools; books

TIDY CRAFTS
1330 Enterprise
Idaho Falls, ID 83402
www.tidycrafts.com
Tidy Trays and organizing accessories

TONER PLASTICS, INC.
699 Silver Street
Agawam, MA 01001
www.tonerplastics.com
Colored plastic art wire

TRANSFERMAGIC.COM
P.O. Box 190
Anderson, IN 46015
United States, 1-800-268-9841;
International, 765-642-9308
Fax: (765) 642-9308
info@transfermagic.com
www.transfermagic.com
Manufacturers just about everything needed
for transferring, including ink-jet Transfer To
Dark paper

TSUKINEKO
15411 NE Ninety-fifth Street
Redmond, WA 98052
www.tsukineko.com
Inks, inkpads, markers, pens

UNITED STATES POSTAL SERVICE
www.usps.com
Commemorative postage stamps

US ARTQUEST, INC.
7800 Ann Arbor Road
Grass Lake, MI 49240
www.usartquest.com
Perfect Paper adhesive

WALNUT HOLLOW FARM, INC.
1409 State Rd. 23
Dodgeville, WI 53533
1-800-950-5101
www.walnuthollow.com
Unfinished wood products, wood burners,
oil color pencils

XYRON INC.
15820 North 84th Street
Scottsdale, AZ 85260
www.xyron.com
Laminating and sticker machines
and cartridges

Contributors

Cynthia Atkins
Diamond Street Productions
P.O. Box 197
Lexington, VA 24450
(877) 764-3033
diamondstreet@go.com
www.postpicasso.com

Betty Auth
14719 Earlswood Drive
Houston, TX 77083
(281) 879-0430
bauth@houston.rr.com

Kathy Cano-Murillo
4223 W. Orchid Lane
Phoenix, AZ 85051
(602) 444-8618
kathymurillo@hotmail.com

pj Dutton
(636) 931-2613
pjstamps@aol.com

Paula Grasdal
65A Dana Street, Apt. 10
Cambridge, MA 02138
(617) 441-0286
paulagrasdal@earthlink.net

Dawn Houser
(210) 930-0373
howzr@aol.com
www.dawnhouser.com

Susan Jaworski Stranc
(978) 465-9896
stance@mediaone.net

Anita Y. Mabante Leach
nitaleach@yahoo.com

Barbara Mauriello
231 Garden Street
Hoboken, NJ 07030

Sandra McCall
(626) 967-6527
mccalls@aol.com

Livia McRee
62 Church Street, #2F
Wellesley, MA 02482
(781) 431-0783
livia@liviamcree.com

Terri Ouellette
terrioaz@qwest.net
www.terricreations.com

Janet Pensiero
263 Dupont Street
Philadelphia, PA 19128
(215) 487-2553
pensieroj@earthlink.net

Vicki Schreiner
(417) 887-9465
vickioriginals@msn.com

Connie Sheerin
223 N. Maple Avenue
Lansdowne, PA 19050
(610) 626-3622
concraft@aol.com

Philip Welch
Diamond Street Productions
P.O. Box 197
Lexington, VA 24450
(877) 764-3033
diamondstreet@go.com
www.postpicasso.com

About the Authors

CONNIE SHEERIN is a designer, author, and TV personality with 30 years of experience. Connie has been a guest demonstrator on numerous television shows, including *The Rosie O'Donnell Show*, *The Carol Duvall Show*, *Home Matters*, *Handmade by Design*, and *Willard Scot's Farm & Garden Journal*. She is CEO and president of Crafts ala Cart, a business based on teaching crafts to others. She is also a contributor to many crafts magazines and is the author of three other books. She resides in Lansdowne, Pennsylvania. Visit Connie Sheerin's Web sites at www.craftsalacart.com or www.conniesheerin.com.

JANET PENSIERO is an award-winning designer with more than 20 years of experience as an art director, toy designer, and craft artist. Since graduating from Moore College of Art and Design, in Philadelphia, she has designed everything from ads to a sign system for the Philadelphia Zoo to activity toys for children. Most recently, she was senior project designer and art director at Craftopia.com. Her varied background and wide range of experience provide an unlimited source of inspiration for the craft projects she designs and executes. Her work has been featured in several magazine and books, including *Hand Lettering for Crafts* (Rockport Publishers). She lives in Philadelphia, Pennsylvania.

BARBARA MAURIELLO is an artist and conservator who has a bookbinding studio in Hoboken, New Jersey. She teaches bookbinding and boxmaking at the International Center of Photography, The Center for Book Arts, and Penland School of Crafts.

BETTY AUTH is a freelance designer, artist, author, and editor whose interest in art and design has led her through many mediums. She has designed and published projects in the areas of quilting and appliqué, polymer clay, wire and beads, stamping, woodburning, and many others. She has appeared on *The Carol Duvall Show* on HGTV, and was a featured artisan on *Lynette Jennings Design*, on The Discovery Channel. More than 300 of her designs have been published in national craft and general interest publications. She was the author of a regular column for *Arts & Crafts Magazine* entitled "Ready, Set, Go!" where she explored easy, intermediate, and artist projects on many mediums. She is a finalist for Craft Designer of the Year and is constantly surprised and invigorated by the creative impulse that lives within each of us. She may be contacted at (281) 879-0430 or bauth@houston.rr.com.

KATHY CANO-MURILLO is a multi-talented writer and designer. She credits her husband, Patrick, for introducing her to their shared Mexican-American culture. Together they launched Los Mestizos, a business creating Chicano folk art. Her work has been carried in hundreds of shops and museum stores and has been featured in national publications, including *Sunset* magazine, *Gourmet* magazine, and *Latina* magazine. She is a journalist for the Arizona Republic newspaper, writing about movies, music, and pop culture, and producing a weekly craft column that's carried in newspapers nationwide. She appears weekly on a television morning show demonstrating home decor ideas and also maintains a crafting Web site, CraftyChica.com. Kathy was one of "10 Latinas to Watch" in the July 2001 issue of *Latina* magazine.

LIVIA MCREE is a craft writer and designer. Born in Nashville, Tennessee, and raised in New York City by her working-artist parents, Livia has always been captivated by and immersed in folk and fine arts, as well as graphic design. She is the author of two additional books, *Quick Crafts: 30 Fast and Fun Projects* and *Instant Fabric: Quilted Projects from Your Home Computer*. She has also contributed to numerous other books, including *Mosaics Inside and Out*; *The Right Light*; *Ceramic Painting Color Workshop*; and *Simple Elegance*.